USER EXPERIENCE IN THE AGE OF SUSTAINABILITY

USER EXPERIENCE IN THE AGE OF SUSTAINABILITY: A PRACTITIONER'S BLUEPRINT

KEM-LAURIN KRAMER

AMSTERDAM • BOSTON • HEIDELBERG • LONDON
NEW YORK • OXFORD • PARIS • SAN DIEGO
SAN FRANCISCO • SINGAPORE • SYDNEY • TOKYO
Morgan Kaufmann is an imprint of Elsevier

Acquiring Editor: Steve Elliot
Development Editor: Heather Scherer
Project Manager: Jessica Vaughan
Designer: Alisa Andreola

Morgan Kaufmann is an imprint of Elsevier
225 Wyman Street, Waltham, MA 02451, USA

Notices
Knowledge and best practice in this field are constantly changing. As new research and experience broaden our understanding, changes in research methods or professional practices, may become necessary. Practitioners and researchers must always rely on their own experience and knowledge in evaluating and using any information or methods described herein. In using such information or methods they should be mindful of their own safety and the safety of others, including parties for whom they have a professional responsibility.

To the fullest extent of the law, neither the Publisher nor the authors, contributors, or editors, assume any liability for any injury and/or damage to persons or property as a matter of products liability, negligence or otherwise, or from any use or operation of any methods, products, instructions, or ideas contained in the material herein.

Library of Congress Cataloging-in-Publication Data
Kramer, Kem-Laurin.
 User experience in the age of sustainability : a practitioner's blueprint / Kem-Laurin Kramer.
   p. cm.
 Includes bibliographical references and index.
 ISBN 978-0-12-387795-6
 1. Product design—Environmental aspects. 2. Sustainable design. 3. User interfaces (Computer systems)
 4. New products—Environmental aspects. I. Title.
 TS171.4.K73 2012
 628—dc23

                                  2012000747

British Library Cataloguing-in-Publication Data
A catalogue record for this book is available from the British Library.

ISBN: 978-0-12-387795-6

For information on all MK publications
visit our website at *www.mkp.com*

Printed and bound by CPI Group (UK) Ltd, Croydon, CR0 4YY

Transferred to digital print 2012

Typeset by: diacriTech, Chennai, India

Working together to grow
libraries in developing countries

www.elsevier.com | www.bookaid.org | www.sabre.org

ELSEVIER   BOOK AID
            International   Sabre Foundation

TABLE OF CONTENTS

PREFACE

User experience professionals are at the apex of a new and exciting field that may one day be termed *sustainable user experience design and research*. Understanding how to puzzle together the pieces and make sense of the wide field of sustainability, as well as combine user research knowledge, has been my personal passion. Over the last few years, much time has been spent questioning the role of user research in design and development. Moreover, I spent a lot of time thinking about the role we play as solution providers that consider ecology as a key factor in design, whether it is something as simple as advocating for a service-based subscription over the design of another piece of hardware, driving more efficiency in workflow, or advocating for better eco-conscious out-of-the-box solutions. The solutions to these seemingly simple design decisions address such issues as dematerialization, efficiency in design that in its aggregate form may result in energy savings, or providing users with an out-of-the-box experience that provides them with recyclability information. To date, I have been unable to find much published in the field of user experience design and sustainability that spoke to my peers and me about such matters. Therefore, this book is a practical exposition that engages user research professionals and addresses what they need to know about sustainability to begin some level of engagement.

I have collected and consolidated all my research and think it is a timely book, as many of my peers are on similar wavelengths looking for ways to grow their careers in new and exciting places with true meaning and purpose. Many designers can design solutions that are for the most part commoditized; the key differentiator is providing products and solutions that are not only beautiful on the outside but on the inside, ones that consider the environment, the people, as well the business.

User Experience in the Age of Sustainability zeroes in on the user experience community and situates our practice at the center of the sustainable design movement; it is a view of sustainability through the prism of user experience that enables the empowerment and practice of this field with bottom-line appeal, focusing on the need for measures and metrics.

BIOGRAPHY

Kem-Laurin Kramer is a user experience researcher and designer with 13 years of experience in the field. She has worked both as a manager and individual contributor in a number of market fields, including mobile user experience, web design, logistics, and assembly; energy and automation; information and communication networks; and medical imaging and health information systems (financial and clinical), to name a few. More recently, she has been engaged in designing user experiences for the following GIS, courts and justice, permitting, licensing and compliance, and freedom of information in the space of citizen-centric solutions.

Kramer is also a pioneer of formal user experience research practice at Research in Motion (makers of Blackberry), championing the building of the company's first ever usability lab and creating traction for the field to evolve at RIM. Since then, the UX practice has been embedded into the company's practices. Previously, she was the first UX researcher hired at Siemens Corporate Research, in Princeton, NJ, working in the field of medical, logistics and automation, telecom, among other Siemens business operations, where she used her unique background in media, usability, and communications to drive this practice. Today, she is a senior user experience designer at CSDC and occasionally speaks at local events on the topic of user experience and sustainability.

Apart from being active in the local user experience community, extolling the virtues of embracing sustainability UX analytic practices, Kramer has given lectures and talks at local universities, as well as written for *Johnny Holland*. She also coauthored a chapter in Nuray Aykin's *Usability and Internationalization of Information Technology: Travel Planning on the Web: A Cross-Cultural Case Study*.

Kramer earned an undergraduate degree from The University of Ottawa and a graduate degree from the University of Waterloo, ON, Canada.

ACKNOWLEDGMENTS

First, I thank Rachel Roumeliotis from Elsevier, who made this book possible and saw a need for a book about user experience and sustainability as part of the Elsevier bookshelf. In addition, David Bevans and Heather Scherer from Elsevier both made the task of writing a book seem so easy, with their guidance through the process and being on point in terms of quick response turnarounds.

Second, I thank all the folks who have been so helpful in sharing their sustainability stories and sending me resources used throughout the book to make this all possible. Most notable of the "thank-yous" goes to April McGee, vice president, eastern region at Human Factors, a true inspiration and gem of a UX professional; to Parul Nanda, who was my partner in pioneering, when we forged the formal practice of user research at Research in Motion—thanks for all your help with edits, reviews, and overall contribution. In addition, I thank Rahwa Haile, who has been instrumental in making me think about a practice of sustainability UX from a business strategy perspective. User experience research has often had the stigma of not having a strong foundation in measures and metrics. Providing me with a business perspective from her background in business and banking was most useful. Moreover, to Ian Chalmers, key principal at Pivot Design Group, thank you for all your help and support, the images, and discussions we have had. There are so many people to mention but the short list includes Nikolay Markov, Tom Liang, and Christer Garbis.

Aside from these, I thank those folks not mentioned explicitly, including all those authors who laid a foundation for me thinking about this book, even though I have never met you: Adam Werbach, Janine Benyus, and Nathan Shedroff especially.

Lastly, I also thank my family, who put up with half attention over the last year. I hope to spend much more time with you all to catch up.

CHAPTER 1

SUSTAINABILITY, USER EXPERIENCE, AND DESIGN

INFORMATION IN THIS CHAPTER

- Sustainability and User Experience
- Sustainability Strategy through the Design Lens
- Sustainability and Businesses
- The Impact on Companies
- Greenwashing, Customer Perception, and the User Experience
- Carbon Footprints
- Signs, Symbols, and Visual Ratings of the Eco Age
- Sustainable Design Ethics

INTRODUCTION

User experience has gone through a transformation over the past 15 years, from a unique, customer-centric, value-added service in the realm of system, product, and service design to a commoditized offering that is part of the development cycle. Designing the optimal user experience, whether for a financial services firm or a small business website, creates value by delivering the company's brand, its value proposition, to its clients. The emergence of multiple digital distribution channels and the consumers' use of these channels has made delivering a company's value proposition a necessity, rather than an added value, such that the business case for user experience has become a commoditized offering rather than a value-added service.

User experience, which elevates and places a focus on customers and their interactions with systems, products, and service solutions, is strategically positioned to change itself as a value-added offering by incorporating a sustainability approach in how it translates and transforms the user experience.

Today, customers' heightened awareness of ecological issues and their resulting expectations form one of the major trends and drivers of sustainability as a business approach, and user experience has the chance to transform itself from a commoditized offering into a value-critical service by incorporating a sustainability lens into its framework.

An overview of the rise of sustainability as a corporate necessity due to the convergence of business needs, the regulatory environment, consumer expectations, and other drivers is covered and how that compares and contrasts with the need for user experience. Furthermore, the trends and challenges for sustainable practices are examined in addition to how strategic planners can make a business case for adopting and implementing a sustainability framework that incorporates user experience. The key success factors for implementing a sustainability-led user experience is a foundational goal of this book, which takes readers from the basic and tactical and drives toward more strategic means of engagement.

SUSTAINABILITY AND USER EXPERIENCE

Sustainability is a loaded word that means different things to different people; so, before any fruitful discussion can begin, it is important to decide on an operational definition, as well as the scope and context of application. Therefore, I target the scope of this book to address primarily the field of design. To be exact, I refer to the general field of user experience, with which many subgroups of designers may identify. This may include user experience design (UX), visual design (VD), industrial design (ID), interaction design (IxD), and other related design fields with similar job activities. Situating the topic of sustainability in the space of design and allowing for some fruitful discussion is the goal of all subsequent discussion.

Today, many great books are written on the topic of sustainability; they range from strictly environmental to sociopolitics to economics and most recently to strategy. However, not much attention has been paid to providing practical guidance to the creators of products and services, even though those very products and services subsequently affect the environment in many detrimental ways.

Designers, like makers of products and services, are key stewards of our world, because the products and services they design influence the ways in which we live. Therefore, it stands to reason that, as the field of sustainability ripens into a practice, we need to take a deeper look at our world and anchor ourselves solidly on this large and amorphous field called *sustainability*.

Sustainability is not a fad; it is here to stay as both a concept and a viable field of practice driven by growing regulations. It will continue to drive key initiatives at every level of society and may soon govern some of the changes within our own profession. Consider that, over just a few years, the Global Reporting Initiative (GRI; n.d.a), an organization driving reporting initiatives, has seen an upward trend in the number of companies and countries reporting on their sustainability initiatives. Recent KPMG research revealed that 74% of top 100 U.S. companies published corporate responsibility (CR) information in 2008,[1] either as part of their annual financial report or as a separate document.

Against the background of the growing criticism and the negative social and environmental implications of globalization, many companies have become active in reporting on activities undertaken to prevent these externalities of production. The trickle-down effect that will eventually give all layers of industry some level of responsibility have led to an onslaught of new job titles such as these Amazon job posts: senior sustaining engineer, sustaining product design engineer, product design sustaining manager. On the reporting front, in Europe and Japan, sustainability reporting accompanies regulatory requirements and government encouragement. The number of reports that now include social issues alongside financial ones has increased considerably. Understanding and viewing the wider sustainability initiative through the lens of our own practice is important to evolve user experience and design as fields of practice and remain relevant as key decision drivers in the product life cycle. At its core, the design of everyday products and services is often the problem that underlies the environmental issues we face in general. Whether it is the design of a poorly built product that breaks down because of poor material selection or the decision to design a product over a comparable service subscription solution, which uses less to no material, are decisions that eco-conscious user experience researchers and designers face. At the heart of it, design is part of the environmental problem and therefore should be a central in finding solutions that produce more sustainable creations.

Many of us will read this book while wrestling with nine-to-five jobs, diminished attention spans, and juggling life with work but also wanting to keep up with the trends and redirections of our fields. Given that, this book is written to get you up and running with the lingo and practice of sustainability in as short a time as possible. It will guide you through understanding the building blocks and allow you to visualize and situate yourself at the center of this exciting field.

At the end of this chapter and subsequently this book, you will feel a high level of confidence both in speaking and thinking strategically about sustainability to peers and managers who have influence to help drive change. After all, user researchers and designers are the same folks who extolled and sold the virtues of usability and "good design" through tireless evangelizing making it the mainstay practice it is today.

The Context: The Brundtland Report of 1987

Our Common Future, also known as the *Brundtland Report* (Brundtland, 1987), a report produced by the United Nations World Commission on Environment and Development (WCED), was published in 1987. The key findings of this report established that economic development taking place today could compromise the development needs of future generations if we continue at the same pace. The ideas advocated in the document aimed to encourage people to reflect on the harm that economic development was having on both the environment and society. A few years later, building on this report, the Rio Earth Summit of 1992 represented a major step toward the goal of achieving sustainability, with international agreements made on climate change, forests, and biodiversity. Out of this summit emerged Agenda 21, a blueprint for sustainability in the 21st century. By championing the concept of sustainable development, Agenda 21 provided a framework for tackling today's social and environmental problems, including such things as air pollution, deforestation, biodiversity loss, health, overpopulation, energy consumption, and waste production, among other issues.

In many ways, the *Brundtland Report* can be seen as the beginning of a sustainability consciousness, which has now received global support and is the source of many sustainability initiatives today. The operating definition of *sustainability* had its birth here and focuses on establishing the idea that we need to determine how to meet the needs of the present generations without compromising the ability of future generations to meet their own needs.

Therefore, that brings us back to the most important questions: What is sustainability and why does sustainability matter to designers?

WHAT IS SUSTAINABILITY?

Emerging out of the *Brundtland Report* is the memorable quote that defines *sustainability* as the idea that, for something to be sustainable, it must "meet the needs of the present without compromising the ability of future generations to meet their own needs."

This definition encompasses the *social, economic,* and *environmental* needs of both present and future generations and emphasizes the ideal that what we do today determines what is possible tomorrow.

> Therefore, we can say that *sustainability* is an economic, social, and environmental concept that involves meeting the needs of the present without compromising the ability of future generations to meet their own needs.

Today, this definition has received some traction as it departs from the legacy term *green* and assumes some prominence at a strategic position in industry, alongside corporate initiatives of social responsibility.

In earlier years, the coverall term *green* was used but, due to the loaded quality of the word (tree-hugging activist, hippie, and radical), many thought leaders moved away from it and embraced terms such as *eco* or *sustainable*. Partly responsible for this paradigmatic shift in philosophy is due to the prominent environmentalist Adam Werbach, who in a speech (Werbach, 2008) provided some self-reflexive insight to his earlier work as an environmentalist (which had once added to the loaded term *green*). In this speech, he suggested that the environmental movement was not well suited to solve the challenge of global warming. In his 2008 speech, titled "Birth of Blue,"[2] he proposed using the term *BLUE* to talk about "green" issues and at the same time to shed the baggage of past approaches. This shift from green to blue departed from a tree-hugger view of the sustainability movement to a focus on the kinds of strategies needed to achieve sustainability goals.

Throughout this book, however, I use the term *sustainability* in the interest of providing the acceptable and progressive ideals of the movement and departing from more loaded history of the word *green*.

> "People who are part of the BLUE movement aspire to make a difference through the people and products that touch their lives. It encompasses green issues like protecting our last wild places and reducing our output of CO_2, but it also includes personal concerns like saving money, losing weight, and spending time with friends and family. BLUE is differentiated from green (other than its requirement to be typed in ALL CAPS) by keeping the 'parts of green that have brought us change and innovation, but let[ting] go of the narrowness.' BLUE builds on the foundation that green has laid, but lets go of its baggage." (Werbach, 2008)

WHY DOES SUSTAINABILITY MATTER TO DESIGNERS?

Over the last 30 years, there has been a growing awareness of the environmental problems caused by exponential growth and human development worldwide. In short, many of these problems are affecting us at rates faster than we can curb and counter them. Some of these specific issues range from such things as high rates of consumer goods wastage to air pollution to energy production to transportation and the consumption of natural resources. These are but a few of the issues with which we have to contend. Some clear examples to illustrate are such things as the high disposal rates of mobile phones and other electronics and,

---

[2]http://www.saatchis.com/birthofblue/birthofblue.pdf.

subsequently, the high amounts of natural resources needed to replace those mobile phones as well as other similar consumer goods being produced to meet consumption rates.

The crisis is reaching epidemic proportions and the natural resources consumption rate is driving many companies to rethink how to accommodate and innovate in the area of design to avoid penalties and detriment to their reputations. Many companies have also gone as far as the overnight formation of a highly visible web presence under the common header of *social responsibility*, *corporate responsibility*, or *green* to highlight, genuine or not, their commitment to curbing the environmental crisis. Look around and you will note this silent revolution. So, too, many governments have begun a massive policy restructuring that involves damage penalties for companies and consumers who are seen as violators to the environment (intentional or not). These penalties help curb and counter the impact of the environmental degradation that has been happening en masse.

Overall, the collective goal of conscious individuals (customers), companies, and government is to help preserve the natural resources needed to maintain future generations while sustaining their own. This lies as the basis of sustainability, as we will discover. For designers, "sustainability" may initially seem like a concept removed from our daily lives. Why should we care, and how can we affect any change, in our limited capacity, within our respective jobs? For deeper insight into this question, it is important that designers of all types begin to understand

1. **The what:** The sustainability landscape.
2. **The context:** What it means to be sustainable in the context of their work.
3. **The theory and advocacy:** How to embrace and advocate for good design.
4. **The practice:** How to begin a practice of sustainable design.
5. **The strategy for sustaining practice:** Lastly, how to maintain traction and momentum to continue to drive change through design.

To achieve what may seem like the impossible, it is also important to remember one of the key tenets of sustainability—*stewardship*. It is the noble idea that we are all caretakers of the environment, society, and the economy; therefore, it behooves us to ensure that both present and future generations can continue to thrive without compromising the lives and existence of either generation.

> Stewardship is the idea that we are all caretakers of the environment, society, and the economy; and it benefits us all to ensure that both present and future generations can continue to thrive without the compromising the lives and existence of either generation.

As designers, we design as opposed to consciously rethink, *re*design, and restore existing designs. These three concepts are, in many ways, at the core of many of the issues we face today. The need to create more versus fixing existing designs solves nothing but it is the standard mode of operation in many manufacturing fields today. The shift in how we think about design takes us through thinking about such concepts as *reduction,*

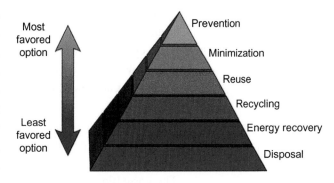

Figure 1.1
The Waste Hierarchy.

reusing, recycling, restoring, rethinking, and *redesigning*—all common phrases derived from the thrust of the sustainability movement, with some foundation in the concept of the waste hierarchy (Figure 1.1). The waste hierarchy is widely used as a basic communication tool for everyone, with the didactic goal of providing guidance to waste management and enabling more sustainable design thinking. The hierarchy shows disposal as the least desirable and prevention as the most favored option of waste management, with recovery, recycling, reuse, and minimization (reduction) as the remaining least to favored, respectively.

The *waste hierarchy* initially referred to a list of approaches (the 3 Rs of reduce, reuse, and recycle), which classify waste management strategies according to their desirability. Initially, the three 3 Rs were meant to be a hierarchy, in order of importance.

However, in Europe, the waste hierarchy comprises five steps: *reduce, reuse, recycle, recovery,* and *disposal.* Today, however, the term *rethink* has been added by some merely as an additional concept to the five, which are seen as more practical in their application. The goal of the waste hierarchy is to extract the maximum practical benefits from products and generate the minimum amount of waste possible as part of the design output. The following are the more mnemonic 6 Rs, which enable better recall and memory:

- **Reduce:** Using less has been the most commonly applied concept and is illustrated in the general area of energy consumption. Estimates show turning down a thermostat by just 1 degree can reduce energy consumption considerably.
- **Reuse:** This refers to recovering value from a discarded item without reprocessing or remanufacture. The adage that one person's garbage is another person's treasure best encapsulates this.
- **Recycle:** This refers to using materials from waste, which have been broken down into raw materials and are reprocessed into either the same product or a new product.

■ **Restore:** This refers to returning an item to its original or usable and functioning condition. A good example is designs made from metal and wood, especially where, with the use of refinishing and restoration, items can be given new life.

■ **Rethink:** This is more concerned with how designers should think about the design process. A design's value and use need great consideration before committing to design it.

■ **Redesign:** This is the application of the rethinking stage and the actual implementation of sustainability principles.

The waste hierarchy, as a concept, is a base toolkit to use before we think about design in the spirit of continuous improvement.

The following examples may better serve the purpose of illustrating some key areas of design issues and how we see our roles.

Figure 1.2

Paper, Plastic, and Beyond.

Paper, Plastic, and Beyond

A commonly cited example is the all-too-familiar paper vs. plastic debate (Figure 1.2), which had its inception in the early 2000s. Recently, a life-cycle analysis of the two (paper and plastic) shows us that sometimes it is difficult to ascertain which product design is the best choice after all. Consider for a moment a partial element of the fuller cycle alone.

Paper bags are made from trees, which are renewable to a certain extent. Plastic bags are made primarily from polyethylene, which is a by-product of the oil refining process. However, many other resources, such as energy and water also contribute to the production of either bag. Here are a few facts worth pondering.

1. Paper vs. Plastic Facts[3] Use-Less-Stuff.com (ULS) issued a report comparing plastic and paper grocery bags. ULS made the following findings: Plastic bags generate 39% less greenhouse gas emissions than uncomposted paper bags and 68% less greenhouse gas emissions than composted paper bags. The plastic bags generate 4,645 tons of CO_2 equivalents per 150 million bags; while uncomposted paper bags generate 7,621 tons and composted paper bags generate 14,558 tons per 100 million bags produced.

2. Plastic bags consume less than 6% of the water needed to make paper bags. It takes 1004 gallons of water to produce 1000 paper bags and 58 gallons of water to produce 1500 plastic bags.

[3]http://www.biotech-products.net/documents/The%20Plastic%20Bag%20vs%20Paper%20Bag.pdf.

3. Plastic grocery bags consume 71% less energy during production than paper bags. Significantly, even though traditional disposable plastic bags are made from fossil fuels, the total nonrenewable energy consumed during their life cycle is up to 36% less than the nonrenewable energy consumed during the life cycle of paper bags and up to 64% less than that consumed by biodegradable plastic bags.
4. Using paper sacks generates almost five times more solid waste than using plastic bags.
5. After four or more uses, reusable plastic bags are superior to all types of disposable bags—paper, polyethylene, and compostable plastic—across all significant environmental indicators.

That said, just looking only at a small part of the process, it is evident that paper may not be overall as environmentally efficient as was once thought. In addition, while this does not illustrate the full life cycle of either product, it begins to erode some of the first impressions that many have had about the plastic vs. paper debate. Over the years, there has been a shift toward reusable bags; they are most often canvas or reinforced nylon material that has become not only reusable but also fashionable. Further, as an incentive to drive users to begin using reusable bags, many stores impose a small fee for those consumers making the decision to go with plastic over purchasing or bringing their own bag. The Swedish furniture store IKEA has also gone as far as completely banning plastic from their UK stores[4] in 2007.

In some supermarkets and even some clothing stores, for example, paper, it seems, is no longer in the running, as many boutique stores are adopting the use of reuseable bags. Recently, I purchased hiking shoes from Northern Reflections and was pleasantly surprised to see that the store provided a reusable tote bag that I could later use for groceries and, in my case, transporting children's day bags on camping or other long trips. The question today for many of us is not simply one of plastic over paper but rather plastic, paper, or reusable bags.

Just recently, I made the grave error of accessing my stash of recyclable and reusable bags only to realize that I have no less than a 30 reusable bags collecting in my kitchen cupboards. This discovery made me think that I failed to remember to carry a bag on hand for unplanned purchases. This realization made me wonder what an ultimate design solution should look like that will incentivize people to

1. Adopt the use of reuseable bags.
2. Remember to take them along on shopping trips.
3. Make it easy to integrate in their travel for impromptu shopping.

---

[4]http://www.guardian.co.uk/business/2007/jul/08/theobserver.observerbusiness3.

Figure 1.3
Baggu Bag.

Have we arrived at the optimal design solution?

Bag designer Baggu may have cornered the market in this area as the designer of fashionable bags that can be compacted for easy use (Figure 1.3). The company's website states the following as an underlying design principle: "Baggu makes simple, high quality bags in many bright colors. They fill many uses so you can own less stuff."

The Baggu bag has not only created an easily collapsible and portable bag solution but also has strong aesthetical appeal for the fashion and eco-conscious shopper. Referred to as the "It bag of the future" by *Teen Vogue,* Baggu has cornered the market in the space of sustainable bagging solutions. The bag is also machine washable and folds up into its own pouch, small enough to tuck into a handbag or pocket; further, it is of nylon and comes in many colors. It epitomizes what is referred to by many as "eco-chic" for those who seek a balance of environmental and aesthetics. Some facts about the Baggu that makes it very popular include

- One Baggu holds the contents of two or three regular plastic grocery bags.
- Six Baggu Bags can contain a cartfull of groceries.
- Baggu Bag handles are ergonomically designed at the perfect length to hold in the hand, on the forearm, or over the shoulder.
- They are made from strong rip-stop nylon weighing only 2 ounces.
- They carry up to 50 lbs.
- They fold into a flat 5 × 5 inch pouch that easily slips in a purse or pocket, making them very unobtrusive and therefore handy.
- Baggu bags have a big gusset in the bottom so they sit flat when they are filled with such items as cartons and milk.

Overall, there seems to be a design direction that builds on the kinds of designs that we see from such eco-chic designers like the Baggu bag company.

Design and Dematerialization

Consider yet another design example that brings to mind the ideals of sustainable and ecological design for many—the design of the popular device the Amazon Kindle (Figure 1.4).

The Amazon Kindle is a portable e-book reader that has grown in popularity over the last few years. This device uses wireless connectivity to enable customers to shop for, download, browse, and read newspapers, magazines, blogs, and other digital media.

The Amazon Kindle stands as a testament to the new wave of design. However, some may still question the sustainability costs associated with production of an electronic device versus books, considering such issues as disposal, reuse, energy consumption and the like. Given the infancy of the shift from paper to electronics, it may be worthwhile to complete a rudimentary cost benefit analysis to determine if, in the short and long terms, we are making sound, ecologically conscious

Figure 1.4
Amazon's Kindle Fire.

decisions. The long-term impact is yet to be determined, for we cannot know the effect that mass adoption will bring, as we have not considered such thing as changes in energy costs that comes along with massive adoption. In addition, some questions surrounding whether or not the device will be serviceable still is to be determined? What will happen to older models as new ones enter the market?

Ultimately, Amazon and other book reader manufacturers need to consider all of these factors to ensure the long-term benefits come at a true eco savings. Further, they need to re-evalute the kinds of solutions they provide, as the relationship with the consumer will inevitably change given the nature of the product—a product with high serviceability potential. Second, customers can download new books and other services instead of always buying new books. However, does that mean that companies like Amazon will rethink their business model and their goals? Will sales of new and novel Kindles continue to be at the forefront of its business operation?

The Amazon Kindle created a new *status quo*, where instead of physical production, books and other published works retain their digital form and delivered only virtually or with minimal hard form production. This eliminates the need for cutting down more trees, consuming printing materials,warehousing, the need for transportation, energy to support the creation and supply chain associated with tangible goods production. The trickle-down effect eliminates a rather complex chain of unsustainable processes and stems the need to destroy many of our natural resources, dematerialization.

> The United Nations Environment Program (UNEP) defines *dematerialization* as "the reduction of total material and energy throughput of any product and service, and thus the limitation of its environmental impact. This includes reduction of raw materials at the production stage, of energy and material inputs at the use stage, and of waste at the disposal stage."

As a practice, dematerialization focuses on improving a product's overall efficiency via reduction, reuse, or recycling materials and products. It entails levels of activity at every stage of the production and consumption that takes into consideration how to

- Save resources in the extraction of materials.
- Drive innovation in the design process.
- Continuously improve the ecological design of products.
- Practice of environmentally conscious consumption habits and patterns.
- Recycle, reuse, reduce, restore, rethink, and redesign.

From a design perspective, dematerialization strategies translate into such activities as

- The conception, design, and manufacturing of a smaller or lighter product, such as tablets instead of laptops.
- The replacement of physical and material goods by nonmaterial and virtual solutions and substitutes (like an e reader over a physical book).
- The reduction in the use of material systems or of systems requiring large infrastructures and such things as irreplaceable energy (ride share or public transportation).

A fitting example here is perhaps a consideration of optimizing work-from-home programs to limit the use of public transportation. One recent example that comes to mind is Turbo Meeting, a web-meeting tool that I recently used with peers from three locations. After using the tool, a true sense of collaboration and presence allowed engaging discussions among the team. Attendees were easily able to take control of the mouse from their remote locations and cohost meetings. Another such tool is WebEx. In these examples, user experience and design is critical in allowing remote users to feel a sense of connectivity to their remote colleagues. While more can be done to improve on the presence of attendees, tools like Turbo Meeting make the possibility of physical transportation of millions of commuters a thing of the past.

Visual, interaction, industrial, and user experience designers all play a role in ensuring that the right user experience, including the optimal visceral experience, captures the imagination and interest of customers. In this role as creators, we can encourage the adoption of these new services, subscription-based designs like the Kindle, while guiding the design principle of dematerialization, if in fact there are benefits in the wider sustainability initiative.

At this point, it is critical to point this out: As the Kindle is a commercial product, I am mindful of obsolescence as an inherent element of the commercialization and manufacturing of the product.

Planned Obsolescence

Recalling the earlier example of paper vs. plastic is another concept—the idea of planned obsolescence, a concept with which many are not conscious but affects us all. It is what I call "the expiration date effect" known in business terms as *planned obsolescence.* Planned obsolescence is a business strategy in which the obsolescence (the process of becoming obsolete) of a product is planned and built into it from its conception, by the manufacturer. This negative business strategy is never far from the minds of companies, which believe they need to evolve by continuing to produce and ensure annual manufacturing of the same product with minor changes to retain their customer base.

> Planned obsolescence is a business strategy in which the obsolescence (the process of becoming obsolete, that is, unfashionable or no longer usable) of a product is planned and built into it from its conception, by the manufacturer. This is done so that, in the future, the consumer feels a need to purchase new products and services that the manufacturer brings out as replacements for the old ones.[5]

The Economist cites a classic case of planned obsolescence, the nylon stocking. The inevitable "laddering"[6] or "running" of stockings made consumers buy new ones and for years discouraged manufacturers from looking for a fiber that did not ladder. The garment industry in any case is not inclined to such innovation. Fashion of any sort is, by definition, is deeply committed to built-in obsolescence. Last year's skirts, for example, are designed similar to the one shown to be replaced by this year's new models, as are last year's pants or shoes or whatever you can think of. The many examples of planned obsolescence is everywhere.

Nevertheless, this is only one of many known examples; ask yourself why many of us feel the need to buy new cars every few years or get a new mobile phone every 6–9 months. Is this a conscious choice or have we been programmed to think that we need new and fashionable designs?

Planned obsolescence, as a topic, always brings to mind my own personal experience, the story of my uncle's yellow Toyota pickup truck.

When I was about 4 or 5 years of age, living in the Caribbean, my uncle Andrew drove a yellow Toyota Hilux (Figure 1.5). The year was 1977, and he had purchased it a few years earlier.

Fast forward to May 2005, I visited my uncle back in the Caribbean, and lo and behold, I was shocked to see the same yellow truck still navigating rough

[5]Taken from *The Economist,* 2009,: http://www.economist.com/node/13354332.
[6]The running nylon when torn resembles the steps of a ladder.

Figure 1.5
Toyota Hilux 1970
Model.

mountainous terrain, still lugging the harvest from his country farm to the city and harbors. After all these years, the vehicle was still operational. Given this experience, the Toyota brand is etched in the psyches of many natives who look down on other brands as simply inferior. Even with the 2009 recall setbacks for Toyota, the brand still has a good legacy. It is easily serviced and practical for life in some of the most challenging terrains of the world as well as in developing nations, which need products that are durable, as people cannot afford to buy new models on a whim. The wonder of Toyota and others like it in the Caribbean was built for easy maintenance and service without the high cost often associated with European brands. In fact, by the time most boys in my family reach their late teens, they knew a thing or two about how to fix the Toyota, as there is no one to help in the event that it breaks down in the middle of the country road leading to the farm.

Apart from my uncle's yellow Toyota, I can add the many other old model Toyotas that I remember as a child and that are still operational today. For inhabitants of countries where funds are low, a vehicle that stands the test of time goes the distance, not only allowing owners to complete the necessary work activities but also in creating solid brands; it becomes etched in the minds and psyche as among the best brands and it remains that way beyond just one generation. Therefore, it was no surprise that my first vehicle after finishing university was a Toyota.

In this case, Toyota earned a gold star for designing a product to last—one that is durable and serviceable at the same time. However, times have changed considerably from when vehicles, like anything else, were made to last and the visual reminders that every year brings new commercials and advertising to encourage newer designs has become, sadly, normal. Inherent in many products' DNA is an eventual death that will trigger images of the "brand new" versions as opposed to servicing what we already have until we really need to replace them.

SUSTAINABILITY STRATEGY THROUGH THE DESIGN LENS

As the sustainability field grows and awareness spreads, it is important for us to step back for a moment and think about how we will create a day-to-day practice around sustainable design thinking.

Presently, in the field of design, many are grasping for practical tools and methods to execute as part of a sustainable design cycle practice. Initiatives such as the Autodesk Sustainability Toolbox[7] are among the growing groups of organizations trying to be responsive to the needs of designers in providing them with evolved design tools that allow them to virtually design and visualize before materially creating design solutions. Still, we lack practical guidance that others beyond visual designers can anchor to as guides to drive their work both theoretically and practically. Over time, this book and others will fill this need and others like it, seeking to formalize sustainable user experience and design as eco-conscious fields of practice.

In many respects, sustainable design as a practice is today at its inception. We are becoming more aware that, when we design, it must be done efficiently and with conscience; but how we do this is still a mystery for many. While the goal will take time, we can already engage certain dimensions and product factors as yardsticks for determining a good design.

Up to this point in time, the "dimension" of energy consumption is perhaps the most easily understandable, although it does not give a full picture of a design's sustainability performance. This example is the one to which most consumers relate when they think of whether a design is ecologically good. If it uses less energy, then for many, this is a marker of its goodness as a sustainable design. However, before we can begin thinking about how we determine a design's sustainability, we need to take a strategic approach.

1. The first step, once we understand the basics of sustainability, is to create a framework that can be operationalized to execute a sustainability design practice. This should be accessible and palatable to those who think in bottom-line terms. Doing this helps to create traction and maintain momentum that can ultimately affect change. To create such a framework, we need to understand what it means to be sustainable in the context of design. This includes looking at such things as new packaging and transportation, in addition to the most commonly used, and energy conservation. All these factors are featured in subsequent chapters (Chapters 3 and 4).

2. We need a fuller understanding of the design areas affected beyond the hard product. This includes such things as the user interface, the interaction design, and user messaging and instrumentation data, all of which come into play when we think about design in the

---

[7]http://thesustainabledesigntoolbox.typepad.com/.

context of software, an area with which many of us are familiar. For example, if we think of energy consumption in the context of user interface and user messaging, there are opportunities for leveraging a system's data to inform users about basic things like energy consumption. This requires some level of user interaction and user interface, where user experience comes into play as a key contributor to the sustainable initiative. While this is one of many examples, it is a way to affect design in reaching our sustainability goals.

3. We need to draw the connection to existing design life cycles, leverage the methodologies we currently employ, and be open to creating new methodologies where needed. For example, a product life-cycle analysis is a perfect example where a proven design methodology in user research can be leveraged but requires further building blocks to give it impact. We may also extend this to see how we can align with existing software development life cycles, which is perhaps the cycle most commonly known to those of us in the field.

4. We need to understand the value of metrics and definitive measures and how to measure them. This is a critical aspect to move away from the "greenwashing" of this field as well as the "touchy-feeliness" that has been one major criticism of the green and sustainability movement. A subcomponent of this step is also to see what data already exist that can be leveraged in the interest of a framework and connected to the wider sustainability mandate across our respective companies at different levels of engagement.

5. Finally, we need to translate our methods and practices into meaningful structures that those in positions of authority can buy into it. This means instituting practices through such things as formalized reporting and product scorecarding based on a defined sustainability rating system. This will go the added distance to formalize and entrench the field into more strategic decision-making venues.

It is also critical to think of measures and metrics as foundational to overcoming some of the criticisms of the green movement, a field often lacking in scientific methods, metrics, and measures. To show value with the transparency of measures enables better tracking, forecasting, and reporting of valuable data with the goal of imminent mandatory reporting, as in the case of what companies are reporting through the Global Reporting Initiative.[8]

For a design to be sustainable, it must comply with a multifaceted definition that considers three key areas: the social, economic, and environmental impact. The threefold definition should be a basis for how, in its finality, twe can assess a product's sustainability value.

Further, the complexity of the definition complicates matters for businesses and creates layers of obstacles in making advances and establishing sustainable

---

[8]The GRI is a network-based organization that pioneered the world's most widely used sustainability-reporting framework. GRI is committed to the framework's continuous improvement and application worldwide. GRI's core goals include the mainstreaming of disclosure on environmental, social, and governance performance. See http://www.globalreporting.org.

design as a viable practice. It is sometimes difficult to begin thinking of where we can begin. How can we measure sustainability in a design?

Directions toward measures will become critical later in this book. However, as practitioners strive to discover more scientific values, a key element is the practice itself. Some questions that peers have asked include

- How do we define a process for sustainable design practice?
- Are there existing tools?
- What do we need to measure and how do we measure it?
- How is it presented and to whom?
- Who cares?
- And, perhaps most important, how will it have an impact for change?

There is a shift dictating new directions in design, and these directions are driven by factors out of our control. A recent U.S. Forrester poll (Mines, 2007) indicates that there are growing "green" concerns, with about 25 million people (approximately 12% of the U.S. population) willing to pay more for green products and a growing 41% who, while they are concerned, cannot afford to pay more.

Consider now, what if the cost of green products were more affordable? How then would design have to change to address this growing demand? In addition to polling, other drivers are quickly mandating changes in how we design. Understanding these general business opportunities can translate into value-added practices for our work.

The Context: Sustainability and Measurement

Hawken, Lovins, and Lovins's *Natural Capitalism* (1999) is a pivotal book that brought to the literary consciousness the significant connection between ecological issues and commerce. Among other topics addressed in the book are the many approaches to sustainability; when it comes to measuring whether something is sustainable or not, we should include four types of "capital": human, manufacturing, natural, and financial.

In a perfect world, this would be a simple task—to measure a product's overall sustainability aligned to these four "capitals." However, as we live in a more complex world of systems within subsystems and so on, where the connection between everything is not always clearly defined or transparent, we need to understand how to formulate an analytical and comprehensive framework that understands the points of connectivity among the capitals as they operate with their respective and collective systems.

(Continued)

Therefore, the challenge is to determine a sustainability analytic approach developed for application and general practice. With this said, we face the task of taking sustainability from a "touchy-feely concept" to a strategic concept, where more businesses can begin to engage. The financial services firm Accenture addresses some of the trends[9] that simplify the sustainability drivers as follows; and it is, in part, our challenge to determine how, from our vantage point, we can come up with solutions address the following societal and market trends:

1. **Consumer demand for sustainable products and services:** People today are making purchases not only as consumers but also as responsible world citizens. By rejecting the indiscriminate consumption patterns of the past and becoming more selective in their choices, they are signaling a shift in consumer attitudes and behaviors that may significantly affect business profitability and growth.
2. **Stakeholder influence:** Globalization and technology give customers and citizens a powerful voice. Businesses and public sector organizations need to extend their reach to a new breed of stakeholders that includes nongovernment organizations, media, academics, and the community at large.
3. **Resource depletion:** Economic growth in developing markets, combined with high consumption in Western economies, depleted natural resources (especially energy and water). Not surprisingly, there is fierce competition for what remains.
4. **Employee engagement:** Employees' commitment and enthusiasm for sustainability are shaping the way we work and live. As the sustainability mandate expands, organizations committed to social and environmental causes are likely to attract the top talent.
5. **Capital market scrutiny:** Sustainability has crept onto the bottom line. Investors now look at sustainability performance when evaluating a company's potential for future returns.
6. **Regulatory requirements:** Ready or not, government and industry regulations are forcing companies in nearly every industry to take sustainability seriously. If it has not happened yet, it soon will.

Last, not added in the preceding list is reporting. Understanding how to design human experiences with many of these constraints and regulations is itself the challenge. Given all these drivers, we need to begin to set the groundwork on how we will grow as a field and niche out to provide meaningful contributions to design as a whole.

---

[9]https://microsite.accenture.com/sustainability/global_agenda/Pages/drivers_of_sustainability.aspx.

With this paradigmatic shift, the need to understand how to support socioeconomic and environmental changes is critical, whether it is the design of a service or consumer product. We are on the cusp of a new age, where design is positioned to become a key player in the practice of sustainability design. The new roles we assume as stewards of our environment, through our design efforts, must be equipped with a wide understanding of the sustainability landscape. Moreover, as the creation and improvement of these goods and services continue, we need a strategic position to prepare for our broadening roles—this should begin with open dialog among our peers and result in strategic and analytical governing frameworks that can help us gauge our progress. Simply put, we need tools that can help us measure how we are doing, so we can better engage with the business side of the effort.

SUSTAINABILITY AND BUSINESSES

Sustainability is a tricky issue for businesses. Companies have to balance against each other their production and advertising costs, user brand perception, and genuine desire to switch to sustainable business practices. There are also so many contentious sustainability issues, which can make choices even more complicated;- for example, take the case of bamboo rayon. Does bamboo's sustainable production outweigh the impact of bamboo rayon's unsustainable manufacturing, or is it an environmental dead end for rayon producers? Is it worthwhile for a business to implement a sustainability strategy that has the possibility of being debunked later on?

When it comes to how sustainability affects the environment, it is important for consumers to understand the impact that conventional business practices have and why they need to change. Some of the specific reasons why conventional business practices have come under fire by environmental groups include an overreliance on fossil fuels, production of carbon, production of toxic waste, production of "heat pollution," and creation of landfill waste. Sustainability also affects the global population, which in itself is a social environmental issue. Here are but some of the general topics becoming areas of concerns for many companies: fossil fuels, carbon, toxic waste, heat pollution, general waste, as well as the growing need for social sustainability.

FOSSIL FUELS

Fossil fuels are fuels formed by the Earth's natural processes, such as anaerobic decomposition of dead organisms. The age of an organism and its resulting fossil fuels are typically about millions of years. Overall, fossil fuels contain high levels of carbon and use of them releases carbon into the atmosphere. Some fossil fuels that contain high percentages of carbon include petroleum, coal, and natural gas. Fossil fuels range from volatile materials with low carbon-to-hydrogen ratios, such as methane, to liquid petroleum to nonvolatile materials composed of almost pure carbon, like anthracite coal. However, many of the products we use make use of some types of fossil fuels.

Fossil fuels are an issue for a variety of reasons. When they are used, they create CO_2, water vapor, and a host of potentially toxic by-products, like carbon monoxide. They are also nonrenewable, so when they are gone, they are gone. Many products that rely on fossil fuels, like plastic items, can be made with other materials, like cellulose pulp, glass, aluminum, or cornstarch polymers. Sustainable practices that reduce a company's dependence on fossil fuels help reduce their production of CO_2 and other fossil fuel by-products, save fossil fuels for the industries that need them the most, and increase demand for green alternatives. Since many power plants still rely on coal as an energy source, companies that want to reduce their dependence on fossil fuels can start by switching to renewable energy, like solar panels, wind turbines, or hydroelectric dams. Companies without the space or means to set up their own renewable energy generators can purchase energy credits from places like commercial wind farms. This helps wind farms invest in more renewable energy technology and expand the number of customers they are capable of serving.

CARBON

Carbon is produced in many ways. One of the biggest offenders is fossil fuel usage, but it is also produced by combustion of other materials, decay, and respiration. Though many consumers laughed at the time, studies on the methane released by cow flatus have given us insight into how many things we take for granted are actually huge carbon producers. Carbon compounds, like methane and CO_2, contribute to global warming. They do this by functioning just like the panes of glass in a greenhouse: They allow rays of sunlight to pass through and contribute heat but do not allow that heat to dissipate back out into space. Sustainable practices that reduce carbon emissions may help slow climate change. Practices that remove carbon from the air, like tree planting programs and algae-based carbon scrubbers, may help curb or reverse it.

TOXIC WASTE

Many consumers envision toxic waste as barrels of green sludge, but a lot of toxic waste looks indistinguishable from clean air and water. Some compounds that are perfectly harmless in small, dilute quantities, like sodium hydroxide, are dangerous in concentrated amounts. When toxic waste is released into the air and water, it can either break down naturally or end up accumulating and causing problems further down the line. The concern about mercury in fish is an example of this. Pure mercury is extremely toxic, but nontoxic mercury compounds are used in all sorts of industries. When waste from these industries makes it to the environment, mercury can be released and absorbed by plants and animals. Fish absorb mercury from the water and from consuming other fish that had absorbed mercury. This resulted in certain types of fish deemed unsuitable for consumption by young children, pregnant women, or consumers with specific medical conditions. Sustainable practices that reduce the production of toxic waste can help protect air, water, and food sources. Some sustainability measures actually allow companies to reclaim raw materials from the waste produced by other industries, which helps keep toxins out of the environment.

HEAT POLLUTION

"Heat pollution" is just what it sounds like, the release of too much heat by manufacturing processes. This might not sound like much of an issue, since heat can dissipate more easily than something like industrial smoke, but it is. It is a particular problem for companies using water-cooling systems that eventually empty into natural bodies of water. Water contains dissolved oxygen, which has an inverse relationship between water's temperature and the amount of oxygen it can hold. When too much heat is released, oxygen levels in water drop. This causes large fish die-offs and boosts the growth of certain types of harmful algae. Sustainability measures that help reduce heat pollution mainly reroute waste heat to ventilation ducts, so it can be used to keep buildings warm, instead of using electric, oil, or gas-powered heating units.

GENERAL WASTE

When it comes to waste, landfills have been an issue for a long time. Ever since life began, things had to be disposed of. This can be everything from food waste to broken or worn out consumer goods. Landfills are a means for consumers to dispose of their waste in a centralized location, which keeps the surrounding area from accumulating mountains of waste. One problem now becomes space; space is at a premium and landfills cannot be used indefinitely, particularly since they are not the ideal setup to encourage decomposition. Most of them are too cool, too cramped, and too dry for waste to break down properly; and they are filled with all kinds of materials that take an extremely long time to decompose. Plastic bottles, for example, retain a recognizable form for over 20,000 years. Some sustainability measures focus on generating less waste by streamlining production methods—the less waste produced, the less of it has to go to a landfill—or by switching to biodegradable materials for products and packaging. Others do it by reusing or recycling things like paper, boxes, and other containers. Still others do it by composting, which creates an ideal environment for biodegradable materials to break down into fertilizer, instead of sitting in a landfill. As manufacturers are in the production business, they are the generator of the many products that ultimately need disposal. Taking a more responsible role in creating products that limit disposal is itself a challenge. One framework we discuss is called *biomimicry*, mimicry of nature. An underlying ideal is that nature finds a way to produce harmless waste, and in the optimized and ideal form, we need to achieve similar feats. This is discussed more in detail in Chapter 2, as we begin to fit together some of the issues and solutions that may exist as steps toward more sustainable practices.

SOCIAL SUSTAINABILITY

Last, social sustainability is another area that has a lot of impact. Many large companies send their production facilities overseas, where they can exploit things like lax child labor laws, human rights loopholes, and low employee wages to discover that sweatshops use can seriously damage a brand's image, and rightly so. Sweatshop workers are routinely overworked, abused, and even maimed by the machinery on which they work, for only pennies a day. By contrast, Fair Trade[10] practices pay laborers a livable wage for their efforts. This helps them improve their lives, send their children to school, and improve their country's economy as a whole. Since many workers getting fair wages produce organic crops and artisan goods, these social sustainability measures also help promote environmentally sustainable production methods.

THE IMPACT ON COMPANIES

Some companies are resistant to enacting sustainability initiatives; sometimes developing workable sustainability measures is a challenge. Things like solar panels, geothermal heating, and eco-friendly production methods are expensive and the cost-benefit analysis dictates that they continue with business as usual. In the current state of the economy, not many businesses can afford to do anything

---

[10]*Fair Trade* is a social movement and market-based approach that tries to help producers in developing countries achieve better trading conditions or fair trade opportunities for the goods they produce. As a practice, it is social and economic sustainability.

that cuts deeper into their profit margins. Therefore, sustainability initiatives are placed on the back burner without realizing the opportunities that lie within reach. Though switching to greener business practices and production methods may result in more overhead, it is becoming more critical than ever before for businesses to court eco-conscious consumers.

Surveys of consumers who consider themselves environmentally aware shoppers found that, on average, they tended to be older, have smaller households, and have higher incomes than the average consumer. A 2009 Deloitte study surveyed green consumers and reported that they bought more than they intended to roughly 29% of the times. Cultivating the kind of brand image that green customers are likely to take an interest in can net companies a base of higher paying shoppers that are not likely to stray. These shoppers are likely to increase a company's profits and provide for long-term growth.

Businesses can use several inexpensive measures to improve customers' perception of them and their products. Recycling can be done off-site, at a municipal recycling center. Internally, companies can do things like reuse printer paper as scrap paper, switch to recycled paper restroom products, and switch out disposable items for reusable ones (see Chapter 5). Not only do measures like these help reduce the amount of resources a company uses and the amount of waste it generates, they can help cut costs, too. Many businesses are also able to turn cost-cutting measures into sustainability programs that help improve their image among green consumers as well as employees. This has to be done with care, however; things that make a company look eco-friendly without actually having a quantifiable, beneficial impact on the environment are considered greenwashing.

While many of the issues listed reside in the domain of business operations, it is important to understand them, so we are prepared to engage at meaningful levels as we try to change the mindset of business practices in our own way, being aware of such pitfalls as "greenwashing."

GREENWASHING, CUSTOMER PERCEPTION, AND THE USER EXPERIENCE

As we become more acquainted with sustainability and it begins to enter common vernacular, we should also become familiar with another term, *greenwashing*.

Greenwashing is the environmental equivalent of corporate whitewashing and refers to the methods that some companies use to foster the idea that their products, production methods, or business practices are more environmentally and socially responsible than they really are. Anything that creates the illusion of sustainability is greenwashing. This ranges all the way from outright lying about a product's ingredients to redesigning logos and packaging to look more "natural." A popular example of corporate greenwashing was a famous oil company's "Consumers Do" advertising campaign. This advertising was directed toward green customers that were previously hostile to the company's business practices. Two years after its inception, surveys found that consumers who had been exposed to the advertising trusted the oil company more than its competition when it came to protecting the environment, even though the company had not actually enacted any sustainability initiatives.

Most, if not all, of a customer's experience is based on their perception of a brand. Studies have shown that customers are willing to excuse failings in a product if they like the company well enough. For a long time, greenwashing was a way for companies to keep their current production methods, save money by avoiding the switch to sustainability initiatives, and still court green customers. Greenwashing could be as simple as padding the description of a product using phrases like "Made with organic ingredients" or as complex as conducting in-depth research on what shade of green makes a package look more environmentally friendly.

In the United States, the Federal Trade Commission has the power to prosecute companies that make deceptive environmental claims about their products. This does not stop all forms of greenwashing; however, only instances in which companies actually lie. There are plenty of other greenwashing strategies, usually involving how customers perceive different packaging materials, images, and logos, that can still fly under the radar. However, while they are ethically questionable, they are not technically illegal.

While greenwashing might sound like a win-win solution at first blush (companies save time and money, while customers avoid feeling guilty about their purchasing decisions), it is usually ultimately not worth it. The amount of research that goes into greenwashing a brand can easily be invested in legitimate sustainability practices instead, and customers who find out that a company has dumped them with underhanded tactics can be absolutely merciless when it comes to boycotting and publicly criticizing its business ethics. Several grassroots watchdog organizations are on the prowl for greenwashed brands, and they generally do a good job of keeping green consumers informed.

Sometimes, attempts at greenwashing are pretty transparent. Since a lot of companies end up resorting to greenwashing tactics in the wake of bad press, like oil companies frequently do after spills and other disasters, greenwashing that gets noticed can just make a bad situation worse. Green shoppers are already hesitant to give their business to companies that are directly or indirectly responsible for ecological disasters, they will think even less of them if they feel deceived.

WHAT DOES GREENWASHING MEAN TO DESIGN?

When it comes to a customer or user's experience, greenwashing is one of the worst things that can happen. Greenwashing represents a betrayal of trust—green shoppers try a brand, like it, continue to use it, and frequently even recommend it to like-minded friends and family. They then find out that the "green" merit of the product was merely superficial. They end up feeling foolish for falling for it and guilty for recommending that product to others. Ultimately, though it might seem like an attractive option for businesses that want to court green shoppers, greenwashing is at best unethical and at worst a public relations disaster waiting to happen.

CARBON FOOTPRINTS

One of the ways in which companies and governments determine the impact that people and products have on the environment is thorough a carbon footprint. What exactly is a carbon footprint? Moreover, what is the design connection?

> A *carbon footprint* is "the total set of greenhouse gas (GHG) emissions caused by a person, a product, an organization or an event." It is often expressed in terms of the amount of carbon dioxide, or its equivalent of other GHGs, emitted.

As I researched this book and became more submerged in the activities surrounding sustainability, I was amazed by the variety of processes that companies employ in tracking down the carbon imprint as growing government regulations emerge and solidify into laws. A recent visit to the Apple website revealed that Apple is committed, like many of its industry peers, in finding out its carbon footprint.

Calculating a Carbon Footprint

To measure a company's environmental footprint, it is important to look at the impact its products have on the planet as they go through the cycle from creation to disposal. The standard for measuring CO_2 emissions is collecting the emitted carbon of products at each phase of the cycle of production (Figure 1.6), that is, from beginning to end.

For the past 2 years, Apple has used a comprehensive life-cycle analysis to determine where our greenhouse gas emissions come from (Figure 1.7). That means adding up the emissions generated from the manufacturing, transportation, use, and recycling of products, as well as the emissions generated by its facilities.

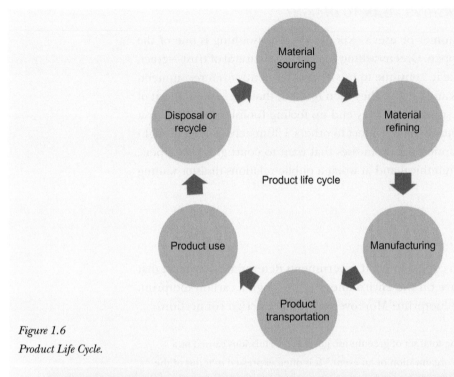

Figure 1.6
Product Life Cycle.

Figure 1.7
Breakdown of Apple's Environmental Footprint.

WHAT DO CARBON FOOTPRINTS MEAN TO DESIGN?

As designers from all walks of life, the most important thing we can do to reduce the environmental impact is to improve product design and in so doing improve the end user experience. At a tangible level, this means such things as designing products to use less material, optimizing packaging, using less toxic materials in the design and creating built-in enhancement that engages the user to embrace more sustainable habits, such as engaging them in energy saving practices or designing products that are serviceable when broken. In many instances, we are not the decision makers, but we can advocate for it. Further, pushing for innovative solutions that limit the use of energy is yet another means. As an interaction or user experience designer, perhaps, this means designing solutions that use the user interface to communicate with users about energy usage of devices and products left in idle states, yet still consuming energy. In addition, ensuring that the things we create are able to be recycled and customers know where to recycle these products. With every new product, we continue our progress toward minimizing our environmental impact.

SIGNS, SYMBOLS, AND VISUAL RATINGS OF THE ECO AGE

As the number of eco, green, ethical, and recycled products and initiatives increase around the world, there has been a bombardment of symbols and trademarks that will affect how we design (Figure 1.8). For now, it is important to

Figure 1.8

Signs, Symbols, and Visuals of the Eco Age.

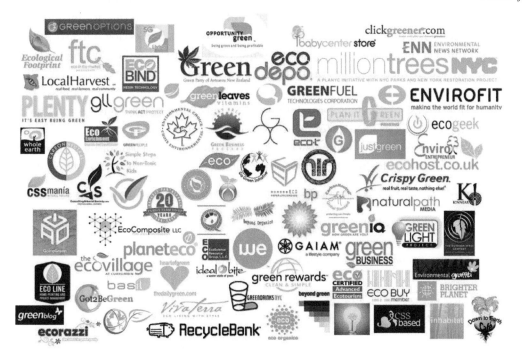

understand their presence and, to some degree, what some of them mean. Today as part of the greenwashing game, some designs that surface or simply used for marketing purposes to draw in naïve green consumers.

Many authoritative websites[11] provide guidance on symbol meaning. Some signs include Fair Trade, Energy Star, and 100% Recycle, but it is important to be mindful of the fact that, just because the logo is green and looks like it is natural, this does not mean that it is. It can be confusing knowing which symbols mean what when shopping for green products, but as legislation increases, we need to make sure our product knowledge is up to date when it comes to knowing which symbol does what and to understand how products we design fit into the eco molds.

SUSTAINABLE DESIGN ETHICS

The understanding that we all play a role in guarding our planet (steward-ship) and making sure the decisions we make do not jeopardize the future of our children and our children's children is rooted in the idea of conscious and sustainable design. This idea is also fast becoming the cornerstone of the value proposition in many industries. If you take a minute to think about recent busi-ness headlines, you will notice that many companies are making a splash about their Green IQ to appeal to users. From Johnson and Johnson to Wal-Mart to Nokia to British Petroleum (BP), across the vertical markets, the trend is becom-ing commonplace. In TV ads, Johnson and Johnson touts its care for the environ-ment, not only with a dedicated link on its website's main page but also a front and center credo, which reads, "We must maintain in good order the property we are privileged to use, protecting the environment and natural resources."[12]

Wal-Mart, likewise, advertises its green commitment in a "Sustainability" web link on its corporate website, letting site visitors know of Wal-Mart's commitment to reducing its carbon footprint. Rebounding from bad press in recent years, Wal-Mart is making a comeback, even going the distance, sponsoring and hosting many events dealing with environmental issues. The company has stated these three main goals:

1. To be supplied 100% by renewable energy.
2. To create zero waste.
3. To sell products that sustain people and the environment.

---

[11] http://www.easywaystogogreen.com/green-guides/guide-to-green-symbols/.
[12] http://www.jnj.com/connect/caring/environment-protection/health-planet.

Nokia, the Finnish mobile phone and software maker, is known for leading the way in thinking about end-of-life practices for disposal of their mobile phones (Figure 1.9). In recent years, focusing on applications that allow users to assess their mobile usage in terms of carbon footprinting has been an added feature of the Nokia phone brand. More and more companies are following this trend and adding this as a main value proposition of their company.

Figure 1.9
Nokia Recycling Initiatives.

In addition, the story of BP strikes fear at many companies' core as to what can happen if their products and processes cause damage to the environment. The company is still recovering from massive fines for oil spills in the Gulf of Mexico and suffers not only a financial loss but that of brand image. Companies now face the reality that, if they mess up, they will pay to clean up. And, this is not only relegated but the fact that is visible for all to see is becoming ever more true as the internet has created a platform for quick information dispersal that can be harmful when social networks and causes emerge to fight companies whose practices are detrimental to society.

Taking another tangent and looking at the dimension of power consumption and the impact of energy guzzling products, flash back to the mid-2000s when Apple received lots of bad press for its energy guzzling iPod, something that was fixed in subsequent models. While the idea of a device that sucked up energy, causing inconvenience to users is one thing, think about how an inefficiently designed system caused users to charge their devices very frequently. Could this defect have been supplemented with better messages in the user interface? Could notifying users of the idle states of their devices and automatic shutting or prompting users to take action?

We may never know.

What is apparent in these cases is that consciousness about what we design and how we design it is paramount, and as players in the field, we need to understand our roles as the paradigm shift is in flux. To create a sustainable world, we need to change our understanding of how the world works. The mechanistic model, stemming partly from the onset of the Industrial Era, which saw the world as a fixed, immobile thing, made up of isolated parts that interact in simple cause and effect relationships is being toppled on its head.

To create a sustainable balance, we need to understand that the world is interconnected and everything exists in communities. From this has emerged a key component of design thinking that purports, if we take cues from the natural world around us, we will find many of the design solutions that have survived in perpetuity as a source of inspiration. This concept is one that every designer should notice and is the first main concept for understanding the connection between the things we design and the world in which we live.

WRAPPING UP

Sustainability is not just about the environment; it is about the whole and not the parts; it is about everything—what we do, how we do it, where we do it, and with what. Sustainable design is the philosophy of designing products, processes, space, and services to comply with the principles of economic, ecological, social, and cultural sustainability, as defined earlier. It is also the idea that, when we design, we do so with an awareness and conscience that the products we create do not take away from the quality of existence for future generations as well as our own. An understanding of this basic principle and ideal is important as we think about our work from the practical perspective.

LOOKING THROUGH THE DESIGN LENS

The process by which we design influences human behavior; in other words, as we design, we create experiences for human beings. Often, we are goaded to think mainly of consumer products and their brands. Nevertheless, as the field grows, it embraces service and process experiences as well. There is a growing need to think about the experiences that we create and the collective impact on our social, economic, and environmental structures in the long and short terms. This unfolding revelation heralded a new and exciting niche for design professionals of all backgrounds, be it interaction, visual, industrial, or user experience.

IN THE NEXT CHAPTER

Chapter 2 focuses on the existing approaches and framework that can help in understanding sustainability from a design process perspective. These approaches help better situate and equip us with a theory as well as practice in employing a process to advance more sustainable design.

APPROACHES TO A SUSTAINABLE USER EXPERIENCE

INFORMATION IN THIS CHAPTER

- Approaches to Sustainable User Experience Design Practice
- Natural Capitalism
- Biomimicry
- Global Reporting Initiative
- Life Cycle Analysis
- Cradle-to-Cradle & Cradle-to-Grave
- Dow Jones Sustainability Index

INTRODUCTION

When we think of sustainability and user experience design as intertwined concepts, the key emerging principle is that a sustainable user experience design should exercise the key principles of sustainability and consider its three tangential ideals: economic, social, and ecological sustainability. What exactly does that mean?

A sustainable approach to design considers the impact of each design choice on humans beings in the present and future, on the environment, present and future, as well as the financial spheres. A sustainable user experience design considers that, once a design is conceptualized and created, it too resides in the system of dependencies. Its life, conception to disposal, is not separated from the system in which it resides, so that they all must operate as collectives and integrated entities.

For the most part, the practice of sustainability is in its infancy but also primed to explore the intersections at which concepts of user experience design and sustainability can engage in even more meaningful ways with the tangible structures that help us not only theorize but practice.

To date, we lack the tools, processes, methodologies, frameworks, and guiding models to drive a user experience–sustainability practice based on measures. However, the opportunities to align the two practices and create well-formed data gathering structures are there. There are opportunities to conjoin some of the approaches we encounter in the field of sustainability and map those back to our established toolsets and methods to create a powerful fusion practice that has impact. Consider a simple example on the research side of our practice: Most of the carbon emitted by a product in the "usage" phase.

User experience design is all about a user-centric approach to design. We use our skills as master ethnographers and contextual researchers every day to observe and gather data to inform design. In our role as researchers, we can already extend our work to gather the product's sustainability as input to more informed design. For example, if users are frustrated because physical designs do not last or are not durable, this is a clear and direct data input that can be tabled for discussion with materials handling and industrial design teams for improved product durability. Alternatively, if a product, like a camera, cannot hold a charge, users are inclined to dispose of it in favor of better models. When users dispose of products because of poor designs that break or simply do not meet their needs the waste impact is great. Collected unit data can help us formulate more compound data that can forecast usage churn rates. When we can measure this unit impact, we can extrapolate and measure compound impact. It is through measures that we are able to create any level of traction to get higher level buy-in for advancing sustainable design thinking in industry.

Those who have been in the field of usability for a while know of the initial struggles of evangelizing and trying to demonstrate usability and design return on investment (ROI). While sustainability is slightly different, in that it is initiative driven more rigorously by the current environmental imperatives and regulations, we will encounter similar challenges when weaving it into our daily practice. However, as mandates by government authorities and consumers demands become the norm, the emergence of guiding models and methodologies will be necessary to enable measures.

In this chapter, I use the words *framework* and *approaches* interchangeably to subsume the terms *methods, tools, approaches,* and *models* as a language to discuss the concept of frameworks that we can use to exercise a sustainable design practice. Following are some of the evolving approaches used in the field of sustainability; they are explored in detail in the next section of this chapter.

APPROACHES TO A SUSTAINABLE USER EXPERIENCE DESIGN PRACTICE

I always have some trepidation in beginning to talk about sustainability frameworks, because I strongly believe that to talk about one approach inherently deflects and seemingly negates others. When it comes to most things in life, the perfect solution always lies somewhere in the middle, and so the frameworks that follow are merely a sampling of the current and more widely known ones that can form some base for thinking about our field. Each framework can be seen as a menu of inspirations for discovering even more applicable ones for your needs.

In Nathan Shedroff's pivotal book, *Design Is the Problem* (2009), he references a few of these frameworks or approaches, as he calls them, from a high level design perspective. He goes further to outline how these frameworks may be applied in the design and development life cycle. These frameworks or approaches are later discussed in Chapter 4 alongside the design and development lifecycle for more relevance to the work we do as user experience practitioners. While many frameworks are taking shape in the wider field of sustainability, I focus primarily on those more suited for our field with some shorter introductions to the more remotely applicable ones as a context and point of reference. The following are some of the key sustainability approaches and their significance in context of user experience and design:

1. **Natural capitalism:** Founded by Hawken, Lovins, and Lovins (1999), this framework provides some founding principles and is a manifesto for modern day sustainability design thinking. Natural capitalism, the concept, is described as a system of four interlinking principles, where business and environmental interests overlap and in which businesses can satisfy their customers' needs, increase profits, and help solve environmental problems all at the same time. It entails a change in the form of business transactions from occasionally making and selling things to providing a more continuous flow of value and service. This model seeks to change the relationship between the businesses and the customer, so instead of having contradictory interests, they have completely aligned interests.

2. **Biomimicry (aka biomimetics):** Popularized by Janine Benyus (1997, 2002), this framework appeals to designers looking for innovative and creative sources for design patterns and inspiration from nature. The framework purports that animals, plants, as well as microbes are the consummate engineers and that they have much to offer in the space of research and development (R&D). Much as we can query a system for solutions, we should look to the first R&D lab (nature) as a source of inspiration for design. After all, nature amassed over millions of years data on survival; it knows what works, what is appropriate, and most important, what lasts here on Earth. Accordingly, this approach consults with nature (organisms and ecosystems) and applies the underlying design principles from nature to our innovations. This approach has also introduced a new realm for entrepreneurship that contributes to designs and solutions with nature as the guide to design thinking.

3. **Total beauty:** Formalized by Edwin Datschefski (n.d.), this framework translates the often qualitative concept of "beauty" into quantitative language and demonstrates how it

connects to the ideals of sustainability. The framework asserts that sustainable products are those that are the best for society (people), business (profits), and the planet. The founder of this framework asserts that products are the source of all environmental problems, such as pollution, deforestation, species loss, and global warming. Further, those ecological and social issues are becoming more important than ever before. The role of design and therefore designers is becoming even more vital. Many beautiful-looking products have an underlying and hidden ugliness, but there should be some revelation of these "ugly" points that have environmental and social impacts redesigned to create products that have a "total beauty."

4. **Life-cycle analysis (LCA):** Popular and prevailing models that look at the product or process life cycle and the issues of waste (a key factor and by-product of design). Life-cycle assessment evaluates the environmental burdens associated with a product, process, or activity by identifying and quantifying energy and materials used and wastes released into the environment. The assessment includes the entire life cycle of the product, process, or activity: encompassing, extracting, and processing raw materials; manufacturing, transportation, and distribution; use, reuse, and maintenance; recycling; and final disposal. As an approach, LCA holds tremendous opportunities for a close alignment to user experience design as a practice. It also enables us to view the process of a product's existence in phases, where we can better view the factors along the continuum and more readily set up a framework to drive assessment.

5. **Cradle-to-cradle (C2C or cradle-2-cradle):** A fusion approach that embraces LCA and biomimicry, it assumes that a product should not have a "death" and that waste or nutrients must be managed. In this approach, McDonough and Braungart (2002) argue that an industrial system that "takes, makes, and wastes" can become a creator of goods and services that generate ecological, social, and economic value. Total beauty design is a framework for designing products and industrial processes that converts materials into "nutrients" by enabling the formation of cyclical material flow metabolisms. In many ways, it has some features similar to biomimicry. In this design approach, waste is food for another product or process. For example, the proponents of this approach have assisted in the design a Ford SUV that is fully recyclable in 5 years. Essentially, the vehicle is leased out, it is returned 5 years later, and the materials are reused in such a way that maximizes use and minimizes waste that cannot be reused. Another example that exemplifies this framework is the Kindle and other readers. In the case of the Kindle, Amazon going through a paradigm shift where it is enabling the once waste producing and resource consuming market of book production, a new platform where books can be more of a service in the form of electronic books. This is different from cradle to grave (C2G), which is less stringent, in that it assumes that products have a "death" and hence waste, which should be managed. It is therefore more business-friendly and less idealistic than C2C and realistically the most commonly embraced by businesses in transition to a C2C approach.

OTHERS FRAMEWORKS

The following frameworks are more in context, as they are subsumed by the ones mentioned earlier or bear less relevance to our work:

6. **Social return on investment (SROI):** The social return on investment analysis framework focuses mainly on wider social environmental concerns. It is a departure from natural capitalism and seeks to understand the financial value that accrues to society in context of sustainability practices.

7. **Sustainability helix:** First cited in Shedroff's Design is the Problem, the sustainability helix is a strategic tool for businesses and organizations to help "drive sustainability into the companies' DNA." This model builds on the ideals of commitment to monitor a company's progress. The sustainability helix covers three domains of sustainability: social, environmental, and financial.

8. **The natural step:** Founded in 1989 by Dr. Karl-Henrik Robèrt in Sweden (*The Natural Step*, n.d.), this framework focuses primarily on the impact of our activities on the biosphere, at large. It is a comprehensive model for planning in systems that are more complex and is openly published and free for all to use.

9. **ISO 14000:** The ISO 14000 family of guidance documentation addresses various aspects of environmental management (ISO, n.d.). It provides guidance for such things as life-cycle analysis. This approach currently has more traction in Europe, where ISO is more entrenched in business practices. It is much like the ISO guidance on usability with which many are familiar.

10. **Global Reporting Initiative:** The GRI is currently the only recognized international initiative that focuses on reporting an organization's sustainability performance using a hierarchical framework in three focus areas: social, economic, and environmental. It is similar to natural capitalism and this framework looks to cover all the main elements highlighted in Natural Capitalism (Hawken et al., 1999). I expand later on this framework, as it can provide some insight into how we can later configure research findings to help drive some of the reporting initiatives.

11. **Leadership in Energy and Environmental Design (LEED):** Developed by the U.S. Green Building Council (USGBC), LEED provides the building industry a concise framework for identifying and implementing practical and measurable ecologically sound building design, construction, operation, and maintenance solutions.

The next section presents the sustainability approaches, first looking at the basics of each and showing the potential points of connection with user experience and design. The format of this chapter is as follows:

1. Understanding the approach or model: *The what.*
2. Key benefits and shortcomings of the approach: *The benefits.*
3. Application of the model for a user experience practice, how it applies to design and design research and examples of the model, where possible: *The application.*

The Context: The Sustainability Movement

The most critical engagement of the sustainability movement in the psyche of design perhaps started in the 1960s and was rejuvenated in the 1970s. At that point, growing public concern for the environment was inspired by Rachel Carson's book *Silent Spring*, published in 1962. In fact, the book is widely credited with helping launch the environmental movement. Carson's book highlights the dangers of pesticides to both ecosystems and humans. Her book was spotlighted in the *New Yorker* and serialized, thereby entrenching into the art world a need for action.

Later, the scientist James Lovelock wrote his "Gaia hypothesis," positing that the Earth is a self-regulating organism, which can keep its climate and chemistry at a state suitable for life. In the same year, 1968, Bill Andes, while on the Apollo 8, presented the world at large with a snapshot of Planet Earth, a scene never before seen. Only a year later, the environmental group Friends of the Earth was formed, undoubtedly as a by-product of all these preceding publications and events. What emerges out of Lovelock's Gaia Hypothesis and the Andes' presentation of the world was the nothing that the Earth is a living self-regulating entity. In early 1970, Greenpeace was founded. At around the same time, the first energy crisis occurred, further alerting us to the dangers of relying on fossil fuels for our existence. Soon after the "hippie" generation began to voice concern over what was happening, not only in Vietnam but also the world at large. At this time, Victor Papanek (1971) and a small number of other pioneers in the design world started to examine the ways of making products. Victor Papanek was a designer, educator, and environmentalist who became a strong advocate of the socially and ecologically responsible design of products, tools, and community infrastructures. His writings, lectures, and designed products were collectively considered an example of ecologically sound designs and inspired many designers.

From a wider lens, we can view the unfolding in terms of waves, for lack of a better term. I propose here four waves of movement that can easily be mapped to the following general timeframes:

1. The Hippie (1960s and 1970s).
2. The Consumer (1980s–late 1990s).
3. Government (late 1990s–early 2000s).
4. Manufacturing Company (mid-2000s to now).

The first wave arose due to a growing awareness of environmental problems that lead to the emergence of environmental *action groups*, also referred in some circles as the *Hippie movement*. The second wave occurred when *consumers'* collective consciousness started to demand more environmentally friendly products because of concerns over further environmental crises. The third wave can be seen in terms of the growing world awareness and realization that we are in a global crisis. *Government* and other organizations, driven by politics began to hear the voices of the movement and institute laws that would help address the growing list of environmental issues. In the fourth wave, we have the push and traction from regulations driving a change in behavior by many of manufacturing *companies*, which control the means of production and are a key contributor to the production of environmental waste.

To address some of these issues, designers were placed in the proverbial hot seat of the movement, because fundamentally the issues that affect the environment seemed to be rooted in "bad" design. And, if designers could become better informed, then this would be one step closer to addressing some of the issues created by poorly designed products that use natural resources, are designed poorly, work inefficiently, and subsequently end up in the landfill with no counter or curbing action to diminish and eliminate the waste created.

The emphasis on design, to date, is on the creation of material, in the form of consumerism, whereas it should be on products, services, and systems that meet human needs, in other words, sustainable design. This ideal is reflected in the Kyoto Protocol of 1997, which set the goal for the reduction of greenhouse gas emissions. In 2002, the second World Summit on Sustainable Development was held. Although decisions were made on a number of issues, it was agreed on that progress toward sustainable development was slower than expected.

In the same year the Kyoto Protocol was approved (2005), designer John Thackara's book, *In the Bubble: Designing in a Complex World*, was published. It called for a change in design culture. One of the main problems designers had to face was where to start.

In his book, Thackara pushes the ideals of dematerialization. He asserts that the design focus is on services not materials. At the core of *In the Bubble* is the belief that ethics and responsibility can inform design decisions without hindering social and technical innovation.

The Kyoto Protocol provided some guidance in this regard. The Kyoto report highlighted six themes seen as problem areas suitable for design to solve: "quality of life, efficient use of natural resources, protecting the global commons, managing human settlements, the use of chemicals and the management of human and industrial waste, and fostering sustainable economic growth on a global scale." It was at this critical juncture that designers became engaged at a higher level to play a role in the movement. Many of the approaches that follow in this book bear remnants of the Kyoto Protocol. More recently other books that have brought to light the problem of design in context of stainability is Shedroff's *Design is the Problem* which reiterates Thackara's call for a change in the culture of design.

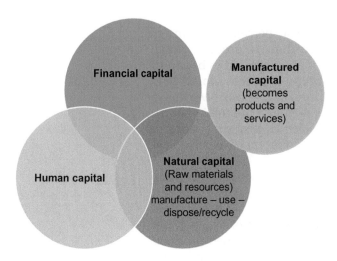

Financial capital

Manufactured capital (becomes products and services)

Human capital

Natural capital (Raw materials and resources) manufacture – use – dispose/recycle

Figure 2.1
Natural Capitalism Framework.

NATURAL CAPITALISM

Natural capitalism, one of the concepts mentioned briefly in Chapter 1 is a forerunner of the approaches, which was popularized in the book of the same title, *Natural Capitalism*, by Hawken, Lovins, and Lovins (1999). At its core, natural capitalism, as an approach, is most applicable in the context of business practices, rather than directed at design in the sense in which we understand it. The authors, however, mention the adoption of biomimicry as one of the shifts that could be embraced to begin more sustainable design and development overtime.

Natural Capitalism, the book as well as its emanating principles (Figure 2.1), asserts that most businesses still operate according to outdated production principles and not much has changed since the Industrial Revolution, when natural resources were abundant and labor was the limiting factor of production. Today, however, there is a surplus of people but natural capital (resources as well as the ecological systems), which provides vital life-support services, is in decline and very costly. Hence, the approach, as a framework, can be viewed as one that looks at design and development (as part of the production process) as having an impact on the overall depletion of social and natural resources.

This model explicitly asserts that, for something to be considered sustainable, it should be gauged not only on its environmental impact but the social and financial effects as well. Hawken et al. identify four types of capital that can be used as foundational to any measure to determine a whether the business activity of "production" is sustainable: *human, financial, manufactured,* and *natural,* defined as follows by the author:

1. **Human capital** is in the form of labor and intelligence, culture, and organization.
2. **Financial capital** consists of cash, investments, and monetary instruments.
3. **Manufactured capital** includes infrastructure, machines, tools, and factories.
4. **Natural capital** is made up of resources, living systems, and ecosystem services.

In addition to these "capitals," Hawken et al., introduce four central strategies of natural capitalism, which enable positive ecological behavior, where all forms of capital are valued. The goals of embracing this behavior are

1. Averting scarcity of resources.
2. Perpetuating abundance.
3. Providing a solid basis for social development, as it is the basis for responsible stewardship and prosperity for present and future generations.

Strategies That Can Halt Degradation

1. **Radical resource productivity:** Natural capitalism emphasizes that radically increased resource productivity is the cornerstone of natural capitalism, because using resources more effectively has three significant benefits. It
   a. Slows resource depletion at one end of the value chain.
   b. Lowers pollution at the other end.
   c. Provides a basis to increase worldwide employment with meaningful jobs.
   The result can be lower costs for business and society, which no longer has to pay for the chief causes of ecosystem and social disruption. This point holds a lot of current relevance, as we have seen the British Petroleum (BP) catastrophe of 2010.[1]

   Nearly all environmental and social harm is a by-product of the uneconomical, wasteful use of human and natural resources. Therefore, "radical" resource productivity strategies can nearly halt the degradation of the biosphere, make it more profitable to employ people, and thus safeguard against the loss of vital living systems and social cohesion.

2. **Biomimicry:** Popularized by Janine Benyus, biomimicry is seen as a way in which humans can eliminate the wasteful throughput of materials by optimizing design through mimicking nature. The idea here is that nature does not "by nature" create waste—humans do. This is accomplished by redesigning industrial systems on biological lines that change the nature of industrial processes and materials, enabling the reuse of materials, and often the elimination of toxicity.

3. **Service and flow economy:** This calls for a fundamental change in the relationship between producer and consumer (end users), a shift from an economy of goods and purchases to one of *service* and *flow*. The change entails a new perception of the value of things, where we shift from the acquisition of goods as a measure of affluence to an economy where the continuous receipt of quality, utility, and performance promotes well-being. This concept offers incentives to put into practice the first two innovations of natural capitalism by restructuring the economy to focus on relationships that better meet customers' changing value needs and reward automatically both resource productivity and closed-loop cycles of materials use, meaning essentially a no-waste cycle.

4. **Investing in natural capital:** This works toward reversing planetary destruction through reinvestments in sustaining, restoring, and expanding natural capital, so that the biosphere can produce more abundant ecosystem services and natural resources.

---

[1]The BP oil spill in the Gulf of Mexico, which flowed for 3 months in 2010, is to date the largest accidental marine oil spill in the history of the petroleum industry.

All of the preceding are interrelated and interdependent and all four touch on the four capitals and help enhance them in some way or another: creation of jobs, economies (money), improvement of environment, as well as having great social impact.

What Does It Mean to User Experience and Design Practitioners?

Taken individually, these "shifts" in behavior may not seem like much in terms of influencing changes in our collective practices. However, as part of a wider puzzle, we can situate ourselves as designers who embrace more ethical design thinking as well as ones who not only look for the common approaches to problem solving and design but are open to solutions within the sphere of more natural means, such as biomimicry.

> When engineers speak of *efficiency*, they refer to the amount of output a process provides per unit of input. Higher efficiency thus means doing more with less, measuring both factors in physical terms.[2]

Benefits and Shortcomings of Natural Capitalism

Overall, *Natural Capitalism*, the book as well as the framework, is a great manifesto for the practice of sustainable design. It also provides a fundamental landscape for containing how we speak about the overall design and development impact (the capitals). As many user experience firms begin to embrace sustainable design at various levels of engagement, it is likely that such tools as heuristics and processes to help quickly gauge product performance in terms of adhering to sustainable design principles or heuristics will transpire. This may be years in the coming, but as regulations emerge, as inevitable they will, user experience and design could one day be a gatekeeper contributing to sustainability design scorecards that enable and drive wider reporting.

Natural capitalism also provides a high-level framework that helps companies think strategically about their approach to production. Of note, one of the world's largest flooring companies, Interface Corporation, already embraces this framework in practice. Interface Corporation chairman Ray Anderson, a well-known advocate of sustainability or eco-friendliness, provides a top-down management lesson in driving home a new way of thinking in business. Concepts such as *rethink*, *reuse*, and *recycle* are real elements of the production process. Moreover, the company has gone from selling just carpet (which generally ends up in waste landfill) to leasing "floor-covering surfaces." This allows it to reduce both waste and costs and to improve its bottom line (more sales via the leased covering) and overall green IQ scoring in the eyes of its customers.

---

[2]*Natural Capitalism* (Hawken et al., 1999).

BIOMIMICRY

The term *biomimicry* was popularized by Janine Benyus in her 1997 book *Biomimicry: Innovation Inspired by Nature*, in which she defined the term as a "new science that studies nature's models and then imitates, or takes inspiration from these designs and processes to solve human problems." She proposes looking to nature as a "Model, Measure, and Mentor" and emphasizes sustainability as an objective of biomimicry. Concisely, the key operating principles of biomimicry is that it could be used as a model, measure, and mentor to help measure and gauge the design.

1. **Model:** The emulation of nature's forms, processes, systems, and strategies to solve human problems sustainably.
2. **Measure:** The use of an ecological standard to judge the sustainability of innovations. After 3.8 billion years of evolution, nature has learned what works and what lasts.
3. **Mentor:** The reviewing and revaluing of nature to introduce an era based not on what we can extract from the natural world but what we can learn from it.

Benyus presents nature as the source of over 3.5 billions of years of research and development, which we can use as inspiration and a model for design. She views nature as an R&D lab with 10 million species to mimic.

> Biomimicry is the mimicking of life using biological systems.[3]

The notion that humans are not the first designers is clear and humbling; she also asserts that design processes should consider welcoming biologists to the design lab, as they can be useful in guiding the design process to include more biometrics in the decision-making process.

Shown in Figure 2.2 is the Woodpecker Axe, inspired by a woodpecker. A woodpecker hammers out 25 pecks per second, hitting a tree trunk with an impact that would rip out the brains of other birds. Consider that the woodpecker, a master chiseler, which typically weighs a pound, uses its entire body for each blow: The tail acts as a brace and spring, and the configuration of spine and skull helps distribute the impact.

---

[3] http://dictionary.reference.com/browse/biomimicry.

Figure 2.2
Woodpecker Axe, Inspired by Nature.

Researchers studying the woodpecker's biomechanics found that its body is designed specifically for this movement. Woodpeckers brace themselves with their tails, which function as springs, taking advantage of both their center of gravity and their skull-bone configuration to absorb considerable stress. In other words, the woodpecker does not hammer on the wood by using its neck. And so the axe consists of an inner core of titanium into which is inserted an adjustable aluminum point. These two parts are attached by a hinge inspired by the two valves of a mollusk, another nature inspired solution. Special attention was given to the handle. Rather than designing it to be straight, it incorporates a slight curve, again taking the body of the woodpecker as a model. When completed this improves the efficiency of the blow.

"Organisms have figured out a way to do the things they do, while taking care of the place that's going to take care of their offspring."[4]

Benyus also points out a few basic principles of nature and their application to design thinking.

Many of these principles directly affect the design process and do not need much explanation. Though sometimes decisions are beyond the control of designers and user experience professionals, there are opportunities for us to engage and illustrate these biometric principles. With time and focused evangelism, we may help drive a paradigmatic shift in product design and manufacturing altogether and at all levels of a company's production and process design. Some biometrics principles follow:

1. Nature runs on sunlight.
2. Nature uses only the energy it needs.
3. Nature fits form to function.
4. Nature recycles everything.
5. Nature rewards cooperation.
6. Nature banks on diversity.
7. Nature demands local expertise.
8. Nature curbs excesses from within.
9. Nature taps the power of limits.

These same principles are the basis on which many biomimicry design consultants spearheaded a growing field of new design thinking. For designers, the connection between design and biomimicry is a direct and apparent one,

---

[4]http://www.ted.com/talks/janine_benyus_shares_nature_s_designs.html.

as the physical and more tangible aspects of a designer's work makes it easier to practice natural design and see inspiration in the natural environment.

Some other, more commonly known examples of biomimicry as it pertains to design follow, including the design of Velcro.

Velcro fasteners were designed by Swiss engineer George de Mestral in 1940, who observed how the hooks of the plant burrs adhered to his clothing and his dog. Observation of this under a microscope showed him numerous tiny "hooks" belonged to the plant. This discovery resulted in design of Velcro as we know it today.

Another very similar invention is Gecko tape, which was designed by Manchester University scientists. This design was inspired by the gecko lizard's ability to adhere to walls as it climbed. The gecko feet with its adhesive lamellae was used as the inspiration for Velcro fasteners. As in the Velcro case, the gecko foot (Figure 2.3) has tiny hairlike structures, called *seta*, that enable this temporary binding quality and can be released with an easy pullback.

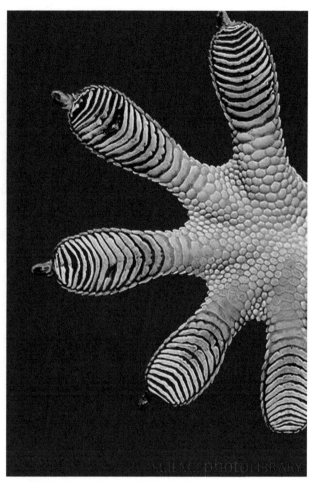

Figure 2.3
Gecko Foot.

To help us think about more concrete biomimicry applications, the biomimicry site, http://www.asknature.org, created a database where users can go in a query how nature has dealt with certain designs. Here, designers, specifically, can query the site's database to see how nature designs specific solutions (Figure 2.4).

In thinking of biomimicry as a general topic, it seems fitting to also spend some time on a the related field of natural user interfaces as well as some of the principles that have a foundation in nature.

Natural User Interfaces

Natural user interfaces (NUI) is a field of interface design where natural human abilities are leveraged to weave in technology. Tangential to biomimicry, NUI, an emerging field in human-machine interaction, leverages some of the natural human abilities and builds on them to integrate artificial technology woven into learned human interactions. The word *natural* in this context is used because most computer

Figure 2.4
Ask Nature.org.

interfaces use artificial control devices whose operation has to be learned. An NUI relies on a user being able to carry out relatively natural gestures that are quickly discovered to control the computer application or manipulate the onscreen content.

NUI is an area that focuses on traditional human abilities, such as vision, touch, speech, handwriting, motion, as well as cognition, creation, and exploration to replicate real world environments to optimize interaction between physical and digital objects.

In terms of the connection of NUI to biomimicry, we can look at it in terms of using the natural world around us as inspiration. In pure biomedics, we look to nature as a "mentor" and "model." In NUI, we look at the natural abilities of humans to inspire and model to generate new modes of interaction. In both cases, nature provides us an array of solutions for many complex design problems—the quest to learn from nature in this way is biomimicry and NUI design. Both have as a founding principle leveraging nature and the natural to drive design. Both consider the efficient and diminished use of natural resources as well, a concept introduced earlier, called *dematerialization.*

While NUI is one area in which dematerialization is sometimes a key benefit, where artificial components are woven into the human frame (Figure 2.5), the long-term effects are not yet known and therefore should be viewed with caution.

What Does It Mean to User Experience and Design Practitioners?

In terms of the multidisciplinary approach, user experience, as a field of study, is one step ahead of many fields, because we already embrace a multidisciplinary approach to our work. Our scientific practice is created through the meshing of various disciplines, flushing out more objective solutions than fields with one approach.

In fact, user-centered design firms, like Boston-based IDEO (Figure 2.6), are already at the forefront of including biomimicry as part of their design process, aligning biomimicry and sustainable design practices alongside development life cycles. And this is perhaps only the tipping point of what will ensue, as user experience has a legacy of interdisciplinary practice and innovative and creative ways to address design problems.

In my 12 years as a user experience professional, I have come across a myriad of professionals practicing in the field of experience, including mathematicians, architects, neurologists, and those from other seemingly unassociated disciplines. Despite distinct contribution to the field, user experience becomes less pliable by embracing an interdisciplinary perspective of design for any design problem. Lessening the pliability makes for more objectivity in design, thereby adding to the overall reception

Figure 2.5

Microsoft Skinput Turns an Arm into a Touch Screen.

Figure 2.6

Biologists joining the IDEO design team, Courtesy of IDEO.

by those who prefer evidence based on more scientific measures. Therefore, an increase in the user experience professionals with biomimicry training is advantageous for our filed; ultimately, it will create more opportunity for growth of our field. While there are many courses now in the area of biomimicry,[5] we should begin to ask ourselves as we solve design problems:

1. Are there similar patterns in nature?
2. What are they?
3. How is it done?
4. How does nature get rid of the waste created in designing similar systems?

A living website database, www.asknature.com, has been created by the Biomimicry Institute to help designers find solutions for design problems. In Benyus's book and her many talks, most notably a renowned TED talk done on the topic (Janine Benyus Shares Nature's Designs, n.d.), she talks about the offerings of nature's principles to the design process and mentions 12 of these principles.

In many cases, we are not the decision makers who ultimately decide what materials and processes contained and created by the output of our user experience and design work. However, we use of research to determine whether a solution is viable through testing with representative users, essentially seeing what is natural to our users. Further extending our research to see how we can optimize designs to respond to real user needs and, at the same time, infuse designs with smarter, more sustainable solutions would entail looking in our natural environment to see if nature's solutions can help curb some of the problems created by our designs. In addition, as many of us work in virtual design spaces, we also need to be acutely aware that, as we create virtual solutions, many of these solutions existed once in some form in the physical world and harnessing this knowledge can be very beneficial for their virtual counterpart.

Facebook's Privacy and Security and Security Model–Biomimicry Challenge?

A year before the Facebook security fiasco, I attended an innovation session on privacy and security. At my table of six designers as well as legal teams well placed to capture Intellectual Property. I commented that Facebook would face major issues in the near future because its model of how a *friend* is defined and who gets access to personal information. Facebook's model of "friendship" assumed that everyone had the same degree of relationship and therefore should have full access to all aspects of a user's Facebook life, including links to view other friends.

When you think about the physical world, the same does not hold true. We have friends and acquaintances from different realms—private and public, work, and other life activities—and many of us desire that they never coincide. Some of our friends and acquaintances have access to our private lives and some have access to our public life profile, some are business and some are family, and so on. However, in the Facebook model, the world is turned upside down—in fact all jumbled. There seems to be an equidistant relationship with all friends, with no difference in terms of how the user feels about the closeness of that relationship. In addition, "friends" could access each other via the user's Facebook page as a connector. On Facebook, the degree of separation was scarily close, especially for those of us who guard our private lives a bit more than others.

It was, and still remains, a complicated model in many respects and a challenge for user experience designers to come up with a privacy model for a social networking site that can be aligned with a magical algorithm taking into consideration the many complexities of real life relationships.

What is clear is that, on many levels, the Facebook model of privacy and security is flawed.

Recently, I had a conversation with a friend, who happens to be a professor. He recounted how his Facebook had become "weird." On Facebook, he now has other professors, his ex-wife and her family members, an ex-girlfriend as well as a new girl-friend, and his students as friends. He would like to "unfriend"[6] a few people but his gentle nature makes it awkward. Therefore, he has imposed a self-banishment and "hiding" in the Facebook world that has become awkward and hard to manage. This example is a recurring theme of the many who are seeking virtual refuge by taking down their Facebook accounts or simply hiding by creating fake profiles.

On the popular site www.mashables.com[7] over 5000 Facebook users were surveyed. They were asked: Why are you trying to leave Facebook? And, 42% of those surveyed indicated it had to do with issues of privacy and security of their personal information (30% do not trust Facebook with their personal information, another 10% believe Facebook sells their information, and 2% do not want people seeing their chats and messages).

How could a model that had looked so promising have gone so wrong? While still popular on some levels, the company is losing the cache afforded to more business-minded social network sites, like LinkedIn, which is used by many as a virtual resume and network tool.

The Facebook model made me think of my own life, growing up in in the Caribbean in what is often called the *colonies*, for lack of a better and more politically correct term. As a child, my family had many unspoken house rules limiting the

---

[6]This is the term used for Facebook users who delete "friends" from their account.
[7]May 2010: http://9.mshcdn.com/wp-content/uploads/2010/05/Screen-shot-2010-05-25-at-3.19.26-PM.png.

access of certain people who would come to the house. This practice seemed so indoctrinated and institutionalized in our daily lives that I never gave it a second thought. Like many better-off homes in the Caribbean, farm workers always were in the vicinity as well as other helpers, such as housekeepers and other laborers. Implicit in our day-to-day living were all these unspoken cues to assert one's privilege over less privileged. Some people had access only to the "house" and could use the house restrooms, while others were never allowed in the bedrooms or bathrooms. I remember having certain friends from school who were prevented access into the house beyond the kitchen and the living room. The grownup relatives around kept a sharp eye on who was inside and outside. They justified it by saying that they may "take something" or gossip about our family and that you could never be too careful, especially in a small village, where privacy was almost nonexistent.

Much later in life, I revisited the Caribbean after living years abroad and I was exposed once again to some of the old ways. It got me to think of privacy and security, in the context of Facebook.

On this visit, I spent some time on my uncle's estate, where many workers were moving around but very interested in my husband and me. It was not every day they had guests at the farmhouse. Then, my uncle mentioned how important it was to maintain old ways or else everyone "knows your business," they become overly familiar, the "proper" social boundaries are violated, and you can "never go back" to the relationship as it was.

The context that spurred this discussion follows: One of the new farm workers had found his way nearer to the house and started a conversation with my husband about what it was like living in a "cold" country. Snow and just all things foreign fascinated him. Just then, my uncle and his wife joined us. The worker, trying to be nice, remarked that the Burberry perfumes we gave, as a gift, to my aunt-in-law smelled wonderful; he had never smelled anything like it. All but my uncle enjoyed the encounter, which resulted in my uncle reprimanding him, telling him to get back to work, and essentially not to attempt to communicate with us. Personally, a part of me was embarrassed for the worker; another part was repulsed by this colonial ideal. Moreover, while we did engage the worker in conversation many times afterward, it was very awkward for my Dutch husband, who simply found the postcolonial mindset very uncomfortable. He seemed to have spent lots of time moderating and self-censuring himself when in contact with the workers.

While sitting at the innovation session, I drew an analogy of this encounter with the Facebook model and began thinking of nature's examples and how they can be used as a foundation for design. I began to think that, while this grotesque postcolonial model endured for generations, it might hold cues for how a privacy and security model can be redesigned to maintain more desirable and realistic definitions of what friendship could look like.

Adopting this colonial model could allow some insight into controlling the level of distancing and exposure of "friends" to each other as well as the degrees of access to themselves. This "house access" and access to people should be very much the same as understanding the wider community access and spoke to me as a model on which Facebook could have built a better system altogether.

I subsequently closed my Facebook account because of the inability to define clearly virtual boundaries with my "friends." The idea that my boss could be in the same virtual room as my precocious 14-year-old cousin and my not-so-politically correct uncle was rather disturbing. Essentially, if I threw a party, I would be horrified if they were all together. The full extent of my life was exposed with little control over my privacy and security. Adopting a model seen in nature (the house access), though not biological in the true sense, was the first inkling of how we can begin to look outside the realm of known design patterns to think about design solutions that can sustain overtime.

As I neared the completion of this book, Google launched Google Circles, a social network solution that takes into consideration some of the shortcomings of Facebook. This includes such features as warnings when information shared within small circles is reshared outside the initial circle. Second is the ability to create small circles of networks; third is an ability to create richer definitions of *friendship*, so that not all "friends" hold the same degree and level of importance to you as the nexus of your own circles.

Undoubtedly, as we learn about the true nature of networks, an ultimate solution will evolve that suits the virtual renditions of friendships.

Toward a Biomimicry Design Process

The Biomimicry Guild proposes a process by which designers can begin to assess their design against natural principle of design (Figure 2.7). It will be very familiar to user experience and design processes that many of us, when designing and evaluating a design.

The following steps, taken from the Biomimicry Design Guild website, outline the fuller checklist of biomimicry principles as a gauge for good design:

1. **Identify:** Develop a design brief of the human need.
   a. Include specifics about the problem to be resolved.
   b. Break down the design brief to identify the core of the problems and the design specifications.
   c. Identify the function you want your design to accomplish. What do you want your design to do (not what do you want to design?)? Continue to ask why until you find the underlying cause of the problem.

1. **IDENTIFY**
Function

2. **DEFINE**
Context

3. **BIOLOGIZE**
Challenge

4. **DISCOVER**
Natural Models

5. **ABSTRACT**
Design Principles

6. **EMULATE**
Nature's Strategies

7. **EVALUATE**
Against Life's Principles

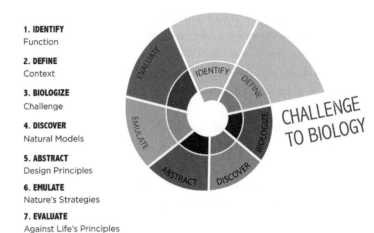

BIOMIMICRY DESIGN SPIRALS

© 2011 Biomimicry 3.8

Figure 2.7

Biomimicry Design Spirals.
(C) 2011, Biomimicry 3.8.
Courtesy of Biomimicry
Institute.

  d. Define the specifics of the problem:
    i.   Target market: Who is involved with the problem and who will be involved with the solution?
    ii. Location: Where is the problem, where will the solution be applied?
  Interpret **(biologize) the question:** What would nature do?
  a. Translate the design function into functions carried out in nature. Ask, "How does nature do this function? How does nature *not* do this function?"
  b. Reframe questions with additional key words.
  c. Define the habitat or location.
    i.   Climate conditions.
    ii. Nutrient conditions.
    iii. Social conditions.
    iv. Temporal conditions.
3. **Discover:** Observe and examine the "champions" in nature who have solved your challenges.
  a. Find the best natural models to answer your questions.
  b. Consider the literal and metaphorical.
  c. Find champion adapters by asking, "Whose survival depends on this?"
  d. Find organisms that are most challenged by the problem you are trying to solve but are unfazed by it.
  e. Look to the extremes of the habitat.
  f. Turn the problem inside out and on its head.
  g. Open discussions with biologists and specialists in the field.
4. **Abstract:** Find the repeating patterns and processes within nature that achieve success.
  a. Create a taxonomy of life's strategies.

   b. Select the champions with the most relevant strategies to your particular design challenge.

   c. Abstract from this list the repeating successes and principles that achieve this success.

5. **Emulate:** Develop ideas and solutions based on natural models.

   a. Develop concepts and ideas that apply the lessons from your natural teachers.

   b. Look into applying these lessons as deep as possible in your designs.

     i. Mimicking form.

      1. Find out details of the morphology.

      2. Understand scale effects.

      3. Consider influencing factors on the effectiveness of the form for the organism.

      4. Consider ways in which you might deepen the conversation to also mimic the process or ecosystem.

     ii. Mimicking function.

      1. Find out details of the biological process.

      2. Understand scale effects.

      3. Consider influencing factors on the effectiveness of the process for the organism.

      4. Consider ways in which you might deepen the conversation to also mimic the ecosystem.

     iii. Mimicking the ecosystem.:

      1. Find out details of the biological process.

      2. Understand scale effects.

      3. Consider influencing factors on the effectiveness of the process for the organism.

6. **Evaluate:** How do your ideas compare to life's principles, the successful principles of nature?

Benefits and Shortcomings of Biomimicry

Biomimicry offers some basic ideas for how designers can begin to engage in measures and metrics. Companies like IDEO are already benefiting from the approach as inspiration for design. Undoubtedly, a research-facing aspect will follow, as many companies see value in making research-driven design a core to their practice.

To the designer it offers much more, primarily to visual and industrial designers, who have more flexibility in engaging with the visceral quality offered by nature. Biomimicry is based on observation and replication, or mimicry, as the name suggests. This makes it more difficult to put through a rigorous process to generate measurement. What it provides, however, is inspiration to help drive more innovation through an understanding that nature itself is an R&D lab laden with ideas and direction for just about everything, even seemingly remote concepts like Facebook privacy and security models.

Biomimicry Design Principles

A sustainable product design experience takes into consideration a number of key principles; it must

1. **Follow nature's principles:** Nature teaches us to build from the bottom up, self-assemble, optimize rather than maximize, use free energy, cross-pollinate, embrace diversity, adapt and evolve, use nature-friendly materials and processes, engage in symbiotic relationships, and enhance the environment. By following the principles nature uses, we can design products that are well adapted to our environment.
2. **Perform well:** In nature, things just work well, as they have learned from 3.8 billion years of R&D; this is a good guide to design.
3. **Conserve energy:** Emulating the efficiency energy-saving strategies seen in nature can dramatically reduce the energy use in a product.
4. **Use just the materials it needs:** By studying the shapes of nature's strategies and how they are built, biomimicry can help designers minimize the amount of materials while maximizing the effectiveness of their products' patterns and forms to achieve their desired functions.
5. **Recycle its waste (nutrients):** By mimicking how nature converts biological waste, designers can learn how to transform technological waste to minimize (ideally eliminate) by-products of design, thereby closing the loop on the design cycle.
6. **See the product in different light:** Biomimicry helps designers see obsolete concepts and envision new ideas, therefore creating an opportunity for innovation and rework of designs that are not sustainable.

TOTAL BEAUTY

In 2001, Edwin Datschefski popularized the total beauty framework in the book, *The Total Beauty of Sustainable Products*. In the book, Datschefski asserts that products are the source of all environmental problems, a thought echoed by Shedroff and Lovins in *Design Is the Problem*.

Major issues, such as pollution, deforestation, species loss, and global warming, are side effects of the activities that provide consumers with food, transport, shelter, clothing, and the endless array of consumer goods on the market today. Ecological and social issues are becoming more important than ever before, and a vital new critical role is opening up for designers.

Datschefski promotes the idea that sees beauty not as a subjective thing after all but more as an objective thing. Therefore, the quantification of beauty is possible using a formulaic assessment. Beauty is therefore not in the "eyes of the beholder" but can be assigned a beauty IQ, of sorts, he goes on to say that, many "beautiful"-looking products have an underlying ugliness hidden to the consumer and often invisible to the designer as well.

To expose the inherent beauty in some of the ugly products could be beneficial to sustainability as a whole. Design should show the complete or "total beauty" of a product—a product's design should reveal the environmental and social effects and show their sustainability compliance both inside and outside, the "total beauty." While a product may look sustainable, it can be so only when it is best for the people, business profits, and the planet collectively.

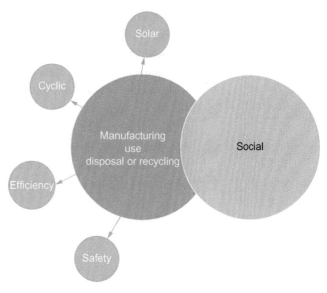

Figure 2.8
Total Beauty Framework.

Fabrication, Form, and Function

One prevailing issue is that most designers focus on improving form and function but they pay less attention to the expense of *fabrication*, how products are made, not only from the outside but also from the inside.

Total beauty, as a concept and design approach, presents a more controversial and radical yet simple framework for sustainability (Figure 2.8). The terms *cyclic, solar, social, efficient,* and *safe* emerge at the key pentadic principles of this framework, an easy-to-understand protocol for understanding products' sustainability.

In this framework, all of the points of the pentad are given a numeric value, except for social, to determine whether a product holds up to the definition of total beauty.

Calculating Total Beauty

Datschefski redefines the "beauty" of design by calculating the total impact of products and services as it relates five criteria:

1. **Cyclic**: This refers primarily to the manufacturing cycle. The idea that the manufacturing process should have a closed-loop material sourcing (all materials should be recyclable or recycled; they should also be compostable, organic, or acquired in a sustainable manner).
2. **Solar**: This calculates the level to which a design uses safe, renewable sources or renewable energy, during both the manufacturing process and use. This is also an area that is part of life-cycle analysis when calculating a product's carbon footprint.
3. **Safe**: This looks at the design and its use of nontoxic materials (a design should not negatively affect plant life, human life, animal life, or the environment in general). This is also an underlying principle of all of the approaches—it is rooted in *natural capitalism* and its model of the same name, as well as has a similar goal to many of the other approaches to date.

4. **Efficient**: Using the year 1990 as a benchmark, this refers to setting a goal that would require 90% less materials, energy, and water than 1990 standards.

5. **Social:** This focuses on the social dimension of what it means to be sustainable. This requires that all materials are manufactured under fair labor conditions, overall supporting human rights and "natural justice."

The "total beauty" of products or services is calculated as an equation for each category except for "social," because products and services that rate poorly on the social scale would fail using this formula. The scoring also includes "ugly points," which are taken out for poor performance, certain materials use, as well as energy inefficiency.

> Only 1 in 10,000 products is designed with the environment in mind. Can a product really represent the pinnacle of mankind's genius if it is made using polluting methods?[8]

Datschefski finds that 99% of all environmental innovation for products resides in 11 categories.

1. Cyclicly mined: Increased recycled content or recyclability.
2. Cyclicly grown: Increased compostability potential.
3. Uses alternative energy in use.
4. Uses alternative energy in manufacture.
5. Substitute materials: Replaced with nontoxic ones.
6. Stewardship sourcing: Increases safety and habitat preservation with sustainably acquired materials.
7. Utility: Increases efficiency with multifunction; in other words, points for dematerialization.
8. Durability: Lasts longer.
9. Efficiency.
10. Follows biomimicry principles.
11. Communication: Changes the behavior of the end users.

Benefits and Shortcomings of Total Beauty

This approach is foundational in formulation but provides a way to begin to list elements of design in quantifiable terms. Designers, however, may not be fully receptive to this approach to design, as it provides no option for making decisions based solely on taste. I think here of various challenges that some designers currently have taking guidance on design informed by strict user research and quantification. Socialization of this framework with strict designers may take some work. What can be harnessed from this approach are the fundamental principles: A "totally" beautiful design is beneficial to all.

---

[8]Edwin Datschefski.

What Does It Mean to User Experience and Design Practitioners?
The quantification of a product's sustainable performance using the "total beauty" model can create some difficulties, as it is not as simple to run a design against a simple checklist without a deeper assessment. In this case, beauty is not only skin deep. Nonetheless, it can be used as a guide to understanding the implication of design choice driven by ecological concerns using a first pass heuristic like tool, which many user experience professionals may understand.

CRADLE-TO-CRADLE

The term *cradle* to cradle was coined by Walter Stahel[9] in the 1970s and is based on a system of "life cycle development" popularized by chemist Braungart and his colleagues at the Environmental Protection Encouragement Agency (EPEA).

While Stahel originated the term, Michael Braungart and his colleague architect William McDonough made it popular when they collaborated to write *Cradle-to-Cradle: Re-making the Way We Make Things* (McDough and Braungart, 2002). Here, they define a *cradle-to-cradle design* as one that "refocuses product development from a process aimed at limiting end-of-pipe liabilities to one geared to creating safe, healthful, high-quality products right from the start."

Cradle-to-cradle design (sometimes abbreviated to C2C or Cradle-2-Cradle, or in some circles referred to as the *regenerative* framework) is a biomimetic approach to the design of systems. Sometimes also referred to as the *ecological efficiency approach*, it models human industry on nature's processes, where materials are viewed as nutrients circulating in healthy system.

The cradle-to-cradle approach suggests that industry must protect and enrich our ecosystems and nature's biological metabolism while maintaining a safe, productive technical metabolism for the high-quality use and circulation of both organic and synthetic materials. Put simply, it is a holistic framework that seeks to create systems that are not just efficient but essentially waste free. Cradle-to-cradle therefore advocates that, to become more effective rather than efficient, the design cycle needs to be optimized so that there is no waste at the end of the product life cycle.

> Cradle-to-cradle design refocuses product development from a process aimed at limiting end-of-pipe liabilities to one geared to creating safe, healthful, high-quality products right from the start. (McDonough and Braungart, 2002)

Previous examples of sustainable designs have focused on minimizing environmental damage; however, cradle-to-cradle argues that this does not stop

---

[9]Walter R. Stahel is a Swiss architect who has been influential in developing the field of sustainability.

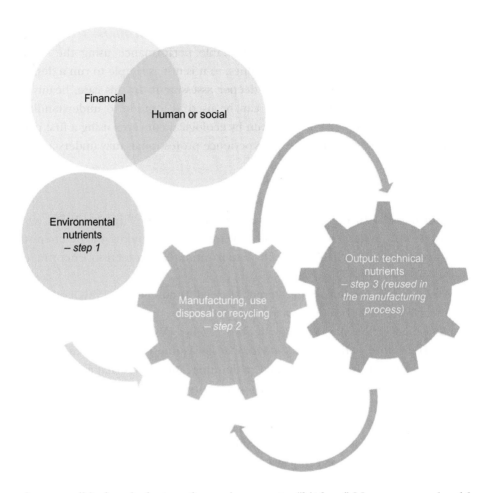

Figure 2.9
The Cradle-to-Cradle
Framework.

damage, all it does is destroy the environment a "bit less." Moreover, we should aspire to eliminate waste all together. The cradle-to-cradle approach (Figure 2.9) takes the whole system view that output (waste) from one system can become input (nutrients) for another product or process in a cyclic system, which is what happens in nature. Cradle-to-cradle departs from cradle-to-grave (cradle-2-grave) in that it has a higher goal. C2G assumes that waste is inevitable; cradle-to-cradle sees a future of no waste, referred to as *nutrients*.

In cradle-to-cradle, there are two types of "nutrients": the biological nutrient cycle and the technical nutrient cycle. The biological nutrient refers to those products designed to return to the biological cycle and that can be composted. On the other hand, a technical nutrient is a product designed to go back into the technical cycle; for example, it may be disassembled and the parts reused.

One of the companies that made waves utilizing this approach is Herman Miller; the chair was designed by Designed by Studio 7.5 (a Berlin based group of designers, for Herman Miller). It has actually gone as far as to create cradle-to-cradle guidelines for use by their designers. In 2003, the firm launched its *Mirra* chair

(Figure 2.10), which was constructed from 96% recyclable material (steel, plastic, aluminum, foam, and textile), the packaging used in delivery of the product is recycled, and the production line for the chair uses renewable energy, a combination of both wind turbines and gas from a landfill. This is a testament to the company, which is concerned not only for the environment but also for its employees.

McDonough and Braungart also collaborated with Herman Miller to take the tenets of cradle-to-cradle into designing a workplace suited to the principles of overall sustainability, addressing the social element of what it means to be sustainable.

Figure 2.10
The Herman Miller Mirra Chair.

From a social standpoint, Braungart and McDonough designed the new office spaces for Herman Miller to give employees a feeling of being in the outdoors, a key aspect that is getting lots of traction in the area of workplace design and a departure from the dull gray cubes that have become commonplace in many companies. The Herman Miller workspace design was so successful that a number of workers who left for higher wages elsewhere returned to work with the company. While the Herman Miller example fits well into the cradle-to-cradle model, it is an aspirational ideal for many other product design and manufacturing companies.

The Cradle-to-Cradle Certification

As part of the cradle-to-cradle design approach, a Cradle-to-Cradle® certification has been created by the authors and is a multiattribute eco label that assesses a product's safety to humans and the environment and design for future life cycles.

The program provides guidelines to help businesses implement the cradle-to-cradle framework, which focuses on using safe materials that can be disassembled and recycled as technical nutrients or composted as biological nutrients, which keeps in line with the no-waste philosophy. The certification program takes a comprehensive approach to evaluating the design of a product as well as the practices employed in manufacturing the product.

The materials and manufacturing practices of each product are assessed in five categories: material health, material reutilization, renewable energy use, water stewardship, and social responsibility. A complete description of certification criteria follows.

At this point, you will begin to see some of the same basic criteria emerging from the various approaches. The following are the base criteria for cradle-to-cradle design certification.

1. Material Health

The cradle-to-cradle plan order calls for materials categorization as specialized or organic nutrients that are safe for human beings and the Earth. Working with the product manufacturer and suppliers, each unit detail is mapped out and broken down into its compound constituents. Through the certificate method McDonough Braungart Design Chemistry (MBDC)[10] teams up with the company's whole supply chain network to guide out each synthetic in the item above 0.01% (or 100 ppm[11]), a procedure that surpasses ecological regulations and mitigates the perils of not knowing all chemicals involved in production.

These chemicals are then assessed in opposition to 19 criteria for human and natural states and given a toxicity appraising of red, yellow, or green. Unlike alternate approaches that essentially measure what destructive chemicals are usually emitted from a unit, the Cradle-2-Cradle certification method tests the toxicity of each material that goes into a result and furnishes a way to make producers enhance unit configuration and protection to humans and nature.

2. Material Reutilization

The cradle-to-cradle approach looks to dispose of the notion of waste and advance recyclability. This model compensates designs that strive to reuse or use renewable materials. At higher levels of confirmation, the company's goal should be to shut the circle on the design through eventual elimination of waste.

3. Use of Renewable Energy

Manufacturers are encouraged to go beyond energy efficiency and commit to the use of solar, wind, geothermal, and other renewable sources of energy during the manufacturing process. Savings made from energy efficiency can then be invested into nonfossil fuel sources of renewable energy.

4. Water Stewardship

Manufacturers are encouraged to operate responsibly and respect the need for all living things to have clean water. A cradle-to-cradle design approach would have the output water of manufacturing leaving as clean or cleaner than it came in.

5. Social Responsibility

Respecting diversity is one of the central principles of cradle-to-cradle. Manufacturers are encouraged to practice business in a way that respects the health, safety, and rights of people and the Earth.

---

[10]The term *C2C Certification* is a trademark protected by McDonough Braungart Design Chemistry (MBDC) consultants.
[11]Parts per million.

Benefits and Shortcomings of Cradle-to-Cradle

Though the cradle-to-cradle approach has high aspirations in seeing a waste-free world, it is one of the frameworks most easily understood and embraced by both businesses and individuals. However, in reality, many companies and individuals practice only a cradle-to-grave approach, where there is no way to close the loop on the product life cycle. For that matter, many by-products of design still end up in the wasteland; whether mobile phones or baby diapers, they are not fully recyclable.

> Design has become the most powerful tool with which man shapes his tools and environments (and, by extension, society and himself). (Papanek, 1972)

What Does It Mean to User Experience and Design Practitioners?

When designing products and solutions, designers should consider how they could create recyclable "nutrients" that do not end up as waste. One such way is by moving away from the creation of products to one based more on services and subscription. The application of the cradle-to-cradle framework in this case requires more than designers. It requires that all the stakeholders in the design process embrace a philosophy of no-waste production. For many of us, this is just not possible at this time in our history. However, what we can do is look for ways to move away from the material-based ideals of creation and focus on how we can build for a service model. An example that I cite in talks and elsewhere is the *Oxford English Dictionary* (Figure 2.11). Today, when you really sit and think of it, even dictionaries may be outdated, thanks to the internet.

In August 2010, Oxford University Press, the publisher of the dictionary, stated that, since so many people prefer to look up words using its online product, it is uncertain whether the 126-year-old dictionary's next edition will be printed on paper at all. From a design and user experience perspective, we are on the verge of something very exciting. We are perfectly situated to think about how virtual experiences can be designed to replace resource-guzzling physical ones. What we are not always conscious of is that this is part of the mandate as eco awareness gains ground and the cost of physical product production is high.

A second, similar effort includes changes already happening the mobile space, where phones are being used as transit cards, credit cards, and coupons, using near field communication (NFC) technology. As in the Oxford example, this helps reduce the need for physical paper- and plastic-based objects.

A third such example is Paper Culture (Figure 2.12), an e-commerce company delivering design through eco-friendly invitations, announcements, and stationery. The company produces virtual solutions that once existed in paper form, including such things as invitations and cards. Although the company still

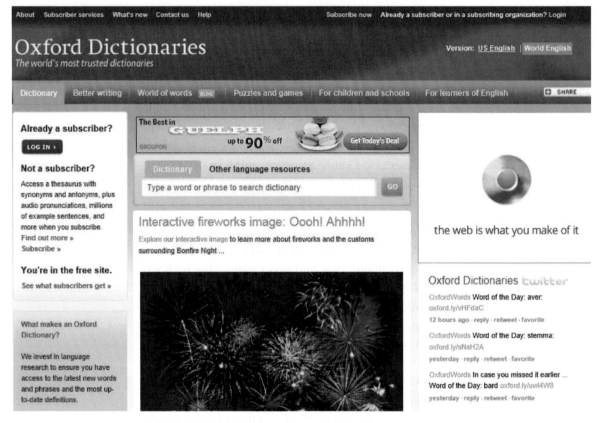

Figure 2.11

Online Oxford English Dictionary User Interface.

uses hard materials in some of its offerings, it sets itself apart by claiming to print them exclusively on 100% postconsumer recycled paper. It goes further to plant a tree for every physical paper order processed; Paper Culture has set out to make giving back to the environment a core part of its business.

In the three examples, we see a shift in how services are delivered, a transition from the physical to providing service-based solutions.

LIFE-CYCLE ANALYSIS

Life-cycle analysis (Figure 2.13) is a technique used primarily to assess the environmental aspects and potential impacts associated with a product, process, or service. This is done by

1. Compiling an inventory of relevant energy and material inputs and environmental releases.
2. Evaluating the potential environmental impacts associated with identified inputs and releases.
3. Interpreting the results to help in making a more informed decision.

Figure 2.12
The Paper Culture Website.

To date, it is the most used framework and the basis of many consultancies in the field.

As a framework, LCA enables the quantification how much energy and raw materials are used and how much solid, liquid, and gaseous waste is generated at each stage of the product's life. For example, in a manufactured consumer product, an LCA involves making detailed measurements during the manufacture of the product, from the mining of the raw materials used in its production and distribution, through to its use, possible reuse or recycling, and its eventual disposal. However, deciding which is the "*cradle*" and which the "*grave*" has been one of the points of debate in the relatively new field of LCA, and for LCAs to have value, there must be standardization of methodologies and consensus as well as assumptions.

Benefits and Shortcomings of Life-Cycle Analysis

There are a number of shortcomings of LCA. The first is that, in conducting a LCA, second-generation impacts are often ignored, such as the energy required for the subsequent life of any product cannot yet be contained for measure. Second, it is hard to find a baseline: There is no scientific base in many instances,

Figure 2.13

Life-Cycle Analysis Framework.

and many of the measures are still merely subjective. For example, there is no way to determine whether the eco cost of trying to close the loop on a product life cycle (by recycling it) actually creates more emissions in the end. This lack of a basis holds true across all of the other criteria when determining how data are analyzed. However, a great deal of work is currently being conducted on this aspect of LCA to arrive at a standardized method of interpreting the data collected.

What Does It Mean to User Experience and Design Practitioners?

In the context of user experience and design it is expected that LCA, as a model, may be a strong starter for understanding other tangible ways in which we can begin to engage in a day-to-day method.

Simply stated, the life cycle of a product embraces all the activities that go into making, transporting, using, and disposing of that product. Some of these phases involve areas where user researchers as well as designers can gain an interface with end users to provide input in the cycle. For example, ethnographic studies already in use are area where we can get close to true data that tells us how a product is used once it has entered the marketplace and how a user actually uses that product. The insights gained from this unique perspective can also provide cues to designers to determine how best to design a product to optimize its use in many ways. As I delve into the later chapters, the application of the methodologies in practice become more apparent. Of note are a few guiding principles, which we later explore, that can be used as a guide to improve a products' life cycle: designing for compliance, disassembly, maintenance, environment, and recyclability.

OTHER FRAMEWORKS WORTH NOTING

The following approaches and frameworks are mention only in brief, not as a means to deflect from them and promote the previously mentioned ones, but instead they are either similar to the other models and are a departure from them or they have indirect application for use in our day-to-day practice. I also provide the respective resource links for further exploration and reading, as many are still in flux.

SOCIAL RETURN ON INVESTMENT

Social return on investment is an approach for measuring the extrafinancial value relative to the resources invested. It is used to evaluate the impact on stakeholders, identify ways to improve performance, and enhance the performance of investments. This approach has had a lot of traction, and in 2008, a network was formed to facilitate the continued evolution of the method. Over 570 practitioners globally are members of the SROI network, to date.[12] The SROI method is standardized and provides a consistent quantitative approach. It is used to understand a project's impact on a business, organization, fund, or its policy. It considers all stakeholders' views of impact and puts financial "proxy" values on all those impacts identified by all the stakeholders that do not typically have market values.

The main aim is to include the values of people that are often excluded from markets in the same terms as used in a market that is money oriented. This gives people a voice in resource allocation decisions. In addition, while it is rather complex in application, it may one day form a base for understanding the overall return on investment for ecological designs and user experience designs.

---

[12]http://www.thesroinetwork.org/.

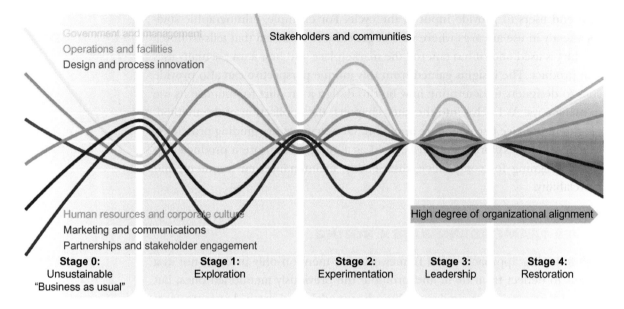

Government and management
Operations and facilities
Design and process innovation

Stakeholders and communities

Human resources and corporate culture
Marketing and communications
Partnerships and stakeholder engagement

High degree of organizational alignment

Stage 0:	Stage 1:	Stage 2:	Stage 3:	Stage 4:
Unsustainable	Exploration	Experimentation	Leadership	Restoration
"Business as usual"				

Figure 2.14

The Sustainability Helix Framework.

SUSTAINABILITY HELIX

The sustainability helix (Figure 2.14) is a model or approach best suited for organizations seeking to infuse sustainability into the "DNA" of their corporate structures and functions. While it does not have a direct applicability to our day-to-day work as user experience practitioners, it is worth a mention for the purpose of getting more insight into the number of approaches and views to the growing field of sustainability. Codeveloped by Natural Capitalism Solutions[13] and graduates of the Presidio School of Management, it tracks efforts in six categories of key business functions through five levels of commitment to sustainable principles and actions. The levels are as follows: no commitment, exploration, experimentation, leadership, and restoration.

The helix helps organizations assess their level of participation as well as ways to integrate sustainability over time and across many organizational functions. The six categories or key business functions listed are

1. Governance and management.
2. Operations and facilities.
3. Human resources and corporate culture.
4. Design and process innovation.
5. Marketing and communications.
6. Partnerships and stakeholders.

---

[13] http://www.natcapsolutions.org/.

While it is still in its infancy and subsumes other earlier models, it is definitely a model worth mentioning, as it includes some direction on design and design processes that may be used at an organizational level and subsequently affect our work as part of a trickle-down effect.

THE NATURAL STEP

The Natural Step framework[14] is a comprehensive model for planning in systems that are more complex. It is openly published to date and is constantly being tested, refined, and developed. The Natural Step as an international organization that serves business, governments, and educational organizations interested in using The Natural Step (TNS) framework for sustainability.

As a practice, The Natural Step framework creates a unifying view of the activities necessary to achieve sustainability. Guided by a board of industry leaders and nonprofit communities, the group tries to translate theory into practice, using logical, practical criteria for consistent decision making. The framework evolved over a period of 20 years and currently proposes five key areas of significance that should exist to execute and practice the framework:

1. **Systems:** Understanding the organization's relationship to the whole, the biosphere.
2. **Success:** Defining what success within this system means before it can be accomplished.
3. **Strategy:** Ensuring a strategic approach to addressing the system's needs, sustainably.
4. **Actions:** Ensuring that all the actions are guided by a sustainable strategy.
5. **Tools:** Being equipped with tools (management tactics and metrics) to monitor the actions to execute strategies and arrive at success within the system.

The Natural Step continues to evolve and provides a structure of operation, which sees a systematic approach to addressing the topic of sustainability.

ISO 14000

Currently dominant in Europe and providing guidance on LCA, ISO 14000[15] is a series of international standards on environmental management. It provides a framework for the development of an environmental management system (EMS) and support of audit programs. As is the case of many of the other frameworks, this model continues to evolve and is modified overtime.

---

[14]http://www.thenaturalstep.org.
[15]http://www.iso.org/iso/iso_catalogue/management_and_leadership_standards/environmental_management/the_iso_14000_family.htm.

GLOBAL REPORTING INITIATIVE

Perhaps the most influential of the frameworks, the GRI framework[16] provides guidance on how organizations can disclose their sustainability performance. The guidelines (G3) are the foundation of the framework. The framework is applicable to organizations of any size, constituency, or location and has been used by many organizations around the world as the basis of their sustainability reporting. In fact, many companies have already begun voluntary reporting with the expectation that mandatory reporting is just a few years away, utilizing the GRI's proposed model as the structure for reporting.

DOW JONES SUSTAINABILITY INDEX

While not a typical framework as encountered in the previous section, it is also worth noting that not all these frameworks lie in isolation from the markets and economic environment. Launched in 1999, the Dow Jones Sustainability Indexes[17] are the first global indexes tracking the financial performance of the leading sustainability-driven companies worldwide. It is based on the cooperation of Dow Jones Indexes and SAM,[18] which provides asset managers with reliable and objective benchmarks to manage sustainability portfolios. In September 2011, following SAM's comprehensive corporate sustainability assessment, 41 companies were added to the Index and 23 firms were deleted from the Dow Jones Sustainability World Index. Again, such activities use some of the frameworks we have seen as the basis of their evaluation.

WRAPPING UP

As we begin to think of our roles as user experience researchers and designers within our respective companies, we may be at a point where we are receiving top-down inquiries about our contribution to the wider sustainability initiatives. Many of us may even be looking for frameworks, processes, tools, and models that we can employ. Whatever frameworks, processes, tools, and models we embrace, it is important that we consider an inclusive approach, where we look at the best features of each and whether or not it has relevance and application for our work, before embracing one exclusively. Very few, if any, of these models are mature enough to be applied exclusively just yet. Further, all the currently proposed frameworks have their weak and strong points; and to counter this, it is best to find a solution at the

---

[16]http://www.globalreporting.org/ReportingFramework/G3Online/.
[17]http://www.sustainability-index.com/.
[18]SAM is an investment boutique focused exclusively on sustainability investing.

Driver for Sustainable User Experience
When my colleagues ask why I am so passionate about sustainable user experience, it is likely to turn into weeks of conversation, but for those who are not convinced and can see only the bottom-line, I often relay a little anecdote.

The field of user experience and usability has still not attained a degree of visibility that feeds into regulations or indexes of any kind; yet, as a practice, it fared financially well for many consultants over the years. The field of sustainability and, subsequently, sustainable user experience will be driven by regulations but, most important, can provide input into mandatory reporting in the short term and long term. Further, the altruistic "feel good" aspect of not creating just any solution or designing just any product but rather environmentally sound ones should be a goal of user experience designers. Accepting the inevitable eco-conscious design directives from all levels (consumers to government) will make it an easier transition for those who are looking to move ahead in the next level of user experience, usability, and design. Situating design and user experience on the sustainability playfield is therefore necessary for the evolution of the field in general.

nexus of it all, where all benefits of the prevailing models converge to offer up a best practice direction for user experience and design in the age of sustainability.

Connecting the puzzle pieces by situating ourselves in the wider picture is of the utmost importance. We are contributors to the problem but also stewards of our planet.

LOOKING THROUGH THE DESIGN LENS

In the mix of all these approaches, product designers and user experience professionals play a key role. We have an impact at the pivotal stages of product conceptualization, where decisions about what inputs are needed for a design, how they must be processed, what the product's life cycle could be, and what its end of life is. Designing for sustainability creates a course that can lock in the benefits from the beginning, whereas leaving environmental impact considerations for late stages of the process is more costly: A midcourse correction is always more expensive. For instance, a product designed for easy disassembly and that enables a user to maintain and service it requires much less effort to convert into recyclable and reusable components than one designed to drive consumerism (to keep users buying) and is energy intensive. Obviously, we have little or no influence over many decisions affecting sustainability. For instance, it is usually not solely up to the designer where materials are manufactured, what packaging is used, or how something is powered. Even so, as a part of the process, we are one notch in the part of the solution.

IN THE NEXT CHAPTER

Chapter 2 has just given you a tour of some of the sustainability approaches in wider use and practice. In Chapter 3, the focus is on looking at the life cycle of product design in context of sustainability. Further, we discuss those touch points where we can latch on to begin practical engagement; that is, those areas used to assess a product's carbon footprint. It is here that many of us will begin to participate and see how we can contribute to this wider initiative of sustainable design. In solidifying a sustainable design practice, from both the research and design sides of things, many of us are interested in such things as how our products measure up in the market in terms of packaging, energy consumption, documentation, and the remaining factors presented in Chapter 3.

PRODUCT LIFE CYCLE AND SUSTAINABLE USER EXPERIENCE

INFORMATION IN THIS CHAPTER

- Sustainable User Experience: Phases and Factors
- Factors of Sustainability
- Manufacturing
- Transportation
- Usage and Energy Consumption
- Recyclability (Reuse and Dematerialization)
- Facilities
- Thoughts about Ethnography, User Experience, and Sustainability
- Framework for a Sustainable User Experience Design Practice

INTRODUCTION

In the previous chapter we looked at some of the approaches that sustainability experts and analysts follow when assessing a product's sustainability performance, for lack of a better term. Regardless of the approach used in any such assessments, some key factors or dimensions are used as a basis for modeling this performance. At the core of the assessment lies the idea that all products have a life cycle, and throughout this life cycle, it affects the environment in some way or another, whether through its use of materials, its energy use, the way it is packaged, or its recyclability and disposal potential. These are some of the areas that experts look at when determining how well a product performs from a pure sustainability perspective. Essentially, how a product goes through its lifespan and the residual impact of its existence from inception to its eventual end or its rebirth.

In the context of user experience, we take it a bit further and situate the end user in this cycle to understand the interplay between product and user, also to understand how user perspective and perception can be used to collect data as part of a comprehensive framework. It is vital to understand that no product exists on its own or is utilized without a user, and the combined effect of product and user, in a specific environment, should form a basis of our sustainability user experience assessment.

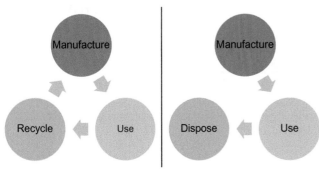

Cradle-to-cradle vs. Cradle to grave

Figure 3.1

Cradle-to-Cradle Life Cycle vs. Cradle to Grave.

To focus in on this chapter's objectives, we look at the typical product life cycle and begin to create a model whereby we can situate user experience as well as collect appropriate user data. I do this using a global brand that has made headway in making its reports transparent and accessible to its users—Apple, the maker of iPhone, among other products.

To collect data in a sustainability assessment, a product is envisioned to have a cradle-to-cradle life cycle or a cradle-to-grave cycle, understanding the product's condition of creation to its eventual reuse or demise. From there we use the cradle-to-grave and cradle-to-cradle models (Figure 3.1) as a base from which to extract the necessary components to get data related to product use in the market and with users. In other words, we lay out a product lifespan from its inception to eventual end or, in the case of cradle to cradle, where the product can be reappropriated, reused, or refurbished.

According to an environmental report put out by Apple on its website: about 97% of Apple's carbon footprint is directly related to its products, from manufacturing to customer' product use to recycling (Figure 3.2). The remaining 3% is related to its corporate offices, distribution hubs, data centres, and retail stores, combined. Apple uses a rather comprehensive yet digestible life cycle analysis to determine where their greenhouse gas emissions come from, and their analysis is a perfect example to demonstrate the junction between sustainability and user experience.

Apple uses a simple model by adding up the emissions generated from the key phases of its production—manufacturing, transportation, use, and recycling of their products—as well as the emissions generated by the facilities in which the products were designed and developed, and/or distributed and stored. It goes without saying that, as the science of carbon footprinting is still not yet fully advanced and approximated, we should also see these values only as close approximations. This distribution can be said to be easily transferable to other, similar consumer products that see a similar breakdown as Apple.

Moving forward in this chapter, we continue to reference the Apple example to illustrate the continuum of a product's life cycle as it pertains to its ecological impact and subsequently how we can collect measures that pertain to user-product interaction. We do so by understanding, first, the carbon emissions associated with each phase of the product's lifespan and extrapolating from this where there is end user impact. This is essentially the point of connection

Figure 3.2
Breakdown of Apple's Product Emissions Distribution.

I propose as a means of engaging user experience as useful contributors of the sustainability practice as it unfolds.

Carbon emission footprint, as defined in earlier portions of this book, is one of the ways in which many organization and governments determine a product's environmental impact. It is defined as "the total set of greenhouse gas (GHG) emissions caused by a person, a product, an organization, or an event." It is often expressed in terms of the amount of carbon dioxide, or its equivalent of other GHGs, emitted.

While this value is seen as an abstraction for many users, it is vital in understanding the distribution of the emissions generated during a product's creation, use, and subsequent end of life. This phase approach also allows the end user to situate him- or herself in the cycle and understand the impact of personal actions on a product's life cycle. However, when a user is presented complex calculations, such as carbon emissions in all its complexity, there is often no sense of personal impact given the abstract view. An end user may understand the value in numeric terms but not have a fuller sense of the contextual implications of his or her role in the process.

Further, it is also essential that users of the product be given some transparency into the impact of their usage on the environment. From a user experience and design perspective, we need to balance this seamless user education without interrupting product usage and design. We can contribute to this heightened awareness by such things as user messages, whether it is in an out-of-box experience (advising users to recycle) or in the product user interface (enabling educational messaging like power save options). These are only a few off-the-top-of-my-mind examples. More case studies of user experience and sustainable design are addressed later in this chapter and in subsequent ones (Chapters 4 and 5).

As an aside and footnote to this: when it comes to user communication, I propose a more simple approach by translating complex concepts like carbon emissions and their impact into percentage and more referential gauges, so users understand the impact of a critical phase like product usage and energy on the environment. In the Apple example, the carbon emissions during the typical product cycle was 46%, and this is attributed to in-market product usage. This valuable representation of a percentile of carbon emissions generated by a product during its life cycle gives users a better sense of their contribution to emissions generated by their usage.

From a manufacturer perspective, users can be given further product information as to how their usage activities translate into environmental impact. This may be a single user (unit) measure or collective usage measure. For example, using the Apple example, a user can be given the following information:

1. On average, 46% of their product's emissions are generated primarily by the of use of their Apple product.
2. This 46% translates approximately to *X metric tons* of carbon in a given year.
3. If *X metric tons* is generated by 1 user, then
4. 1 million users generate *Y* metric tons.

To take this a step further and from a social responsibility perspective, manufacturers need to also provide users with the impact of individual and collective end use in both qualitative and quantitative terms. Essentially, a user should not only understand what this collective usage means for the environment but what behavioral changes need to be made to counter and correct detrimental environmental effect. For example, manufacturers can, in an out-of-box experience, encourage the use of more efficient power supplies; they could also include out-of-box software that allows users to manage power consumption. In the case of electronic consumer products, this can take the form of seamless software integrated into devices to warn users of power usage and help them seamlessly

Figure 3.3
Power Management Software Android HTC.

manage energy use (Figure 3.3). In the case of other products, it could be informational content on product usage included in packaging and labeling.

User experience and design is perfectly situated central to these social responsibility initiatives, and we later explore the various phases of product life cycle and build a framework for data collection.

Becoming active stakeholders in the manufacturing process is a first step into situating design and experience design as a contributing stakeholder in producing more sustainable products. As manufacturing is the first step in the process, it is important to become a contributing stakeholder at this phase to ensure a greater end-to-end contribution and better transparency in the product life cycle.

As part of the process of user education, organizations like Greenpeace have underscored the value of reporting and making transparent how organizations are doing in terms of social responsibility and overall commitment to reducing their carbon footprint. This reporting has an effect on eco-conscious consumers, who utilize such data to help them make decisions about a product. And, while user experience design, in the strict definition, is not explicitly what is being affected from the manufacturing standpoint, there is an implicit consumer effect when companies tout their social responsibility and create the impression that their products are eco-friendly. So, by extension, there is an impact on the experience that users ultimately have with the product. It is here that the practice of user experience can help inform the process by providing real user feedback on the product's usage experience. This could be such things as the product's energy usage, its durability, and other aspects where the data can be collected only by observing groups of users in the real context of product use. This process of ethnography can track the in-market product use all the way up to disposal and provide insightful data and recommendations on closing the design cycle by making the product not only more sustainable but also relevant in context of use.

Many organizations like Greenpeace keep records of companies performance in market. In Greenpeace's latest "Guide to Greener Electronics" (Figure 3.4), the organization's ratings on personal computers, televisions, and mobile phones recognize the efforts Hewlett-Packard and Dell have made to clean up their supply chain. Nokia, the initial leader in social responsibility, also ranked among the top three and BlackBerry maker Research in Motion came in last place. Greenpeace uses a scorecard to rank the company's performance and makes the report available to consumers.

The Greenpeace guide originally set out to encourage companies to stop using materials such as brominated flame-retardants (BFRs) and PVC insulation in their products, and many manufacturers did so between 2008 and 2010. But there is still widespread use of these materials.

While the latest rankings still measure the energy consumption and PVC and BFR content of finished products, Greenpeace is now targeting the way products are made (i.e., the process), asking companies to report on the greenhouse gas emissions and the type of energy used by the factories that make them. Greenpeace is also asking that there be some transparency into the components and raw materials that feed the assembly lines.

This report, seen as the most authoritative reporting of social responsibility, has had such tremendous impact that, on publication of the report, companies such as HP, Apple, and Acer were quick to react. Apple immediately footnoted that their products are now BFR free and the company uses no PVC, except where required by local safety regulations on power cords.

Figure 3.4

Greenpeace Guide to Greener Electronics Dashboard.

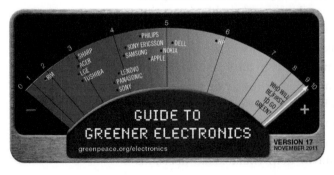

What this report underscores is the mainstream awareness of sustainability and ecological reporting on consumerism. Understanding the current climate of sustainability reporting gives us insight into the issues and orients us on how to contribute. Let us now look at those phases and explore the areas or touch points with which user experience design and research can connect.

SUSTAINABLE USER EXPERIENCE: PHASES AND FACTORS

As we set about the tasks of creating a framework to drive data collection, we need to understand the phases of the life cycle of a product as well as the factors that can generate the data we need collect. I refer to the base of the framework as *factors*, and they can be viewed as elements of the phases. These phases of product life cycle are manufacturing, transportation, use (energy), and disposal or recycling. As noted in the Greenpeace report, these are the key phases and areas that drive reporting. Within each of these phases are areas that enable pointed questioning, which I outline shortly.

The following is a list of the key phases of the product life cycle and the associated questions that form the foundation of these dimensions. This structural approach enables building a framework for end-to-end product assessment. While social, economic, and environmental areas are affected by all these phases, I focus on those factors that affect our actual role as contributors.

1. **Manufacturing:** Reports take a high-level view of the act of the production, including the use of machines, tools, materials, and labor to produce the product. Here we can address the following questions:
   a. Of what materials are the products made?
   b. How were the materials extracted?
   c. Does the product contain hazardous materials?
   d. Was the product manufactured under ethical conditions, such as the extraction and manufacturing process?

2. **Transportation:** This relates to transportation cost associated with the production and distribution of the product. On the surface, it may not seem relevant to design but a slight scratching of the surface shows how redesign of a product, specifically in the area of cube optimization and innovations that limit mass, can affect the product's environmental impact.
   a. What is the transportation costs (emissions) associated with the products production?
   b. How is the product packaged?—how a product is packaged has tremendous impact on the ultimate cost of transportation.
   c. What are the packaging constituents?

  d. Are there associated documentation produced as part of the out-of-the-box experience?

  e. Are products compactable to lower Transportation emissions and cost?

3. **Usage and Energy Consumption:**[1] This relates to primarily to the in-market energy usage. Most of the carbon emission happens here, in the hands of the user. Understanding the context of use can help reinform the process on how to leverage data for improvements in the phase.

  a. How much energy is consumed in the production and use of the product?

  b. If the product has a user interface, is it efficiently designed from a sustainability perspective?

  c. Does the product allow users active management of energy preservation (user messaging and notifications or alerts)?

  d. Does the product provide energy usage management guidance as part of the out-of-the-box experience, for example, a smart usage guide?

  e. What is the performance of the product in market with the user?

  f. What are the user's perceived and real experiences with the product?

4. **Recyclability (Reuse and Dematerialization):**[2] This looks at the product's end life and how the end user and product relationship can help create new opportunities for reuse, serviceability, and other ideas that can help close the waste loop into reduction or complete elimination. User experience methodologies can be used to collect significant data at this phase.

  a. How long does the product last?

  b. Do end users think that the product is durable?

  c. If broken, can the user repair the product easily, is it serviceable?

  d. Can the constituent parts of the product be broken down to create other products?

  e. Are there alternative service subscription options to the product?

  f. Does the product have other hardware dependencies when upgraded?

  g. Are the constituent parts available locally or shipped from other locations?

5. **Facilities:** Facilities, the last of the phases, can refer to a number of spaces including where the product is manufactured, distributed, and sold. It is one that I do not explore in this chapter, as it accounts for a very small percentage of the carbon emissions, given the Apple example of 3%. However, I want to point out that, when we think of fuller sustainability reporting, this phase will be useful in looking at not only the emissions but more social issues and human impact pertaining to the operations of the facilities. But, in a strict sense of product user experience, this phase is not central to the user experience framework we are trying to create. It must be noted, nonetheless, that many companies, such as HP and Dell, use this step as a central gauge of their environmental overall impact. In the context of the user's experience, we do not be considering this aspect, though itis vital for a more comprehensive reporting initiative beyond the user experience.

---

[1] This phase is well-suited for user data extraction.
[2] This phase is well-suited for user data extraction, too.

Using these factors as a base of measures, we can now begin to see how the user experience and the product intersect to create opportunities for data collection. Further, using a point system against these questions, one day, it may be possible to calculate a product's sustainability quotient not only in market use but also from the inception point to end of life.

However, it must be mentioned that, even though we can speak to a products performance based on these specific phases and their factors, it is often difficult to follow a product's supply chain, as many such chains are broken, with no dependable information to support true and comprehensive measures. The reason is that a true supply chain view of most products is not transparent and tangible for many reasons. In some cases, it could be that the unethical procurement of natural resources need to remain hidden from regulators. And, we do not always know what happens to a product after is reaches its end user.

But, to our benefit, what has some transparency is that certain phases of the product's life continuum is known with certainty, such as cost of transportation from source to distribution, actual energy used in market by users, what packaging comprises, and what the average user does with a product during and after use. The touch points of the user experience contribution is there for analysis. So, to situate user experience in the cycle, we focus primarily on the product in market and its use.

Let us turn to the Apple example as a starting point. Apple reported that at least 46% of the carbon emissions occur.[3] This amounts for almost half of product emissions of the product. When doing the assessment for a specific product you need to understand the values associated with that product. Many companies have a social responsibility or sustainability analyst, who may be able to provide you some direction. Also, as more guidelines and regulations emerge, many companies most likely will begin active management of this kind of data, making it more readily accessible for use.

Let us now take a look at each of these factors in more detail. After each section, we use the previously formulated questions to create frameworks for collecting data, where applicable, and extending the user experience practice for more relevance in the age of sustainability. While we focus more heavily on phases 3 and 4, I present each for the benefit of having a fuller picture.

The next section is only a guide to help structure your own framework and build on it with the goal of advancing user experience into different research spheres.

---

[3]http://www.apple.com/environment/#product.

FACTORS OF SUSTAINABILITY

As a user experience professional, I have engaged with many peers on the topic of environmentally conscious product design. The discussions have ranged from how to create more durable products to providing evolved out-of-box experiences with regard to packaging, recycling, and documentation. These discussions continue to mount in light of the wider global initiatives taking place, the formalization of such organizations as Global Reporting Initiatives and a growing customer base demanding greener products and solutions. For the most part, many of my peers are stuck in a loop of tracking user issues or in the lab running sessions that lack realism and an understanding of customer issues. A lot of this may be because the product development life cycle and design cycle exist in solo though many design and development process illustrations depict a closely coupled process, where issues are addressed and the design and development are more holistically tied. But, this is not reality, and one of the features missing is the contextual perception of users and their ever-changing views and goals as they use products. We sometimes neglect to ask whether a designed object (with solid software and aesthetically beautiful design) is housed in durable, serviceable hardware. Or, are users willing to keep buying a product that simply cracks at a drop.

I use my Canon camera as a prime example. For the most part, Canon is leader in point-and-shoot cameras. In 5 years, I have owned three point-and-shoot Canon cameras; my partner has owned one. Overall, I have never had a problem with the overall software or the user experience (how it works) and have found the packages design to be pleasing aesthetically. However, the overall sensitivity of the camera has led to broken hardware in all four instances. Two of the three cameras have zooms that are stuck and the other has a shutter that, for no obvious reason, remain half-open. Moreover, trying to address the problem through online forums reveals that these were known issues with the camera, many software and as many hardware posting of issues. This example is one that demonstrates a recurring end user problem. The product in my case was not durable and therefore missed the mark on sustainability. Moreover, without the warranty, they are now useless cameras that are, for the most part, of no value. I eventually purchased a Nikon with a warranty.

This example also speaks to two other consumer issues that have sustainability impact:

1. Due to the short memory of consumers and limited options in some products, they will continue to try different models of the same product type, hoping one will hit the mark.
2. The built in obsolescence of the product has created a customer tolerance that makes them think it is okay to continue to support manufacturers who produce below-par products.

To these points, a friend of mine, fed up with the poor quality of point-and-shoot cameras on the market today, decided to purchase a Leica camera, a retro camera that has had a legacy of durability and quality. Leica Camera, not to be mistaken with Leica Microsystems or Leica Geosystems,[4] is however not mass produced and expensive and its retro look has less appeal with the wider consumer base. My friend viewed retro with quality, citing that, back then, things were simply made to last. His example demonstrates that some buyers are willing to pay premium prices to get good quality.

The Context: User Experience Sustainability Awakening

While there is an acute awareness of issues concerning the growing ecological issues and a willingness to do something about it, many of us may have felt an overwhelming sense of helplessness and a lack of understanding as to how we can create added value. The incident that propelled me to take notice and become more conscious of sustainable design practices happened over 2 years ago. At that time, I headed a focus group of young mobile phone users to elicit from them what factors determined whether or not they would buy a mobile phone.

At that time, as today, the marketplace was flooded with many "rush-to-market" mobile phones and the race was to capture a young prosumer[5] market. Apple suffered because its popular touch phones consumed so much energy that customers complained of it not being able to hold its charge and sales dropped for that release. No one overtly classified this energy as a sustainability issue but indeed it was such and as well it had an end user impact—users complained in voices that were heard and purchased alternatives or waited for new releases. Overall users' complaints forced Apple to respond by quickly releasing newer models, where part of the marketing campaign centered on improved energy consumption. Ultimately, users were happier with the longer charge of the new model and Apple has since then moved on to capture the market and solidify its claim on the prosumer mobile space.

Another market leader of mobile devices, Research in Motion, had yet another problem with two of its leading devices utilizing trackballs and buttons. It is well documented in forums and online communities that buttons easily came off and the trackballs needed for navigation fell off

(Continued)

---

[4]Leica Camera AG, is a German optics company that produces Leica cameras. The predecessor of the company, formerly known as Ernst Leitz GmbH, is now three separate companies: the others are Leica Camera AG, Leica Geosystems AG, and Leica Microsystems AG. They produce cameras, geosurvey equipment, and microscopes, respectively. Leica Microsystems AG is the owner of the Leica brand, and grants licenses to Leica Camera AG and Leica Geosystems.
[5]*Prosumer* describes the consumers who buy products (mostly technical,) that fall between professional and consumer grade standards in quality.

with little effort. In short, customers were taking notice, and this growing user complaint had become a sticking point for me as a practitioner who often interfaced with users. At that time working as a practitioner in mobile user experience research, many of my user sessions ended up off topic and seemed to have become therapy sessions for many mobile phone users with complaints about their phones breaking down only months after purchase.

For some users, it was not the first time that they had either replaced their mobile phones only to realize that, even before one year was up on their three year contract, they were forced to get new phones. Essentially, what was happening was the phones simply were not durable, yet another end user issue that has a strong sustainability slant to the ultimate solution. Users wanted durable products that were worth the $500 to $600 they paid for these phones. Again, it was clearly another design issue (planned obsolescence), another user finding that should be logged as a sustainability finding—and where better to voice these types of user frustration than in a user experience focus group session. Granted their carrier complaints were fruitless, as the carrier cost increased if they had to give every customer replacement devices because of flawed design. Undoubtedly, one can only imagine the churn rate of devices back to the maker and the impact it has on a company's image when customers are not happy.

At that time, I witnessed many mobile device releases on a four or five per year cycle with the same mobile phone (with minor software upgrades) still having in the same issues: poor quality phones with weak dome sheets, easily destructible buttons and trackballs that fell out with no effort. And the user complaints kept coming as part of the user sessions. Note that, more often than not, I was in user sessions to get unrelated information on a new release or new concept and therefore could only empathized with the complaints but not really have an outlet to report it, as it was not really part of my role.

Parallel to these events I had also just received a new crop of interns completing Human Computer Interaction degrees from their respective universities. As part of their research mandate and on-the-job training, many of them felt strongly that their work should center on some form of eco-design study. This indicated to me that educators had changed their curriculum to include classes on ecologically sound design and students were taking heed.

One of the interns opted for improving the packaging experience of our products as research -coursework for which she would be graded. Her goal was to create an experience that would limit the amount of waste in packaging as well as provide consumers with an out-of-the-box experience guided by principles of cradle-to-cradle, product life extension, and driving higher recyclability. As a case study, she wanted to understand an unexplored phenomenon, why many iPhone and High Tech Computer Corporation (commonly known as HTC) users kept the product package while customers of our product immediately disposed of the packaging. Her findings are proprietary, off course, but rooted in ecological design principles and designing for reuse. She discovered that, in many instances, iPhone and HTC users retained the boxes in which their product was packaged as storage boxes and in 3 out of 12 cases the boxes were used by young children as toys. One 3 year old used the box, which he had kept for over a year, as an everything toy—one day a truck, another a box for imagined presents, for keeping little transient valuables, and so on.

Another student looked into working with our documentation team to envision the creation of an eco-friendly help solution that would eliminate the need for the many booklets that came with our products. In this case, he was disturbed by the fact that, even though he bought this product in North America, he also received documentation in German and Asiatic languages. How could he improve this experience that would save on paper?

What was happening on all sides (end user, educators, and researchers alike) was a societal and generational awareness that we will continue to see with later generations to come. While I had limited means to report on user issues, there was at least some awareness in the next crop of practitioners on design issues that they could affect the overall user experience in a more holistic way.

Reporting the issue to my then manager was a frustrating feat, as there was simply no means to escalate this type of user issue from user session and also a narrow view of user experience as firefighting. As happens in many user experience practices, the sessions become mechanical and eventually boil down to reporting and tracking user issues related to the software. Entering user issues into a repository had become the mode of operation and the only way to communicate to development people. This mode of operation only serves to put the user experience practice in jeopardy, as we are sometimes inhibited from operating beyond our restricted role definition. This limits us in our capacity to connect with users and hear their real issues, specifically those issues that can be logged as product sustainability issues. In retrospect, in many cases, I should have been asking user questions beyond the standard usability questions of

a. Was the workflow efficient?
b. Were the task flows memorable?
c. Were the task experiences effective?
d. Are you satisfied with the workflow?
e. Was the experience enjoyable?

instead of extending the questions to include (in no specific order) questions such as

a. What do you think of the quality of materials that make up the phone?
b. How long do you keep your mobile phone? And why?
c. Do you return your phone to the manufacturer when it is no longer functional?

(Continued)

d. How do you dispose of it?
e. What do you think of the packaging of your product and how do you dispose of it?
f. Do you see any way in which the product can be reused?
g. Are there opportunities to extend the life of this product to keep you using it for a longer period? If so, how?
h. Are you satisfied with the energy consumption levels on your mobile phone?
i. Does the device message appropriately remind you of power saving options?

The usability questions are very task focused and never consider the overall user experience outside the software use cases. In these situations, I felt that the sessions and the research were incomplete.

These traditional questions and measures, in their current forms, have undoubtedly plateaued in their impact on the final design. We can even argue that they are now commoditized. Even collecting new measures as net promoter scores and affective design data also seemed to have minimal incremental impact and do not provide a comprehensive view of product performance in the new environmentally aware zeitgeist.

I propose that we, as researchers, begin to explore beyond the traditional usability data, net promoter, or affective data and include data based on green consumerism. This is an inevitable gauge of user purchasing decisions that will continue to grow over the coming years.

Ultimately, as it was in my observation, in a poor economy, users wanted value for money.

Beyond the cost of mobile plans, users felt frustrated that after purchasing a mobile phone, they faced issues like not being able to hold charges or the phones were easily destroyed. These were some of the real issues of the day. Not whether it took three or four steps to open a music player or whether a user wanted to swipe right or down to access an application.

Therefore, this epiphany, which took place years ago, the participant who stood out to me was a 22-year-old South Asian woman, who indicated that her mobile preference was from a company that respected the environment. She remarked that many of these "useless" phones ended up in the part of the world where her parents grew up. She was also impressed that her then Nokia phone came with information about recycling and other information that showed the company's commitment to sustainability. Other mobile companies did not stand a chance, primarily if the products were not built to last her more than 5 months.

The sentiment that products had to last was re-echoed in so many subsequent interactions that I became more conscious of how I could engage. I recognized that the solution was one that designers could contribute to in their own small way and that user research can help drive with more proactive focus on the users realities.

In a recent study and article published by Greenbiz.com[6] ("Amazon's Purchasing Data Finds US Consumers Going Green"), researchers from Amazon US, one of the largest online retailers in the world, tried to understand the role of ecological design in consumers' purchasing decisions. Their results give a broad sense of the growing trend of green buying. While the results show differences across the country, with California, New Hampshire, and Vermont customers purchasing the greenest products (excluding books) across categories, a map generated from the data of this research shows a gradual trend in America toward greener purchasing. The Amazon research is vital, as it is one of the few neutral studies that do not position any one retailer at the center of the research. It is also significant because it sheds light on user behavior reinforming us as designers of the role of driving toward sustainable user experience design.

I work alongside designers (industrial, visual, and interaction) as well as large documentation teams, whose main duties are to produce without the conscious thought of production. Like many companies in a rush to market, there is little to no time to think about the work we are doing. The only focus is rush to be first and postcourse corrections will repair potential damages—but at what cost? Given that this is the realistic nature of business, we have to work with these constraints, which will most likely not change overnight. How can we add value? Also, we need to take a moment to consider when we perform ethnographic studies, focus groups, or other types of studies collecting user feedback, are we thinking of the product and its users in the context of ecologically sound design? As designers of all shades, it seems that the role of design and how we move toward greener designs are imperatives, and therefore measuring progress is also very important.

PHASE 1. MANUFACTURING

For the purposes of this chapter and its objectives, I do not focus much on the phase of manufacturing but provide some general information about some of the typical questions that we can address when thinking of framework creation in product assessment and modeling.

In the wake of the Global Reporting Initiative and other reporting initiatives, many companies are actively looking to understand the life-cycle impact of product creation. In the case of Apple, our example throughout this chapter, this phase is the first one for which the company begins to report on the carbon emissions of its portfolio of products.

---

[6]http://www.greenbiz.com/blog/2011/04/19/amazons-purchasing-data-finds-us-consumers-going-green?page=0%2C1.

Some of the challenges facing many manufacturing industries are the presence of toxic substances in their products. These include such things as such as lead, arsenic, polyvinyl chloride (PVC), mercury, and phthalates, to name a few. Although most countries still allow the use of these substances; many companies have begun some level of research and goal setting to investigate alternative material substances that would have little to no impact on the consumers and the environment at large. The hope is that, ultimately, these harmful materials will be eliminated from their products. Further, the commitment to understand the ethonomics[7] of their business has also become paramount to many manufacturers, who are now making social responsibility a key added value and business differentiator to their core offering. Companies such as Wal-Mart, Apple, HP, and Nokia are but a few that have made transparent their active roles and initiatives in ensuring that working conditions in their supply chains are safe, and that workers, regardless of geographic location, are treated with respect and dignity and up to the standard of that country's laws. These companies are also looking at such things as their manufacturing processes and ensuring improved environmentally responsible practices. As we begin to build on a framework, some of the question that we can ask here are

a. Of what materials are the products made?
b. How were the materials extracted?
c. Does the product contain hazardous materials?
d. Was the product manufactured under ethical conditions in the extraction, manufacturing process?

These four questions are the essentials that should be addressed at this point. And, while the role of traditional user experience and design is minimal, it is informational and allows us to see the fuller picture. In plotting the data collected from this phase, stakeholders use existing data bases of known hazardous substances that are put out by such government agencies as the U.S. Environmental Protection Agency (EPA).[8] Processes documenting how these materials are extracted, as the ethical aspect of manufacturing, are the by-products contained in the document reports.

---

[7]Ethonomics is the provisional name for the discipline of formally mapping and defining the prioritization of values within value systems, with the intent of understanding differences between seemingly disparate value systems, the people who hold those value systems, and the decisions they make based on those value systems. The intent is also to provide a mechanism for resolving conflicts between value systems through rational analysis.
[8]http://www.epa.gov/.

What Does It Mean to User Experience and Design Practitioners?

In terms of end user impact, we can become advocates and stakeholders in such things as material selection. This role may certainly be relegated to industrial designers, who have a say in the type of materials ultimately selected to design a product. And, while I center mostly on consumer products, as this is where the core of our practice lies, there may be opportunities at this phase for designers of varying types to have some greater impact.

Think of a product and company cited in earlier chapters, the Mirra chair by Herman Miller (Figure 3.5).

The Mirra chair was designed to accommodate both the sitter and the environment. Apart from adapting its shape and form to each individual sitter, it is also made of 94% recyclable material. In this example, we see design as a fundamental ingredient driving production. While this is not the case in all companies, Herman Miller, a leader in engaging its designers in sound eco-friendly design, stands as an example for this phase of manufacturing and can be used in some ways as a model for how engagement of designers can result in optimal product design. Today, this product is on exhibit at the Museum of Modern Art.

To conclude thoughts on this phase, our contribution can be in looking at material selection and understanding the impact of the materials selected. Selecting materials that can be reused and recycled is a good first step into becoming conscious contributors to the overall process.

Figure 3.5
Herman Miller.

PHASE 2. TRANSPORTATION

Transportation, in the context of this chapter, centers around three key aspects: the emissions associated with products being transported from the point of manufacture to the distribution hubs; the means of transportation used, and the role of packaging in transportation. All three are highly interrelated and are at the core of assessments in the phase of transportation. But, to draw this relationship in the user experience context, a simple illustration may be necessary.

Apple claims that, by reducing its packaging of the MacBook by 53% between 2006 and 2010, it shipped 80% more boxes in each airline shipping container, which saves one 747 flight for every 23,760 units shipped. Accomplishing this feat included designers in the process as the out-of-the-box brand and experience has had to be preserved throughout. Apart from the inclusion of designers and developers in the life cycle of this Apple example, I find it also fitting in terms of illustrating to users the impact MacBook redesign had on the wider eco-design initiative that the company has undertaken.

To get some further high-level insight, consider a little bit of contextual information on the transportation types and their impact as they transport the goods to users: Air and rail shipping is costlier than sea cargo and many companies are now beginning to set limits on product transportation cost and use the most efficient transportation means, where possible.

The Adidas-Group, another big brand, also addresses issues of transportation on their website's sustainability page by stating:

> "The fuel used to transport goods to market creates carbon dioxide emissions, a major contributor to climate change. The Adidas Group works each year to reduce the environmental impact of transporting its products around the world. Our policy is to minimise the impacts from transport, in particular minimising air freight shipments. Generally, we plan to ship products by ocean freight. Only when the product is needed faster than planned, for example during sporting events, or in times of high market demand, we consider other modes of transport such as air freight—and then only on a case-by-case basis."[9]

Like Apple and the Adidas-Group, Ikea, another global brand, is actively looking at this transportation phase of a product life cycle as a key phase in which to reduce its carbon footprint. The company is taking it a bit further and trying to decrease the number of car trips to and from its stores by customers and employees combined. Its global goal[10] is that 15% of its customers leave their cars home and use other forms of transportation to get to and from the stores. To achieve this goal, IKEA created pilot programs and initiatives for improved public transportation, environmentally friendly home delivery services, as well as providing free shuttle service to and from their stores. In Denmark, customers can borrow bicycles with trailers to bring their purchases home. In 2009, IKEA reported that it had passed the halfway

[9]http://www.adidas-group.com/en/sustainability/Environment/transport/default.aspx.
[10]http://www.ikea.com/ms/en_US/about_ikea/pdf/ikea_ser_2010.pdf.

Figure 3.6
Ikea Product Packaging to Optimize Transportation.

mark, as 10% of its global customers used a form of transportation other than their cars for store trips.

The company also believes that its continuous focus on packaging innovation will result in a 6.3% reduction in its transportation-related carbon footprint by 2012 (Figure 3.6).

In terms of regulations surrounding packaging and transportation, Germany, for example, is pressuring suppliers to take back packaging materials, while the United Kingdom is setting fines based on the amount of packaging material used to transport goods. Further, the European Union is amending its Emissions Trading Scheme (ETS) to cover transportation; these changes will result in charges being levied based on a product's carbon footprint (through a direct carbon tax).

All of this has not gone by unnoticed, as large retailers, who recognized the cost-cutting opportunity in sustainable packaging, have not waited for regulations to be passed before addressing some of these issues. For example, in 2006, Wal-Mart mandated a 5% reduction in packaging across all product categories by 2013.[11] It even went as far as creating a system to help suppliers calculate their products' carbon footprints. So far, Wal-Mart estimates that over $3 billion in costs has been saved as a result of this initiative.

Overall, what we see in the phase of transportation is how the end packaging of products ultimately affects the user. But, most important, from what key areas can we collect vital information and data to allow us to engage as designers of all disciples:

a. What transportation costs (emissions) are associated with the product's production?
b. How is the product packaged?
c. What are the packaging constituents?
d. Is associated documentation produced as part of the out-of-the-box experience?
e. Are products compactable to lower transportation emissions and cost?

These questions can, to some extent, be addressed by designers, as there is room for engaging on such aspects as how a product is designed and how packaging can accommodate the miniaturization of these designs to optimize transportation and the subsequent emissions that arise.

What Does It Mean to User Experience and Design Practitioners?

Using a concrete example to demonstrate how we can have impact is fitting in this case. In November 2006, Wal-Mart's packaging scorecard (Figure 3.7) allowed suppliers to evaluate themselves relative to other suppliers, based on specific metrics. The metrics in the scorecard evolved from a list of favorable attributes that the company announced as the "7 Rs of Packaging." They are *remove, reduce, reuse, recycle, renew, revenue,* and *read.*

Through consultations with a group of leaders in the global packaging industry, including suppliers, experts, and internal and external stakeholders, Wal-Mart outlined the following metrics for the packaging scorecard:

1. 15% is based on greenhouse gas (GHG)/CO_2 per ton of production.
2. 15% is based on material value.
3. 15% is based on product/package ratio.
4. 15% is based on cube utilization.
5. 10% is based on transportation.
6. 10% is based on recycled content.
7. 10% is based on recovery value.

---

[11]http://www.accenture.com/SiteCollectionDocuments/PDF/Accenture_Simultaneous_Sustainability_and_Savings.pdf.

Figure 3.7
Wal-Mart Sustainability Packaging Scorecard.

8. 5% is based on renewable energy.
9. 5% is based on innovation.

In a few of the above listed scorecard goals or criteria, product and experience designers are perfectly situated to provide input into this scorecard process, particularly items 3, 4, 6, and 9.

- ■ (3) 15% is based on product/package ratio.
- ■ (4) 15% is based on cube utilization.
- ■ 610% is based on recycled content.
- ■ (9) 5% is based on innovation.

These goals can be achieved and monitored through improved design of packaging that has, as its goal, more efficient transportation and subsequently lower emissions. Understanding how the changes in design affect transportation as well as user experience should be the goal of user experience and design engagement in this phase. The redesign challenges afforded by this phase can also be a good innovation driver, as designers become increasingly challenged to find solutions.

In terms of outlining the concrete activities that a designer can engage in at this phase, there is potential for collaboration in terms of

1. Defining and illustrating packaging design criteria.
2. Researching and developing packaging options based on performance needs, especially as it relates to transportation from the manufacturer to the user.
3. Creating packaging concepts (packaging prototyping and research across design teams).
4. Preparing and documenting packaging specifications.

With respect to how the information and data from this phase can contribute to a framework designers can keep logs that enable forecasting of product-to-package ratios and the cube optimization that result from their innovative design solutions. Also, as intellectual property becomes a hot commodity, designers need to become more active in patenting solutions that show their value in the optimization of space and packaging to drive transportation optimization.

PHASE 3. USAGE AND ENERGY CONSUMPTION

As we move along the product life-cycle continuum to in-market product use, energy usage becomes central to understanding how we can begin to engage at critical points with the user and product. Here, user experience designers become integral in effecting change, particularly in the case of electronic design. Using methodology such as ethnography and the data generated can help improve design and user experience based on actual user data. Such real-life observation of users can help drive behavioral changes in users. Some of the kinds of information and data that can be gathered from knowledge of user's behavior include

a. How much energy is consumed in the production and use of the product?

b. If the product has a user interface, is it efficiently designed from a sustainability perspective?

c. Does the product engage users in allowing some active management of energy preservation (user messages and notifications/alerts)?

d. Does the product provide energy usage management guidance as part of the out-of-the-box experience? For example a smart usage guide?

e. What is the performance of the product with the user?

f. What are the user's perceived and real experiences with the product?

g. What is the user's perception of the ecological value of the product, its durability?

With regards to this phase, user experience can contribute by understanding, using ethnographic research, consumption patterns, and behavior.

Figure 3.8

iPhone Energy Management Application.

Understanding real behavior patterns can go a long way in informing subsequent designs that help users manage their energy consumption (Figure 3.8). The ultimate contribution I have seen for design with regard to energy usage is in software design. Here, the system uses data collected while a user is actively using a device and warns users of such things as power-saving opportunities.

This kind of data, as the name infers, is often referred to as *instrumentation data.* Instrumentation data is essentially data harbored by a device as part of the design architecture. Utilizing this repository of data has been a way in which user experience creates messages to users about monitoring their behavior. The actual output of our work here may be helping design something like energy management software that comes as part of the core application;it demands minimalist design and most of all targets the user messages with respect to the user's context. One of the challenges here is how messages and user education can be unobtrusively integrated in the products. In the end, our contribution here though seemingly minimal has great effect when we think of the collective global impact.

This is another application of how user data helps drive user behavior when the users are aware of their consumption.

While working on this book, I had been thinking of the ways in which ethnographic data can be used to drive better user experience as it relates to energy use. As if serendipitously, I received an information sticker from my local power supplier that put some ideals of user experience into a better frame (Figure 3.9). The refrigerator sticker was a *Power Smarter* graphic that showed peak times that

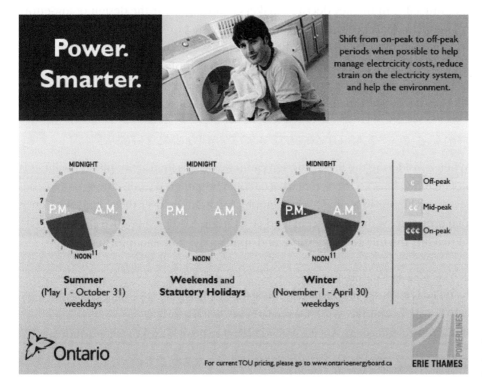

Figure 3.9

Power Smarter Information Guide.

energy use. The data used was based on the company's monitoring of when users were consuming the most and least amounts of energy. The highest peaks of course meant the cost was highest to the user.

What Does It Mean to User Experience and Design Practitioners?

As we focus on this phase, I propose that some of the ways design can play a role here is being the voice to the users by creating awareness where possible and ultimately trying to drive behavioral changes. At a rudimentary level, I propose the following:

1. **Knowledge Gathering:** Understanding the key issues surrounding the design of more sustainable products and services.
2. **Practicing and integrating knowledge:** Implementing, through consciousness of the known issues and the solutions that will help counter and cure these issues.
3. **Driving user awareness:** Making users aware, though the design, of the impact of their behavior and decisions on the environment.

In more innovative companies, user experience and design teams have also had leeway in designing small mobile applications that inform users of their product usage, where there is an emissions impact. Consider how you can situate yourself with the key decision makers to advocate for the design of low-effort user educational applications. This could be done by using instrumentation data, in conjunction with understanding user behavior, and allowing users to modify behavior via advanced user messages. For example, users can be guided to a power-saving mode based on usage data or informed of the cost of talk over text. All these small steps help drive the consciousness of more sustainable solutions.

PHASE 4. RECYCLABILITY (REUSE AND DEMATERIALIZATION)[12]

When considering the impact design can have on this final active phase (facilities is not included here), a lot of in-market data can be gathered using ethnographic studies. As in the previous phase, ethnography can help discover the actual experience that users have with a product in market. In studies, user experience can investigate in real life, the following questions and appropriate data can inform design:

a. How long does the product last?
b. Do users think that the products are durable?
c. If broken, can the user repair the product easily, is it serviceable?
d. Can the constituent parts of the product be broken down to create other products?

---

[12]This phase is suited for user data extraction.

e. Are there alternative service subscription options to the product?

f. Does the product have other hardware product dependencies when upgraded?

g. Are constituent parts available locally?

Findings from these questions can form a basis for improved solutions. In this phase, as user researchers, we can inquire about how products end and are used after the utility is gone? Find out about whether users try to service broken parts, when possible. Provide options to users where, instead of buying new hardware, they can look at such things as software updates and downloads that lengthen the life of their product. Granted, this step is often counter to a company's mandate of increasing sales. Accordingly, this can be addressed by working both with users and the company or client to look for alternatives to keeping products fresh and innovative and ultimately meeting user needs while sustaining their own bottom line.

At the end of the day, the data from these can be normalized to generate trends among targeted user groups. I refer back to the trigger to this book, my experience with a group of mobile users and the endless complaints about the brand of phones a company manufactures. Today, the same issues exist with that mobile phone maker, who incidentally has lost a large amount of market share and had a drop in share prices, as there is a move toward phones made of less destructible plastics and parts that do not easily fall out. Whether or not it is the driving reason, we will never be certain. However, the trend by younger users toward more compact, no button designs is apparent.

What Does It Mean to User Experience and Design Practitioners?

As someone who tries to always find new uses for products that have reached the end of their utility in one form, I often need a momentary pause when I think of how I would redesign something to make it last longer. Here, I think designers of all types can begin their engagement in helping counter the cost associated with materialism.

Consider the example of Maille mustard, which has taken a new approach to the design of their jars. After using the jars many customers appropriate jars for other uses (Figure 3.10). Maille is but one of many companies now looking to extend their brands "stickiness" by selling their products in packages with longevity. Recently I purchased some Creme Brulle from a local store and was pleasantly surprised to find that I could reuse the for glass jars as candle holders. These practices are on the rise and many companies are noting the power of "reusable" as customers remember products that become part of their living environment long after the actual product has been used up.

Further, consider the creative design mind that envisioned the Kindle and the impact on deforestation. Even solutions such as applications that do everything from

Figure 3.10
Maille Mustard Jar
Reuse.

time telling to calendars as opposed to creating and designing the physical objects that add to materialism are the small ways we can show value. The idea that society is also moving to more subscription-based solutions is also another element that we should think about in this age of sustainable thinking. And as more and more applications are designed; less materials are used as the products take on virtual forms. Design will again be a central component in creating these new sustainable solutions.

PHASE 5. FACILITIES

While I added this phase to be as comprehensive as possible, it is for informational purposes only. Typically, this area is part of designing efficient processes and is not strictly an area where traditional user experience plays a role.

CUSTOMER PERCEPTION AND SUSTAINABILITY

While I talk a lot more about customer perception in Chapter 5, this topic, along with some of the issues surrounding customer-company relations is worth a mention at this point. The impact of consumer perception on corporate reality has long since proven to be strong: The increase in the number of companies creating a corporate social responsibility (CSR) presence on their websites speaks to this fact. Further, there is a growing market trend, with auditing and financial services firms creating new business opportunities by providing companies who lack in-house CSR teams with outsourced CSR options. The auditing firm KPMG reported a 30% increase from 2005 to 2008 in the percentage of large companies generating corporate responsibility reports; four out of five (79%) of the world's largest companies now provide this information publicly on their websites.

Clearly, these trends infer that consumers believe that when they support companies, they do more than just shop. They align themselves with the ideals and beliefs of the businesses from which they purchase products and services. From a design research perspective, I see this area as void of user experience practitioners who actively work with corporate responsibility teams, within their organization, and use the research data to help make design decisions based on this dimension of growing significance.

Beyond the questions that can be addressed as part of the start to end phases, some of the other questions that can be included are as follows:

a. What is the performance of the company's products in the market with the user?
b. What are the user's perceived and real experiences with the product?
c. What is the user's perception of the ecological value of the product, its durability?
d. How can the company design solutions and make changes to improve users' eco perception.

These questions require a more bird's eye view on what product and user experience means, including data of all sorts, as well as that of the end user, is a necessary step in building more responsive solutions in an age where eco consciousness.

So far we had a look at the various phases of a product life cycle and need to envision the types of output, such as reports that we use as input for more comprehensive user experience product reporting. Greenpeace's report,[13] "Guide to Greener Electronics," is an example of such a report (Figure 3.11). This guide ranks the leading mobile phone, TV, and PC manufacturers on policies and practices to reduce their impact on the climate; produce greener products; and make their operations more sustainable. Such a model is not only applicable to electronics but can be used for almost every facet of manufacturing within any company. This could be the production of water bottles to paints to bicycles or any product or service with end user usage.

Here we can begin to map potential user experience activities and associated findings, with such questions as

■ How much energy is consumed in the production and use of the product?
■ If the product has a user interface, is it efficiently designed from a sustainability perspective?
■ Does the product engage users in some active management of energy preservation (user messages and notifications or alerts)?

---

[13]http://www.greenpeace.org/international/en/campaigns/climate-change/cool-it/Guide-to-Greener-Electronics/.

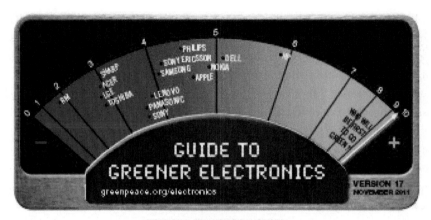

HP, 1st position, 5.9/10

HP takes the lead in the re-launched Guide with 5.9 points. It scores most of its points and is the leader on the new Sustainable Operations criteria, which includes the management of its supply chain. It has the best programme for measuring and reducing emissions of greenhouse gases (GHGs) from its suppliers, disclosing emissions from its manufacturing at 3,500,000 tonnes CO_2-e, with 91 percent of first-tier suppliers reporting estimated emissions in 2009. It also scores maximum points for its thorough paper procurement policy. HP and Dell are the only companies in the Guide that effectively exclude the sourcing of paper from suppliers linked to illegal logging or deforestation. Together with Apple, HP is also a top scorer for its policies and practices on the sourcing of conflict minerals, for publishing its suppliers and engaging effectively in the Electronics Industry Citizenship Coalition's conflict-free smelter program. The only operations criteria where it scores relatively poorly is e-waste, where it needs to expand its take-back programme for consumers in countries without legislation and improve on its reporting of data.

HP is also a relatively high scorer on the Energy criteria, and does especially well for its disclosure of externally verified GHG emissions from its own operations and for setting targets for their reduction, with reductions of 9 percent from 2009, although it needs to address increasing emissions from business travel and to set more ambitious targets to reduce its own GHG emissions by at least 30 percent by 2015 for its operations and to use 100 percent renewable electricity by 2020. Its score for its clean energy plan is average and although its use of renewable energy is increasing it needs to increase this further. HP is also rewarded for its relatively strong advocacy position in opposition to California's proposition 23 in Nov 2010, which it believes was to "impair California's leadership in reducing greenhouse gases".

It scores the least points in the Products category; although it scores comparatively well for its progress on phasing out the use of polyvinyl chloride (PVC) plastic and brominated flame retardants (BFRs) from its product range and is on track to achieve 90 percent of its new goal to phase out BFR and PVC in newly introduced personal computing products in 2011. HP needs to report on the amount of post-consumer plastics it uses as a percentage of all plastics and publicly disclose the length of warranty and spare parts availability for its main product lines, as well as show more innovations to extend product life. HP does not provide a summary of the energy efficiency of its products by giving a percentage of its products that meet the latest Energy Star standards (or other relevant international standard for external power options); this should be published on its website, for each product range. However, HP risks a penalty point in future Guide editions as it is a member of trade associations that have commented against stringent energy efficiency standards; it needs to distance itself from such regressive positions with a strong statement.

HP Overall Score

	ZERO	LOW	MEDIUM	HIGH
Disclose own operational GHG emissions				■
GHG emissions reductions and targets			■	
Clean Electricity Plan (CEP)				
Clean Energy Policy Advocacy		■		
Product Energy Efficiency			■	
Avoidance of Hazardous Substances in Products			■	
Use of Recycled Plastic in Products		■		
Product Life-Cycle			■	
Measure and reduce energy consumption in the supply chain			■	
Chemicals Management and Advocacy			■	
Policy and practice on sustainable sourcing of fibres for paper				■
Policy and practice on avoidance of conflict minerals			■	
Provides effective voluntary take-back where no EPR exists		■		

Figure 3.11

Greenpeace Green Report for Electronics 2011.

- Does the product provide energy usage management guidance as part of the out-of-the-box experience, for example, a smart usage guide?
- What is the performance of the product in the market with the user?
- What are the user's perceived and real experiences with the product?
- What is the user's perception of the ecological value of the product, its durability?
- How long does the product last?
- Do users think that the products are durable?
- If broken, can the user repair the product easily, is it serviceable?
- Can the constituent parts of the product be broken down to create other products?
- Are alternative service subscription options available for the product?

These questions, as you will see, are a subset of the questions generated earlier to help collect realistic user data when conducting something like an ethnographic study. What is noticeable in reading the Greenpeace report is the need to report unit data, which translate to end user data. By understanding the unit value of impact, we can calculate the mass impact carbon emissions and other values that feed into sustainability calculations? Given all of this, what better place to be positioned than as the user experience researchers and designers, who are already positioned to collect such critical unit data from end users as they use a product.

What Does It Mean to User Experience and Design Practitioners?

In solidifying a sustainable design practice from both the research and design sides of things, many of us can begin to think about the work we do and address such key areas as how our products measure up in the market in terms of packaging, energy consumption, documentation use, and the like. We can begin to think about the real possibilities of utilizing our roles as user experience professionals to improve and drive better design, not only on an aesthetical level but on an ecological level as well. While we operate within our respective businesses, designing for user and other environmental constraints, understanding the landscapes gives us clearer insight into positioning ourselves as contributors to enabling sounder ecologically minded practices and becoming part of the new era of designers who design with conscience.

THOUGHTS ABOUT ETHNOGRAPHY, USER EXPERIENCE, AND SUSTAINABILITY

More companies are beginning to recognize the value of ethnographic research and are incorporating this approach into more traditional marketing research methodologies. Ethnography, as we have known it from a usability research perspective, is a comprehensive method that goes beyond the limitations of focus groups by taking marketing research outside the laboratory setting into the real lives of users. Ethnographers observe, interview, and capture users (audio, video) in the context of their everyday lives, where they work, live, shop, and play. Ethnography goes beyond surveys and their standard question-and-answer status quo, and ultimately reveals realities in all its intricacy. Utilizing this method as a basis to evolve the practice of sustainability user experience will go a long way in designing with more conscience and realism.

FRAMEWORK FOR A SUSTAINABLE USER EXPERIENCE PRACTICE

So far we have looked the phases and the kinds of questions and issues that can be addressed as we create framework for practical application. Table 3.1 is a consolidation of the previous sections in a bird's eye view and for quicker reference. It illustrates a listing of the key product phases and the questions that researchers and designers can use as to gather data. It also shows that kinds of tools and methods that can be used

Table 3.1 Table Framework for Sustainable User Experience Data collection

Product Phases	Questions
Manufacturing	a. Of what materials are the products made? b. How were the materials extracted? c. Does the product contain hazardous materials? d. Was the product manufactured under ethical conditions, extraction, manufacturing process?
Transportation	a. What transportation costs (emissions) are associated with the product's production? b. How is the product packaged? c. What are the packaging constituents? d. Is associated documentation produced as part of the out-of-the-box experience? e. Are products compactable to lower transportation emissions and cost?
Usage and energy consumption	a. How much energy is consumed in the production and use of the product? b. If the product has a user interface, is it efficiently designed from a sustainability perspective? c. Does the product engage users in allowing some active management of energy preservation (user messages and notifications or alerts)? d. Does the product provide energy usage management guidance as part of the out-of-the-box experience, for example, a smart usage guide? e. What is the performance of the product in the market with the user? f. What are the user's perceived and real experiences with the product? g. What is the user's perception of the ecological value of the product, its durability?

Product Phases	Questions
Recyclability (reuse and dematerialization)	a. How long does the product last? b. Do end users think the products are durable? c. If broken, can the user repair the product easily, is it serviceable? d. Can the constituent parts of the product be broken down to create other products? e. Are there alternative service subscription options to the product? f. Does the product have other hardware product dependencies when upgraded? g. Are constituent parts available locally?
Facilities	Not covered
Customer perception	a. What is the performance of the company's products in the market with the user? b. What are the user's perceived and real experiences with the product? c. What is the user's perception of the ecological value of the product, its durability? d. How can the company design solutions and make changes to improve users' eco perception?

Using the table, both design researchers and designers can more easily situate their roles in the life cycle and achieve a study based on measures and metrics. To conclude, this proposed framework is meant as an example to start thinking about how we can create frameworks appropriate for our respective fields.

WRAPPING UP

One of the ways in which traditional user experience and usability became an entrenched part of the software development life cycle was in demonstrating, by quantifiable means, a user centric approach to design. At its infancy, the kinds of measures collected were such things as task flow efficiency, product learnability, and user satisfaction. The value of these objective questions bodes well for thrusting user experience into the company's boardrooms and improving communications with respective development teams. Therefore, driving a practice that infuses sustainability issues as part of user experience, it is important to utilize measures and metrics to illustrate value. The key to making impact is to be able to know where we are, what we need to change, and what impact the change has on the products we design. We can do so only through institutionalizing a framework for gathering quantitative data, alongside qualitative data.

This chapter extrapolated some of the issues we should address to create the necessary frameworks for gathering relevant user feedback. As the field matures, so will the information we need to provide more precise measures.

LOOKING THROUGH THE DESIGN LENS

As the general field of user experience design strives to remain relevant, practitioners need to understand the full extent to which a product has impact on its end user and vice versa. The opportunities that lie in ecologically guided design are prime for exploration. As stated in the earlier portions of this chapter, products exist for users. Our role, as designers of all functional shades, is to situate ourselves in the process and address some of those issues that can help limit carbon emissions, within our control. Experience designers, for example, can ask questions such as how to create nonintrusive messages to help users manage their energy consumption. These are but a few of the areas that interaction designers can already begin to address. Visual designers may make their mark by designing solutions that limit the possibility of print and force users' immersion in the virtual version of the experience, for example. Industrial designers, as part of the software design cycle, can also contribute by helping select materials that have longer life and designing in such a manner that products do not fall apart with ease. Last but not least, we can contribute along the continuum of design, engaging industrial, interaction, and visual designs by having face time with end users and ensuring that new approaches to design ultimately satisfy the users. The delta between the older ways of design and new ecologically driven approaches can form the basis for showing improved value and eventually affecting not only a company's bottom line but also our planet's.

IN THE NEXT CHAPTER

Chapter 3 has just given insight into factors of sustainability, those areas used to assess a product's carbon footprint. They are a tangible set of markers that we can use to address a product in pursuit of more sustainable and eco-conscious design. Undoubtedly, it is here that many of us will begin to engage and see how we can contribute to this wider initiative of sustainable design. In the next chapter, we look at the inclusion of the traditional concepts in our field to build our envisioned framework. This includes research concepts and methodologies as well as the persistent software development life cycle that dictates how we have worked over the years. Tying in the traditional with new concepts is the goal of the subsequent chapter.

CHAPTER 4

PULLING IT ALL TOGETHER

INFORMATION IN THIS CHAPTER

INTRODUCTION

In Chapter 3, we examined product life-cycle phases that experts use to assess a product's sustainability performance. We went further to situate the user experience practice alongside this phased approach to drive a framework for collecting user data along the continuum of the product's life, particularly during the "use" phase. In this phase (product use), products emit most of the carbon emission; therefore, the usage data we collect from research with user can be used as unit measure contributing to more aggregate data.

This chapter pulls together concepts learned so far and provides some practical guidance on how we can set sustainability goals to measure performance, given our role as design stakeholders; it also provides direction on the types of sustainability data we can target, given our role in the context of the design cycle.

The chapter further examines the various life cycles of product and software development and ties together the methods, metrics, and knowledge we already have as a base for building a sustainability user experience framework. The goal is to visualize a framework that integrates sustainability data with other types of user and usability data, integrated in known product cycles to enable measuring. Such types of user data collected may include, but not limited to,

- Users product perception.
- Users' expectation of company's social responsibility.
- Energy consumption and usage patterns of a product.
- What happens post usage at the product's end of life.
- Leveraging data from users to determine prolonged usage scenarios of the product.
- Exploring post usage scenarios:
  - How might a product's life be extended?
  - How might a product be used after its utility in one form has expired?

A SPECIAL PREFACE TO THIS CHAPTER

While assembling this book, some of my peers and contributors provided insight into this chapter and its position to best optimize its usefulness for those seeking immediate practical application of the concepts outlined throughout the book. One takeaway from contributors and peers is that, given the nature of how people read today (hyperlinking versus continuous as with a novel), some readers may come directly to this chapter as a point of departure. Therefore, this chapter is tailored for those who feel the need to move ahead in their reading and get right to practice, then to the basics later. It is structured as a thread of discussion that starts with the role of user experience; second, the engagement of users and customers; third, integration of sustainability goals in design and development to achieve optimal sustainable user experiences; and fourth, the research methods that we can use to collect data during the product manufacturing life cycle alongside design and development cycles.

I touch upon the following, in this general order:

- The emerging role of user experience in the sustainable design process.
- User perception and the design process.
- User research as part of the process.
- The design and development life cycle.
- Setting goals as part of the product design and development life cycle.
- Integrating sustainability in the life cycles.
- A proposed framework.
- Reporting.

Following these, we revisit some of the known and established methodologies and practices of user experience to look at how we can use our knowledge base to drive a practice based on measures and metrics. This looks at such activities as ethnography and other forms of user research utilized to collect the data based on sustainability goals set in earlier part of the product design.

EMERGING ROLE OF USER EXPERIENCE IN THE SUSTAINABLE DESIGN PROCESS

User experience refers to a customer's total experience when it comes to interacting with a product, from how users feel about the product to the brand image, to acquiring it, to using it, and even just having this product as part of their living environment. It is a given that good design results in an overall positive user experience, while poor design universally results in a negative experiences. Further, a positive user experience should be the ultimate goal of any kind of product design.

However, what constitutes good product design is extremely subjective; it varies, depending on the product itself, the target market, as well as its competitive landscape. For example, the same design goals and criteria do not apply to designer shoes as to computer keyboards or water bottles, for that matter. Attempting to duplicate the experience would result in a product that has lost sight of its user experience goals. However, based on some of the designed products in market, one can argue that some companies have lost sight of their initial product goals. Unfortunately, this is not the only way that companies miss their user experience objectives. It is very easy for designers, and for that matter developers, to lose sight of the intended goals of the product.

Today, as we need to think of additional goals during the specification phase (such as eco-conscious design principles and sustainability goals), the challenges are even greater. However, as we think about design in the context of such things as software development and design cycles and mapping back to an optimized user experience, we need to track back to the drivers and triggers for designs in the first place.

WHY PRODUCTS EXIST

The primary reason why designed products exist is the need of people to achieve a specific goal, whether it is the design of a chair for sitting, a phone for connecting with others, or a refrigerator to keep things cold. All these products meet a need and help us achieve our goals. In turn, companies assume the role to meet those needs by designing products and solutions to this end. We need to take a step back to think of the prespecification phase to ensure that the initial needs of users are not lost in translation as we move through the cycles of product design. We now need to consider these factors as well as postdesign phases needed for continuous and sustainable product design. We also need to "toe the line" and work within the constraints of business goals. Sometimes, features over functionality and sustainability are the mode of operation. While we have very little control over the role that consumerism plays in this this cycle, we can contribute by being aware of the product in all its stages: from user goals and needs to how it is created to how it performs and cyclically how we can use the usage data to improve subsequent cycles of the same design. This means we need to consider

- How users perceive a product.
- How they would like to use the product.
- How we should optimize and reset product goals to meet user needs, and how to drive more sustainable user behavior.
- How to meet environmental needs as well as business needs all at once.
- How the various design and development cycles intertwine and support sustainability goals.

In synthetizing all these factors, we can achieve more sustainable design by thinking of the cycle of events that drive a product's creation and the goals and needs that we need to keep in mind at every part of the cycle. These goals now extend to sustainability goals.

THE USERS' PERCEPTION AND PRODUCT EXPERIENCE

Today many businesses face increasing difficulties when it comes to product user experience. This is because, even though companies try to build in an experience, end users bring their subjective view to the process, creating a new and unintended product perception that overrides the intended marketing perception. The perceptions that customers have of the company, whether imagined or real, are important input for how we design. If a product has an experience legacy of not being durable or not holding its charge, this user experience perception information needs to be cycled through subsequent iterations of designs. These perceived experiences have a lot to do with the experiences that users have had in the past, as well as the subconsciously pushed experiences users have. A past product experience, or the simulated experience presented via commercial marketing helps form our perception of the product experience. While many may never be able to afford a luxury car, the vicarious experience from commercials influences our perception that the experience is a pleasurable one. When consumers make purchases, the visual aesthetics of a product is their first encounter, which either attracts or repels them. However, today, it is not enough to have beautiful product. Think back to one of the sustainability frameworks encountered in Chapter 2, the idea of total beauty. This framework is based on the ideal that surface-level beauty is not enough, today. Users, today, look beyond the surface to such things as product value, durability, manufacturing, and company practices. The total beauty framework uses a technique to score a product so that companies know where to focus their improvement efforts. Scoring is based on whether a product is efficient, cyclic, uses solar, is safe, and social all at the same time. In terms of the product's "total beauty," consumers are better informed, and as the spread of environmentalism takes it course, users are asking questions such as

- What is the battery life?
- What are the company's takeback program initiatives?
- What are the company's social responsibility practices?
- Are the materials used in the product ethically sourced?
- Is the product durable?
- Is the product too heavy; is it portable?

All these perception questions map easily onto sustainability goals that we can set at the onset of design by having this level of psychographic understanding of our users through user research. Today, the push for more eco awareness in society and subsequently in design has created a new class of consumer (user), one whose core values align with such things as

- Avoiding pollution.
- Conserving natural resources.
- Eliminating wasteful products.
- Being energy efficient.

Today, consumers have different criteria for their product experiences; they are demanding integration of their core values, not only in the final products but also in the design process. Understanding this paradigmatic user trend is the role of user experience in the age of sustainability.

How can we respond to the changing user needs and goals and how can we tie this back to our role in development and design?

We must engage at the tactical and strategic levels to translate the changing relationship that businesses have with customers to ensure we meet a new standard of user experience. The growing base of informed and eco conscious users care not only about functionality but impose their core values on the products they purchase and chose to use in their daily lives.

PERCEIVED PRODUCT VALUE AND THE USER EXPERIENCE

One concept often overlooked as part of the design cycle and the work we do as user experience researchers is the "perceived value" of a product. A product's perceived value is the value consumers assign to it, based on things like how it looks, of what it is made, and how it is priced. Oftentimes, however, value and sustainability go hand in hand. Take for example a pair of shoes built to last for 10–15 years. In many cases, it means that the manufacturer chose the materials used to make the shoes with the goal of durability and stayed clear of *planned obsolescence* as a product marketing strategy. This also results in less waste in the landfills. The perception that users have of a product being of a certain quality therefore goes hand in hand with how soon they dispose of the product. This perception of lesser value is a critical element that we have to factor in when redesigning, another opportunity to define goals based on user perception.

When consumers are faced with two products, one of which is cheaper and made of inferior material and the other of a higher price but made of superior quality products, the choice is often easy. Perceived value plays an integral part in the design process when it comes to such activities as selecting materials. Many manufacturers seek to optimize cost savings by using inferior products. However, this choice is one that user experience designers need to actively think about when collecting user data and informing design. Some materials have an intrinsically high perceived value. For example, metal and glass as more valuable than plastic, silver is more valuable than copper, and so on. Therefore, as part of driving for more sustainable design practices, it is advisable that, when we collect user data to inform design, the perceived product value be included as part of the data set and designers engage in material selection that increases perceived value. The eventual goal is waste reduction, because when customers feel that something is more valuable, they are likely to retain it for longer periods.

How do we as user experience professionals create this sustainable user experience, given this insight?

The user experience can be viewed as a number of related cycles: First, the users' cycle (from the phases of purchase, usage, and ownership to disposal). Second, the design and development life cycle is another cycle that often seems disconnected from the user's cycle. While the user and usage cycle comes after the design and development cycle, it also is a cycle that offers opportunities for infusing built-in design and development elements that influences and help define the products overall user experience. The third cycle is the product cycle itself in terms of a stainability. It can be seen as an overlay of stainability performance along the continuum of design and development. In terms of a product's sustainability performance. This last cycle is the opportunity for looking at the design and development cycle with respect to infusing "inner" beauty of the product, its sustainability points. For example, a well-built product that lasts and is serviceable ties in with sustainability and, at the same time, gives users an impression of overall quality. Therefore in a practical example making design and development choices that foster such stainability points as serviceability and durability only serves to give users a more postitive experience.

In the next sections, I touch on the latter two cycles, as it is fair to say user experience practitioners have been socialized on the ideals of the first cycle, the user cycle, and much attention has already been give the purchase to usage stages, though not to the sustainability aspects that enhance usage in a more socially and environmentally driven manner. The goal now is to integrate the sustainability goals and gather more data points for improved design and development.

THE USER, THE RESEARCH, AND THE FINDINGS

In an earlier example (focus group research example), I discuss a project where the research goal was the collection of affective design data. In this example, the company's focus was on ensuring that its product was visually on par with the two main competitors. However, what happened was that the issues users had were unrelated to the product's visual appeal. In fact, users were relatively satisfied with the visuals of the graphical user interface; they had come to accept the company's visual look and feel as standard brand and the reliability of the company's software was notable. The issues were related to the poor hardware quality, which was incongruent with the brand image of "solidity," "reliability," and "durability." The product was a premium mobile and email solution priced above the rest, but the recent hardware seemed incongruent with the brand value. Product components (such as trackballs and buttons) were so poorly designed that they fell off easily, leaving users with an unfavorable product experience: The perceived value of the product when set against the pricing left users bitter. Further, the inferior dome sheet of the phones chipped very easily and the product looked much older than it was, after only 3 months of use.

As researchers, it can sometimes be frustrating when a study's goals are overshadowed by issues that are out of scope of the research, particularly if these are issues of which you too are aware but helpless to address, given your role and research scope. In many cases, as user researchers, there is no way to convey such critical data because of the endemic silos typically found in large organizations. Nevertheless, the data need to be included in the reports simply for data integrity preservation, and it may eventually receive some recognition when companies are more engaged on every level as to the impact of unsustainable design practices.

The findings in this focus group were later confirmed by churn rate reports, divulged by phone carriers and consumer reports, relaying much the same information as the earlier focus group users divulged. However, the damage was uncontainable at that point, given the nature of the internet and how quickly information spreads. In the near future, social networks may be the source of on-the-fly data product data. This can supplement such moderated activities as focus groups, and we can gather more general and detailed insight into the true issues that users face when using products. User reporting may confirm that many of the issues with products have to do with quality that can be resolved with a sustainable approach to design.

In fact, the concerns and problems that consumers face today spearheaded such initiatives by organizations like the Go Green foundation.[1] To empower people to make more "green-aware" purchases at point of purchase, Go Green and Climate Counts came together to provide access to thousands of environmental scorecards and ratings of recognizable consumer brands in industries such as clothing, consumer electronics, and fast food. In the case of the Go Green Initiatives, using simple text messaging, users can instantly receive the ratings about the companies and brands they purchase as well as contribute to the product data by entering their experience data.

Following this focus group, the company in question created a sustainability department, loosely aligned with user research. The department uses a rudimentary product eco scorecard incorporated in its reports, shared with vendors to counter some of the similar scorecards that the vendors themselves generate on the same products. In this case, the company responded to the vendors' scorecard to counter and supplement others' view of their products. Nevertheless, the eventual goal of all is a more tightly coupled report of sustainability issues, stemming from usage and user experience research.

Parts of these types of initiatives (sustainability departments) come from Europe, where there is more consumer awareness of environmental issues and active engagement in sustainability initiatives. These eco-savvy consumers are demanding transparency of the products' virtues, and this is served up to them in the form of scorecards. In the case of the company's initiative to develop a sustainability department, mobile carriers in Europe went as far as placing eco scorecards alongside each product for consumers to peruse, a common practice today. The company was displeased with the scores and used the internal team to "repaint" the eco image as a supplement to the external scorecard. For the vendors, presenting products' scorecards is a way of assisting consumers to make wise, ecologically sound purchases, a trend more entrenched in Western Europe today and gaining wide traction in North America as well. On the other hand, the company in question had a different goal, which some may define as "greenwashing." However, the strong eco trends driving

---

[1]The mission of the Go Green Initiative is to provide schools, homes, businesses, and organizations of all kinds with the tools and training they need to create a "culture of conservation" within their community. Its goals are to conserve and protect natural resources for future generations and protect human health through environmental stewardship.

markets will eventually undermine any greenwashing attempts by businesses wishing to adopt a Band-Aid approach to solving eco delinquencies.

BUSINESSES, TRENDS, AND SUSTAINABILITY STRATEGIES

While I do not spend a lot of time on strategy, as better books exist (see Adam Werbach's *Strategy for Sustainability*, 2009),[2] we need to spend some time on understanding some of the trends that will be the tipping point for many companies to latch on to this powerful initiative. In 2010, Forum for the Future,[3] a nonprofit organization working globally with business and government to create a sustainable future, held its annual meeting. It does so by creating partnerships and developing practical innovations in the aim of transforming key sustainable issues. At the 2010 meeting, the forum cited a number of sustainability strategies that businesses should engage in making headways. The following are among these top trends:

1. Focus on low-carbon opportunities.
2. Drive value by embedding sustainability into core strategy.
3. Build greater resilience into supply chains.
4. Integrate "reverse innovation," innovation originating in emerging markets, into business models.
5. Engage in two-way dialogue with customers to build trust and generate valuable market insights.
6. Collaborate across the full value chain to cocreate new products, services, and business models.
7. Map biodiversity-related risks and opportunities.

Each of these strategies offers a myriad of opportunities for improvement; however, of note is item 5, which lies at the core of user experience.

The user experience practice, which elevates and places a focus on customers and their interaction with systems, products, and services, has the opportunity to make the leap and refashion itself as an added value, by incorporating a sustainability approach in how it translates and transforms the user experience. Customers' heightened awareness of eco issues and their resulting expectations are major trends and drivers of sustainability as a business approach, and user experience has the chance to transform itself from a commoditized offering into a value-critical service by incorporating a sustainability lens into their framework. An overview

[2]http://www.strategyforsustainability.com/book/.
[3]http://www.forumforthefuture.org/about.

of the rise of sustainability as a corporate necessity due to the convergence of business needs, regulatory environment, consumer expectations, and other drivers covered how that compares and contrasts with the need for user experience.

The subsequent proposed framework that emerges in the rest of this chapter is intended to fulfill the need for more layers of product reporting beyond the usual measures of: learnability, efficiency, effectiveness, and the currently popular affective design research trends. Incorporating opportunities to extract sustainability data as part of user contact is necessary in reshaping the overall design of products and solutions.

PULLING TOGETHER TRADITIONAL TOOLS AND NEW IDEAS

Today, many user experience practices have an in-house repository of tools, methodologies, and activities that they use to evaluate and design products, depending on the phase of the product life cycle. This may include anything from heuristic evaluation forms, scorecards (to track task performance) to ethnographic procedures (such as a protocol for collecting in-field data etc., usability-testing procedures). As we move ahead and integrate new concepts of sustainability, we need to mesh our existing knowledge base with the product life cycle phases encountered in the previous chapter: from manufacturing to energy usage (in-market use) to recyclability. In many ways, it is an alignment of known product development cycles and our own methods and tools to what we can term the *sustainability framework*. Aligning our traditional knowledge base with a framework that speaks to collecting targeted use data by product design phases is the goal to collecting comprehensive user data. You may be asking yourself:

a. How does all of this map to the software design and development structures that I use?
b. At what points do I use traditional or new tools to include user data throughout the product life cycle?
c. What methodologies can I use to collect the data associated with in-market use of the product?
d. What kinds of data do I need to support a product's improved sustainability?
e. How do I integrate these findings into a report?
f. How do I report users' comments on such things as product durability?
   And so on.

At first, the many questions may be overwhelming. However, they must be seen within the product life cycle context, incorporate existing knowledge and tools, as well as integrate new ideas and concepts from the field of sustainability. Let us take a moment to look at the Product design and development life cycle, as many of us know it today. Do not be too concerned if the graphic is not exactly as you know it in the specific context of your work, as there are many renditions of this illustration and concept. Using this as the base of knowledge, we build from here by overlaying the proposed sustainability framework and show points of connectivity to models we already know and use. This includes the software development life cycles and product design, respectively.

LIFE CYCLES: CONNECTING DESIGN, DEVELOPMENT, AND SUSTAINABILITY

Many companies currently use some kind of product life-cycle process for managing a project's progress. Rather than establishing a new process for executing and managing sustainability, it is fitting to integrate known sustainability frameworks into the existing process cycles. We need to be able to overlay the varying cycles and see where we have touch points and opportunities for setting sustainability goals and collecting sustainability metrics to drive the process in a sustainable design direction.

The concept of cycles is not applicable exclusively to product and software life-cycle processes. Much as we encountered when we looked at the cradle-to-cradle approach, we can begin to think about how a framework integrating seemingly complex cycles can work. For this reason, sustainability specifications should be included with other product performance specifications that are normally tracked in the product development process.

While they are complementary, the product life cycle process should not be confused with the life-cycle assessment (LCA) as we have encountered earlier. In the case of the product development cycle, I refer to the phases of product development—ideation, concept development, prototyping, detail design and production. While a design cycle is normally subsumed by the more extensive software cycle in some companies, I mention both separately for readers more familiar with one over the other as the Product cycle is often referenced to product design while software cycle to software development.

THE PRODUCT DESIGN AND SOFTWARE DEVELOPMENT LIFE CYCLES

The software and product development life cycles (SDLC and PDLC), for the most part, have similar features when thinking of the model (Figure 4.1). The software cycle, sometimes referred to a *system design cycle*, consists of the following steps that we can align to the product cycles we explored in Chapter 3 ("Product Life Cycle and Sustainable User Experience"). In Chapter 3, we discuss cycles in terms of the process of product life end to end, from manufacturing to disposal.

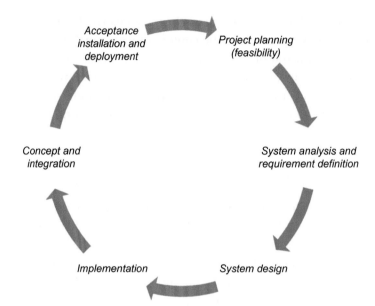

Figure 4.1

*Software Development
Life-Cycle Model.*

For those not too familiar and reading this book, I outline in brief the basic steps in software and system design, which is for reference only, as we set out laying out a wider framework, where we can begin to engage and practice sustainable design, specific to software. The phases are

1. **Project planning and feasibility study:** In this step, stakeholders establish a high-level view of the intended project and determine its goals.
2. **Systems analysis and requirements definition:** This step is the definition of the project goals into defined functions and operation of the intended application to be designed. This step analyzes end-user information needs.[4]
3. **Systems design:** This step describes desired features and operations in detail, including screen layouts, business rules, process diagrams, and other documentation.[5]
4. **Implementation:** This step is the building of the application.
5. **Integration and testing:** This step brings all the pieces together into a special testing environment, then checks for errors, bugs (quality assurance), and interoperability (does it integrate with other systems?
6. **Acceptance, installation, and deployment:** The final stage of initial development is where the software is accepted, installed, and deployed for use.
7. **Maintenance:** The maintenance stage considers such things as updates, changes, improvement, additions, for example, platform migrations and the like.

---

[4]This is an opportunity for user experience practitioners.
[5]Designers and researchers engage here as well, to provide support and design direction.

For those of us more in tuned with the design of product, the following termi-nology is perhaps better suited to describing product design (Figure 4.2):

1. **Ideation:** This is the phase of discovery of an idea for design. In this phase, the idea may be researched, recorded, and patented.
2. **Conceptualization:** In the conceptualization stage, there is often a brainstorm session that helps fine-tune the design. Results from this brainstorming may include such things as drawings and other concept artifacts.
3. **Design and development:** In the design and development stage, many designers may work with some form of virtual tool to begin a modeling of their concept, ensuring that such things as ergonomics are well tested and practical.
4. **Prototypes:** Next, the virtual prototypes are given shape in the form of working prototypes. Oftentimes, user experience designers are heavily involved, as these designs need some form of user validation.
5. **Testing:** The testing phase may take the shape of user sessions or focus groups. Input from users may result in redesign, rework, and respecifications.
6. **Marketing:** In the marketing phase, the project is on its way to being used by users. This is another stage where user experience design plays an instrumental role in ensuring that the product meets the needs of the users.

What is common is that each cycle provides the opportunity for us to think about our role as experience designers and how we can infuse the sustainability principles and practices amassed so far in his book.

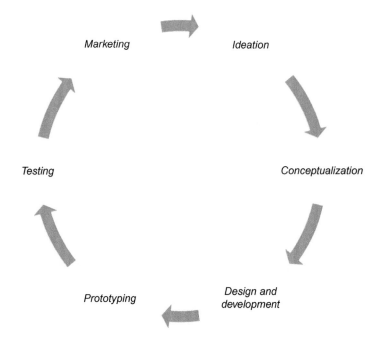

Figure 4.2
Product Design Life Cycle.

As we consider the process of design, we have to include all of these cycles as we think consciously and responsibly about design.

THE PRODUCT LIFE CYCLE (USED IN LIFE-CYCLE ANALYSIS)

Now, as we think about sustainability, we move to the life-cycle assessment internationally recognized and accepted as one of the most popular life-cycle design techniques for evaluating environmental performance of a product. The life cycle in the LCA context of the product (Figure 4.3) refers to the life of the product from cradle to grave. This includes the activities such as materials sourcing, refining, manufacturing, assembly, transportation, usage, and finally, end of life of the product. This cycle of assessment, weaved through design and development, enables us to begin thinking of the process of design in an ecologically conscious manner.

Integrated life-cycle thinking aims to combine these two processes (LCA and software and product development), respectively (Figure 4.4).

In viewing the three cycles as congruent and relational, we can better align the respective goals and consolidate a sustainability plan that addresses each phase in turn.

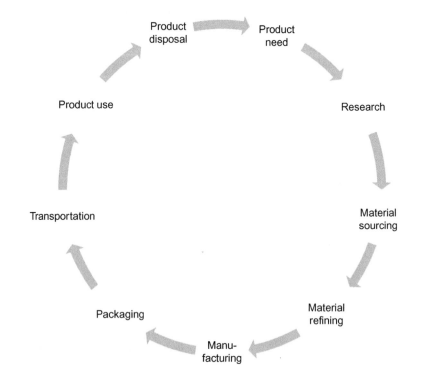

Figure 4.3

Product Life-Cycle (Used in LCA) Model.

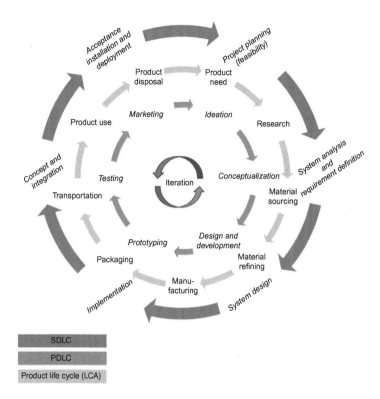

Figure 4.4
SDLC, PDLC, and LCA
Cycles.

PRODUCT AND SOFTWARE DESIGN LIFE CYCLE AND SUSTAINABILITY

Typically, product design and development begins in earnest with several con-cepts. The process starts with several loosely defined concepts. The concepts are then refined through iteration, and elimination until it is optimized for develop-ment. At earlier stages, the feasibility of meeting performance targets also is clari-fied. However, many companies wait to evaluate sustainability performance until later stages of the process, due to the perception that it is difficult to evaluate sus-tainability metrics on vaguely defined concepts. However, this perception arises because sustainability tools such as LCA require sophistication and accuracy. For example, the performance of a computer cannot be fully defined until every component is identified; yet, teams are able to select and define concepts early, based on performance through their experience, best practices, and guidelines. Like other performance metrics, best practices and guidelines for sustainability targets need to be developed during this stage.

> We are searching for some kind of harmony between two intangibles: a form which we
> have not yet designed and a context which we cannot properly describe.[6]

---

[6]Alexander, Ishikawa, and Siulverstein, A Pattern Language, 1977.

In locating user experience as part of the design cycle, we can provide some insight into connecting the loose dots and driving a closer coupling of design with sustainability. We have amassed a growing base of knowledge about measuring sustainability, today; we can also begin to use experience, best practices, and guidelines as a base to setting goals and integrating sustainable practices in the design cycle. We can look to many of the guiding principles of the learned frameworks as guidance and input at this point.

In Shedroff and Lovins's book *Design Is the Problem,* they propose some of the frameworks and strategies that can be used in the phases and subphases when designing. Table 4.1 serves as a great quick guide for designers and developers alike. It is also an adoption of Shedroff and Lovins's guide but tailored to meet the needs of user research professionals to enable identification:

Table 4.1 Framework and Strategies by Development Subphases

Software and Product Phases (SDLC and PDLC)	Referential Sustainability Framework	Sustainability Goals and Strategies
SDLC: Project planning and feasibility study PDLC: Ideation	Cradle to cradle Biomimicry Natural capitalism Sustainability helix*	Design for efficiency Transmaterialization Interoperability Localizations Informationalization Interoperability (think systemically vs. systematically)
SDLC: Systems analysis and requirements definition PDLC: Conceptualization	Cradle to cradle Biomimicry Natural capitalism Sustainability helix*	Design for efficiency Transmaterialization Interoperability (think systemically vs. systematically) Localizations Informationalization
SDLC: Systems design PDLC: Design and development prototyping (may be virtual proof of concept) and iterative before actual design	Biomimicry Total beauty Natural step Life-cycle analysis Cradle to cradle SROI*	Design for use Dematerialization Material substitution Design for efficiency Transmaterialization Interoperability Design for disassembly Design for serviceability Localizations Informationalization Design for durability Avoid planned obsolescence Design for reuse Design for effectiveness Design for all (universal access) Design for safety Design for aesthetics (users keep beautiful things)

Software and Product Phases (SDLC and PDLC)	Referential Sustainability Framework	Sustainability Goals and Strategies
SDLC: Implementation PDLC: Design	Biomimicry Total beauty Natural step Life-cycle analysis Cradle to cradle SROI*	Design for use Dematerialization Material substitution Design for efficiency Transmaterialization Interoperability Localizations Informationalization Design for durability Design for disassembly Design for serviceability Avoid planned obsolescence Design for reuse Design for effectiveness Design for all (universal access) Design for safety Design for aesthetics (users keep beautiful things)
SDLC: Integration and testing PDLC: Testing	Life-cycle analysis SROI* Cradle to cradle Total beauty (All of these frameworks can be used as testing options for determining the product's sustainability performance)	Design for durability Design for reuse Design for effectiveness Close the loop on design Design for disassembly
SDLC: Acceptance, Installation, Deployment PDLC: Marketing	Life-cycle analysis SROI*	Design for reuse Design for users, ensure users know what they are buying, how to recycle (out-of-the-box information) Design for recyclability (takeback programs, compostable, recycle)

*These frameworks involve more strategic business involvement from upper management.

Utilizing and building on such a guide enables discovery of potential sustainability target goals, such as but not limited to

- Design for use and reuse.
- Design for serviceability.
- Design for efficiency.
- Design for durability.
- Designing for disassembly.

One example is making design decisions to ensure that parts used can provide disassembly out-of-the-box information to users. Another is engaging in the selection of materials and stress testing materials to ensure that products are not easily destroyed. In the case of software, another goal may be task optimization. For example, a task that took users 3–4 minutes to complete can now be done in 30 seconds. The latter example is one with which I have had experience with users unable to set a simple ringtone and assign individual ringtones to their contacts. In studies, this task has taken upwards of 4 minutes with users who are intermediate in their mobile phone usage. Consider the efficiency that can be built into workflows to affect one user as well as collective users. The end value is not only retaining customers, users hold on to things that work. At another level, the energy savings from creating efficient workflows can be astounding when aggregated.

Every design decision we make can change results in a product's sustainability performance, which may also result in the adjustment of targets. This requires evaluation to compare the performance of past and present design. Good documentation eases the effort required to track and re-evaluate sustainability metrics. Further, sustainability metrics can be continually refined over time and can later be fine-tuned to address every phase. Consider the ease of later reporting and the diminished evaluation effort as well as the generation of rich marketing data. Apple has already embraced such practices, as we saw earlier, and undoubtedly, many more companies are taking notice (cube optimization of products, for example) that may be used for marketing.

One final point as we think of the element of goal setting and collecting sustainability performance data: The life cycle of the product does not begin with component procurement; it begins with materials sourcing and all the processes necessary to make and deliver the component. This means the impacts on sustainability metrics extends to suppliers and vendors outside of a company. Further, after the product is marketed, it is placed in the user's care for usage. Extending our view of the product life cycle is therefore critical. It is also here that user experience again is useful in ensuring a continuous engagement of goal setting and data collection. This extends to providing sustainability specifications and guidelines for reporting sustainability metrics at many instances.

Integrating sustainability into a product development process may seem like an overwhelming task. For user experience and usability, this also was once considered difficult. However, with the advent of user experience analytics, many companies have implemented sophisticated processes for specifying, integrating, communicating, and ensuring user experience metrics. It is feasible to expand product design to include sustainability. The cycles and frameworks exist; it is just a matter of identifying goals and methods for integrating sustainability into them. This integration can result in increased traction, broader acceptance, and faster integration at all levels of product engagement and design.

Earlier we discussed the SDLC, the established model for how software is designed; we also looked at the PDLC, the product design equivalent. For many in the field of user experience, this knowledge is foundational. Therefore, the leap is introducing the sustainability frameworks and models alongside an SDLC and the PDLC and their interrelationships in an easy to understand and usable framework.

As mentioned earlier, do not be concerned about the previous illustrations used for SDLC, they are not completely identical to the ones you use. The concept of models is to create a relatable abstraction for communicating and, in this case, laying the life cycle of software alongside the sustainability model is a good approach. As we move forward and enable the adoption of sustainability, it is critical that

- We adopt a life-cycle approach that can be laid over existing cycles.
- For each life-cycle activity, sustainability goals should be addressed and methodologies employed to ensure sustainability is incorporated not as a guide but rather in its metrics and measures form.

SDLC, PDLC, and Integrating Sustainability Specifications

During the product specification stage, product managers and other stakeholders begin to set the characteristics of the new product. It is here the designers and user experience researchers can also play a part in supporting the definition of products by deriving more sustainable design. This stage is where an idea takes its form before entering into development. Just as performance goals are set based on consumer user needs and market opportunities, sustainability goals can be set based on higher-level organizational goals and stakeholder interests. In this case, the interests can be positioned as sustainability and social responsibility ones that lie in line with an overarching company mandate. Very rarely does a product specification consider the underlying values on the company, especially those companies that claim to have social responsibility as a core value. It is important to establish sustainability performance goals and metrics when establishing all other specifications of a product. Follow-on stages have better ability and more opportunity to meet goals established at this stage in the life cycle in a cost- and time-effective manner. It also reduces reactively changing a design to add sustainability later. Some of the specification goals that can be defined at this stage relate back to some of the guideposts set by earlier frameworks. For example, does a design make use of reusable parts? Is it durable? Understanding the goals and how they are measured is important to maintaining a continuous collection of relevant data. In the next section, we look a bit closer at some goals that we can use as a basis of measuring, because after all, if we can measure it, then we can set a baseline and determine how we are doing over time.

Setting Sustainability Goals

Before product design begins, the challenge is identifying product performance goals and, more specifically, sustainability goals. This can be driven by data that are collected in the field as well as other stakeholder groups' contributions from their points of view. Since we cannot realize nonmeasureable goals, this step includes first defining metrics for assessing these goals. Teams must first implement identifiable, quantifiable, and measurable performance metrics. However, to keep driving continuous improvement, product development should revisit performance metrics often to confirm their validity and ask if the metrics continue to make sense, given the current state of the product design; if not, what metrics should be revisited for improvement. This activity also applies to us as user experience designers and researchers.

Many of us understand such concepts as functional performance, ease of use, usability, and efficiency. However, like any of these other product performance metrics, all measurements of products, as well as the systems in which they are created, extends to sustainability performance. We can contribute to performance metrics that can make products more sustainable. For example,

- Reduce the carbon footprint over last year's product.
- Reduce the use of toxic material compared to similar products.
- Provide energy-saving messages at defined points.
- Minimize overall ecological impacts.
- Provide users with out-of-the-box information regarding takeback programs.
- Reduce dangerous emissions throughout the product life.
- Help reduce landfill waste by providing suitable user information in web form over hard copy alternatives, where possible.

These are important features of sustainability. All products use resources and lead to emissions; therefore, a 100% sustainable product is not a feasible objective, but in increments, in the spirit of continuous improvement, we can achieve better and more eco-conscious designs. In addition to establishing sustainability goals, it is important to identify the relative baseline for all the goals identified. The specification phase offers the chance to establish or adhere to uniform and similar goals across all product lines and allows for reuse later on.

The nature of sustainability considerations in the development life cycle and the subsequent effectiveness varies widely. Some products may eliminate substances considered harmful to people or the environment, while others include technology to reduce a particular impact. This could involve such things as the replacement of a physical product with a subscription online solution that uses no materials. What is important to take away is that sustainability goals aim to be less harmful, more sustainable for people and the environment. The means of implementing sustainability may vary, but they are most effective when goals are set and metrics are included in the original intent of the product design. However, it is not enough to start out intending to design a more sustainable product; sustainability metrics should be maintained throughout the product life cycle. A life-cycle approach should be incorporated into all aspects of product development.

A PROPOSED FRAMEWORK

Up to this point, we have a bit of an anchoring in the traditional model of the software and design development life cycles, so we can begin to think about positioning these known cycles into a proposed framework. Much like the many renditions of the software development life-cycle framework, the proposed sustainability framework is designed as a guide to allow you to begin thinking of frameworks within the context of your work. While we talked about cycles, the information here is best contained in tabular format for improved readability (Table 4.2). Undoubtedly, as the field of sustainability ripens, we will be able to build beyond this model; but for now, we are able to integrate cycles and visualize evolved cycles where we think of product design with built in sustainability measures.

Table 4.2 Sustainability User Experience Frameworks

Product Phases	Questions	User Research Methodology
Manufacturing	a. Of what materials are the products made? b. How were the materials extracted? c. Does the product contain hazardous materials? d. Was the product manufactured under ethical conditions, extraction, manufacturing process?	Out of scope for user research but possible through product research and adds to user researcher and designers product knowledge for understanding the product beyond usage.

Transportation	a. What transportation costs (emissions) are associated with the product's production?
	b. How is the product packaged?
	c. What are the packaging constituents?
	d. Is associated documentation produced as part of the out-of-the-box experience?
	e. Are products compactable to lower transportation emissions and cost?
		Ethnography
		Surveys
		User sessions
		Panels and forums
		Questionnaires and surveys
		Contextual inquiry
		Focus groups
		Workshops
		End-user interviews
		Data collected using these methods can feed into understanding how to design more efficient systems that focus on such things as
		    Product cube optimization (making things compact based on user needs)
		    Dematerialization: Migrating a service-based solution to replace solutions that require product transportation. See the Chapter 5 case studies.
		    Transmaterialization
		    Informationalization

(Continued)

Table 4.2 Sustainability User Experience Frameworks—cont'd

Product Phases	Questions	User Research Methodology
Usage and energy consumption	a. How much energy is consumed in the production and use of the product? b. If the product has a user interface, is it efficiently designed from a sustainability perspective? c. Does the product allow users active management of energy preservation (user messages and notifications or alerts)? d. Does the product provide energy usage management guidance as part of the out-of-the-box experience, for example, smart usage guide? e. What is the performance of the product in the market with the user? f. What are the user's perceived and real experiences with the product? g. What is the user's perception of the ecological value of the product, its durability?	Ethnography Surveys User sessions Qualitative vs. quantitative research methods Cultural probes and photo ethnography Fly-on-the-wall observation Panels and forums Questionnaires and surveys Competitor analysis Contextual inquiry Focus groups (workshops) End-user interviews
Recyclability (reuse and dematerialization)	a. How long does the product last? b. Do end users think that the products are durable? c. If broken, can the user repair the product easily, is it serviceable? d. Can the constituent parts of the product be broken down to create other products? e. Are alternative service subscription options to the product available? f. Does the product have other hardware product dependencies when upgraded? g. Are constituent parts available locally?	Ethnography Surveys User sessions Qualitative vs. quantitative research methods Cultural probes and photo ethnography Fly-on-the-wall observations Panels and forums Questionnaires and surveys Competitor analysis Contextual inquiry Focus groups (workshops) End-user interviews
Facilities	Not covered	
Customer perception	a. What is the performance of the company's products in the market with the user? b. What are the user's perceived and real experiences with the product? c. What is the user's perception of the ecological value of the product, its durability? d. How can the company design solutions and make changes to improve users' eco perception?	Ethnography Surveys User sessions Qualitative vs. quantitative research methods Cultural probes and photo ethnography Fly-on-the-wall observation Panels and forums Questionnaires and surveys Competitor analysis Contextual inquiry Focus groups (workshops) End-user interviews

EXPLANATION OF THE FRAMEWORK

The first column displays the product life cycle; the second column depicts user-centered data that can be collected; and the third lists the methodologies we can employ (see end of this chapter for methodologies). Most readers, however, are familiar with these methodologies. At each phase, we can also look at the various goals that we can set. We can use this as a guide to determine what methodologies can be used at varying points in a product lifecycle.

Table 4.2, along with Table 4.1, can supplement each other to collect, measure, and set goals that help integrate sustainable design thinking in the design and development life cycle as well as looking at the product life cycle through the user research lens and using basic user research methodology and tools to collect additional user data.

At this point, I do not propose what the data representation should look like in specific cases, except to say that, as the field is still at its infancy, there is a need to temper qualitative data with strong quantitative data that can be collected using the current methods. As well, user researchers have already amassed the skills of determining how data currently collected is presented. Some examples follow, for the benefit of helping readers think of the presentation of data.

KEEPING TRACK: SUSTAINABILITY REPORTING

There are many sustainability-reporting initiatives today but the most notable is the Global Reporting Initiative, which is discussed in Chapter 2. While I cannot endorse any one reporting framework, the GRI is today the most comprehensive and widely adopted and will most likely be the framework of choice adopted by most companies when mandatory reporting becomes law. A brief contextual reintroduction is offered for ease of reference. See Chapter 2 for more on the GRI framework.

GLOBAL REPORTING INITIATIVE FRAMEWORK

The Global Reporting Initiative is a self-described network-based organization that produces a comprehensive sustainability-reporting framework widely used around the world. The goal of the GRI is to affect the continuous application and improvement of the sustainability reporting framework (Figure 4.5). The organization's core goals include disclosure of companies' environmental, social, and governance performance. The GRI's reporting framework was developed through a consensus-seeking, multistakeholder process and is therefore well suited as a guide for any peripheral fields of practice that seek to contribute to the wider initiative. Participants in the GRI are drawn from global business, civil society, labor, academic, and professional institutions that bring a multidimensional view of what a comprehensive framework should look like.

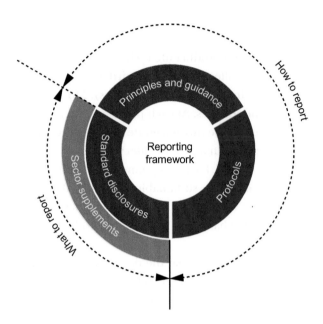

Figure 4.5
GRI Reporting
Framework.

The framework itself comprises comprehensive documentation that provides a guideline for the component of the actual report. The guideline document covers such key sections as protocols, principles and guidance, sectors and supplements, and standard disclosure. The structure has room for companies that wish to provide more granularity than the framework provides.

Currently, companies are not mandated to report on their operations; but it is fully expected that this will be required in the coming years and each year more and more companies are reporting on their own initiative. The reports combine the three spheres that make up the definition of: social, economic, and environmental performance. Given that companies exist to produce a product or service, it may arise that more granular data, sourced from such things as in-market usage (user research), will be included to provide unit impact of the products and services they produce.

It must be noted that the GRI sustainability reporting framework provides guidance on how organizations can disclose their sustainability performance and allows for flexibility in what can be reported. Therefore, some companies provide more granularity than others, depending on the entrenchment of the practice.

The GRI framework itself consists of the sustainability reporting guidelines and principles and is suited to include product data, as the reason that many companies exist is to sell a product. In addition, an understanding of the product's overall impact seems fitting to include in any comprehensive report. The GRI framework is applicable to organizations of any size or type, from any business sector or geographic region, and has been used by thousands of organizations worldwide as the basis for producing their sustainability reports.

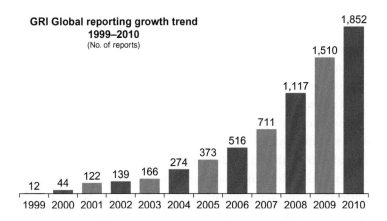

GRI Global reporting growth trend
1999–2010
(No. of reports)

1999	2000	2001	2002	2003	2004	2005	2006	2007	2008	2009	2010
12	44	122	139	166	274	373	516	711	1,117	1,510	1,852

Figure 4.6
GRI Graph Showing the Trend in Reporting, 1999–2010.

To name a few notable companies reporting, though not all to the same degree: Apple, BAE Systems, Barclays, BASF SE, Bayer, Bell Canada, Best Buy, Bloomberg, BMO Financial Group, Bombardier, Chrysler Group LLC, Royal Bank of Canada, Clorox, Coca-Cola Company, COSCO, Daimler, Dell, Deloitte, Heineken N.V., HSBC Group, IBM, Kellogg, Nestle, Siemens, Tyco, and Volvo.[7] However, what is important is the growing traction of the initiative and its influence on how companies will operate in the near future. Moreover, another element not immediately evident is the supply chain and affiliation effect. As a company needs to disclose supply chain reports, it will seek to align with other manufacturers that also practice sustainability as a fundamental company value. The association of environmentally negligent companies is one thing of which companies are keenly aware today. Take for example Greenpeace's *Guide to Greener Electronic* report, where HP topped the list but lost points for its affiliations. The report cites:

> "HP and Dell are the only companies in the Guide that effectively exclude the sourcing of paper from suppliers linked to illegal logging or deforestation . . .
>
> However, HP risks a penalty point in future Guide editions as it is a member of trade associations that have commented against stringent energy efficiency standards; it needs to distance itself from such regressive positions with a strong statement."[8]

Therefore, the trend of reporting will continue (Figure 4.6), as companies wishing to play in the eco-conscious marketplace need to improve their initiatives, without greenwashing.

The types of companies reporting are varied and come from every conceivable industry the marketplace. Even a number of world cities, educational institutes, and other organizations are joining this trend.

---

[7]http://www.globalreporting.org/ReportServices/GRIReportsList/.
[8]http://www.greenpeace.org/international/Global/international/publications/climate/2011/Cool%20IT/ greener-guide-nov-2011/guide-to-greener-electronics-nov-2011.pdf.

WHAT DOES IT MEAN FOR USER EXPERIENCE?

The role of user experience is positioned to contribute in two distinct facets: the data collection and in achieving designs driven by sustainability principles and well-placed goals in the product life cycle. We have a unique point of contact with end users and an exclusive visibility into a product life cycle as it passes through its usage phase. Here, the carbon emissions of most products take place and methodologies, some unique to our practice, can be used to collect data about the behavior of users with the product in market.

It is important to understand that, before we concentrate on the complex, we need to understand the simple; understanding the unit measures that enable more complex measures is an area to which user researchers can contribute. The mobile phone example cited earlier references realistic data that can be observed and gathered directly only from end users in context of use. For example, in the real context of use, we can garner valuable user data.

While we can rely on users in some instances to self-report, it is critical that the methodologies we use combine some level of longitudinal and observation studies as well to give a truer picture of the product usage and context with the user environment:

a. What do users think of the product's durability?

b. Are users able to service products that are broken?

c. Are products designed to optimized energy use?

d. Are users recycling products as they were intended?

e. Do users feel that companies are providing enough out-of-the-box information about proper disposal of a product if it is not recyclable?

There are many more questions of this nature that only anthropological methodologies can answer. For companies to venture a guess as to what these answers may be is not a good basis for driving improvements and being fully socially responsible or realistic about the use of their product. It is also critical to collect unit level data, correctly answer the preceding questions, and build an honest picture of a product's life cycle assessment. Later in this chapter, we revisit the questions and look at what data reporting and representation can look like in its final report.

To speak in more familiar terms, our goal as practitioners is to think of how we can present user data that shows us the wider sustainability initiative in its unit bits and further feed into the overall reporting initiatives. The proposed framework is intended to serve as an approach for reporting on product and service performance as affected by end user use. Both researchers and designers can use it as an awareness gauge that helps us think actively of the kinds of products we design.

THE GOAL OF REPORTING

The GRI describes the goal of reporting as follows:

> "Sustainability reporting is the practice of measuring, disclosing, and being accountable
> to internal and external stakeholders for organizational performance towards the
> goal of sustainable development. 'Sustainability reporting' is a broad term considered
> synonymous with others used to describe reporting on economic, environmental,
> and social impacts (e.g., triple bottom line, corporate responsibility reporting, etc.).
> A sustainability report should provide a balanced and reasonable representation of the
> sustainability performance of a reporting organization—including both positive and
> negative contributions. Sustainability reports based on the GRI Reporting Framework
> disclose outcomes and results that occurred within the reporting period in the context
> of the organization's commitments, strategy, and management approach. Reports can
> be used for a variety of purposes, including:
>
> a. Benchmarking and assessing sustainability performance with respect to laws, norms,
>   codes, performance standards, and voluntary initiatives;
> b. Demonstrating how the organization influences and is influenced by expectations
>   about sustainable development; and
> c. Comparing performance within an organization and between different organiza-
>   tions over time."[9]

The same goals should hold true for user experience as we drive toward evaluating product use and providing realism and relevant user data that ultimately
improves the overall user experience of products. While we focus here on the GRI
framework that can help organize how reports are presented, a recent Greenpeace report (November 2011) provides very relevant insight into the kinds of
information that user experience practitioners can identify with in terms of situating themselves in the practice.

While not a GRI report, the Greenpeace initiatives are intertwined and connected with the GRI. This is an example of the top scoring company (HP) this
year and the abstract content of the report. In reading this, we can see tremendous opportunity for user driven data:

> "HP takes the lead in the re-launched Guide with 5.9 points. It scores most of its points and
> is the leader on the new Sustainable Operations criteria, which includes the management
> of its supply chain. It has the best programme for measuring and reducing emissions of

[9]http://www.greenpeace.org/international/Global/international/publications/climate/2011/Cool%20IT/
greener-guide-nov-2011/guide-to-greener-electronics-nov-2011.pdf.

greenhouse gases (GHGs) from its suppliers, disclosing emissions from its manufacturing at 3,500,000 tonnes CO_2-e, with 91% of first-tier suppliers reporting estimated emissions in 2009. It also scores maximum points for its thorough paper procurement policy; HP and Dell are the only companies in the Guide that effectively exclude the sourcing of paper from suppliers linked to illegal logging or deforestation. Together with Apple, HP is also a top scorer for its policies and practices on the sourcing of conflict minerals, for publishing its suppliers and engaging effectively in the Electronics Industry Citizenship Coalition's conflict-free smelter program. The only operations criteria where it scores relatively poorly is e-waste, where it needs to expand its takeback programme for consumers in countries without legislation and improve on its reporting of data.

HP is also a relatively high scorer on the Energy criteria, and does especially well for its disclosure of externally verified GHG emissions from its own operations and for setting targets for their reduction, with reductions of 9% from 2009, although it needs to address increasing emissions from business travel and to set more ambitious targets to reduce its own GHG emissions by at least 30% by 2015 for its operations and to use 100% renewable electricity by 2020. Its score for its clean energy plan is average and although its use of renewable energy is increasing, it needs to increase this further. HP is also rewarded for its relatively strong advocacy position in opposition to California's proposition 23 in Nov. 2010, which it believes would 'impair California's leadership in reducing greenhouse gases'.

It scores the least points in the Products category; although it scores comparatively well for its progress on phasing out the use of polyvinyl chloride (PVC) plastic and brominated flame retardants (BFRs) from its product range and is on track to achieve 90% of its new goal to phase out BFR and PVC in newly introduced personal computing products in 2011. HP needs to report on the amount of post-consumer plastics it uses as a percentage of all plastics and publicly disclose the length of warranty and spare parts availability for its main product lines, as well as show more innovations to extend product life. HP does not provide a summary of the energy efficiency of its products by giving a percentage of its products that meet the latest Energy Star standards (or other relevant international standard for external power systems); this should be published on its website, for each product range. However, HP risks a penalty point in future Guide editions as it is a member of trade associations that have commented against stringent energy efficiency standards; it needs to distance itself from such regressive positions with a strong statement."[10]

Some of the glaring references to product usage and user facing items include

1. HP has no takeback program for consumers.
2. HP needs to report on the amount of postconsumer plastics.

---

[10]http://www.greenpeace.org/international/Global/international/publications/climate/2011/Cool%20IT/greener-guide-nov-2011/guide-to-greener-electronics-nov-2011.pdf.

3. HP needs to disclose the length of warranty and spare parts availability for its main product lines and add more innovations to extend product life.

4. HP does not provide a summary of the energy efficiency of its products by disclosing the percentage of its products that meet the latest Energy Star standards (or other relevant international standard for external power systems); this should be published on its website, for each product range.

The listed items are some of the areas that have direct user facing impact where solutions require user involvement. To address these, we need to consider such things as

1. Improved out-of-the-box experience that makes transparent to users the takeback initiatives of the company from which they purchase products and validation thereof.

2. Collecting user data that truly reflects whether they follow up on the takeback initiatives.

3. Providing insight into the *planned obsolescence* of the products. This issue digs into the inability of users to service their products to extend the product life.

4. Providing users with the information they need to make wiser and ecologically minded purchasing decisions.

The Context: User Experience and Sustainability Reporting—In-Roads to a Framework

User experience, in its current form, is driven by understanding the users of products in the context of product use. In the process of design, the user is the focal point and driver of how new solutions can best serve their existing and future needs more efficiently.

A variety of research methodologies and practices have been utilized over time in gathering information about users. They range from qualitative to quantitative and from direct to indirect contact with users. In the effort to drive a user-centered design practice with sustainable design as the key goal, we must consider that, while the user has been at the center in design, it is even more critical to capture those behavioral nuances that encourage more sustainable and conscious behavior. The maxim that the "user is always right" needs to be noted and tempered by a more eco-conscious strand of thinking: While the user may always be right, designers should "design responsibly to encourage more sustainable behaviors." In the final event, if we do not design sustainable products and solutions, then users will not use them sustainability, thereby eradicating this maxim that the user is always right. We need to understand the users' context, their aspirations, their limitations, as well as the collective human experience and try to configure and design solutions that guide, inspire, and seamlessly educate users into making sustainable usage practices natural in the end.

CONNECTING THE USER EXPERIENCE DOTS

Connecting our own field of practice to the goals of such initiatives as the GRI, we can, in the future, look toward extending our current reporting of user experience and usability and feed into wider reporting structures. We have an extensive inventory of tools and methodologies that can position us to provide input to wider initiatives. Most of these have had a long history in user experience and can be extended as we evolve traditional user experience into a more sustainable theory as well as practice.

USER EXPERIENCE METHODOLOGIES AND PRACTICES MEET SUSTAINABILITY

Many user research methods can be used. However, regardless of what names they are given, methods should be chosen that are suitable for the situation at hand. Using these methods, it is possible to tweak into collecting the kinds of information that can be part of a sustainable user experience report.

The following lists the main user research methodologies and activities partitioned into two main categories:

1. **Direct user contact**: The researcher interacts directly with the end user, be it in a lab or field environment.
2. **Indirect user contact**: The researcher uses user research or observes without direct interface with the end user.

Direct User Contact

The following list of research methods can be integrated into gathering user data to enable designs that are more effective.

End-User Interviews

Perhaps one of the most traditional methods used in the field is the basic interview. Sometimes referred to as *in-depth interviews*, this method is practiced in the users' environment, where the activity to be researched takes place in a semi-structured interview: We have a set of questions to guide us, or we could keep it completely open, as an "unstructured" interview. In the case of sustainability data, this method is well suited to also gather product usage data. End-user interviews can capture individual as well as collective normalized information to determine how a design can be optimized. Users can be asked about their preferences and behavior as well as expected use of a product.

In this type of research, some of the kinds of data that can be collected are qualitative, given the observational element. If, however, it is combined with surveys and can be normalized with results from a valid sample group, then the data output can also be quantitative. In the context of product use, research can validate and collect information pertaining to

1. How much energy a product consumes while in use.
2. Observational patterns of use of the product, expected usage vs. optimized or ideal usage.
3. How a user disposes of the packaging components.
4. Whether users have devised postuse utility for products. Are they reused for something else, for example?

The information gathered here can provide insight into such design improvements, like

1. Adding push messages to allow users to control energy use.
2. Creating instrumentation triggers that allow some self-awareness from the product perspective to go into Power Save.
3. Looking for opportunities to educate users and create layers of transparency about their carbon impact when using the product.
4. Providing disposal instructions of product in a socially responsible way, return to manu- facturer programs, for example. Capturing user inspired data that can help give products new life, for example, by creating aesthetically pleasing packaging that a user my use as something else, such as Maille mustard jars that are used as beverage glasses when empty or mobile phone boxes that are used as storage cases.

Focus Groups (Workshops)

Small groups of about six to eight people with a facilitator or guide on a specific topic(s) can be a good way to gather "pulse" information about a product's performance (Figure 4.7). I use the word *pulse* here as a way to describe that gut feel that can be captured from a group dynamic and verified through further group interaction. This can be as formal or as informal as you wish. Often this method has received a lot of criticism as, inevitably, there are often stronger and weaker personalities in a room and it is important that all voices be given the same level of credence and no one be allowed to override the other. Managing the group can sometimes be difficult and peer pressure can affect the answers given (known as *group think*). The social interaction can also elicit more information than if you interview each person individually. They are good for idea generation, brainstorming, and comparing alternative designs. However, they are not always appropriate, as you cannot see how people do what they do, only what they say they do, which is not always the same. A focus group or workshop needs facilitation by a skilled researcher, who can guide and neutralize group think

Figure 4.7
Focus Group Setting.

issues as he or she sees fit. In many ways, it is much like an interview, but notes are taken to represent a group sentiment, rather than that of the individual.

Again, the same kinds of data can be gathered as in the in-depth research.

Contextual Inquiry

Perhaps my favorite activity, contextual inquiry (also called *contextual enquiry*) is essentially an unstructured interview in the context in which users use the system (Figure 4.8). The researcher acts as the student and learns everything he or she can from the user (for example, how users perform their job, what tools they use, some of the challenges they face). As with many direct contact research methods, it is not so much about what you find out about a particular product but more about getting access to users who represent the "real" end uses of the product. Understanding even a small sample sets in-depth use issues that can provide valuable insight into how users expect to use a product and whether or not a product lives up to the expectation of the user.

Ethnography

Ethnography is the practice of immersing oneself in the world or culture that one is studying (Figure 4.9). This means going into the field to observe users behavior in its "natural setting," and assuming the subjects' perspectives when analyzing and reporting. Ethnography, in whatever shape it may take, is direct contact of immersion and collecting data without upsetting the natural order to which users would adhere if researchers were not present.

Figure 4.8
Researcher Conducting
Contextual Inquiry.

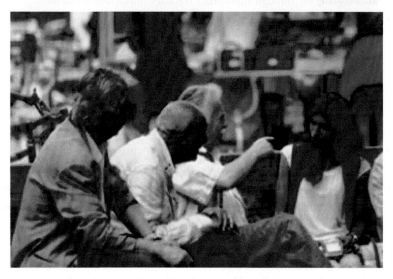

Figure 4.9
User Researcher
Conducting Ethnographic
Research.

Taking photos in the field is an excellent way to document the environment and behavior of the users. Documentaries or "ethnographic films" are a natural extension of this concept and help capture the real situation of users. They are a rich and emotive form of communication, particularly useful when presenting research findings to project stakeholders and allowing them to experience what users do in a near to firsthand format.

Using ethnography is a great way to explore unspoken opportunities for creating designs that are in tune with real needs. Tempering this with the consciousness of sustainable design only serves to create with the spirit of creating designs that work, thereby reducing waste.

Indirect User Contact

Heuristic Evaluation (Audit)

In this methodology, a person assesses a product using a list of heuristics, or guidelines, based on usability best practices and design conventions. In this case, the heuristics would be sustainability best practices drawn up as part of a product goal exercise that we encountered earlier in this chapter. These may include predefined questions that speak to key sustainability issues (e.g., energy, recyclability, and reuse).

A formal heuristic evaluation involves the use of a comprehensive checklist of heuristics used by multiple assessors, who score the product individually, for methodological validity and objectivity. Some of the typical heuristics (taken from Jakob Nielsen) commonly used today are

- "**Visibility of system status:** The system should always keep users informed about what is going on, through appropriate feedback within reasonable time.
- **Match between system and the real world:** The system should speak the users' language, with words, phrases, and concepts familiar to the user, rather than system-oriented terms. Follow real-world conventions, making information appear in a natural and logical order.
- **User control and freedom:** Users often choose system functions by mistake and will need a clearly marked "emergency exit" to leave the unwanted state without having to go through an extended dialogue. Support undo and redo.
- **Consistency and standards:** Users should not have to wonder whether different words, situations, or actions mean the same thing. Follow platform conventions.
- **Error prevention:** Even better than good error messages is a careful design that prevents a problem from occurring in the first place. Either eliminate error-prone conditions or check for them and present users with a confirmation option before they commit to the action.
- **Recognition rather than recall:** Minimize the user's memory load by making objects, actions, and options visible. The user should not have to remember information from one part of the dialogue to another. Instructions for use of the system should be visible or easily retrievable whenever appropriate.
- **Flexibility and efficiency of use:** Accelerators—unseen by the novice user—may often speed up the interaction for the expert user such that the system can cater to both inexperienced and experienced users. Allow users to tailor frequent actions.
- **Aesthetic and minimalist design:** Dialogues should not contain information that is irrelevant or rarely needed. Every extra unit of information in a dialogue competes with the relevant units of information and diminishes their relative visibility.

- **Help users recognize, diagnose, and recover from errors:** Error messages should be expressed in plain language (no codes), precisely indicate the problem, and constructively suggest a solution.
- **Help and documentation:** Even though it is better if the system can be used without documentation, it may be necessary to provide help and documentation. Any such information should be easy to search, focused on the user's task, list concrete steps to be carried out, and not be too large."[11]

These traditional heuristics need to be extended to include additional heuristics formulated to gather data on general sustainability with end-user touch points. These extended heuristics need to address a broad set of issues such as, but not limited to,

- Product energy usage.
- Product durability.
- Recyclability.

What an eventual sustainability heuristic could look like depends on the product. Nevertheless, in its final form, it can take its departure from the frameworks used as assessment tools, for example, the total beauty framework that already uses a point system for product assessment (Figure 4.10).

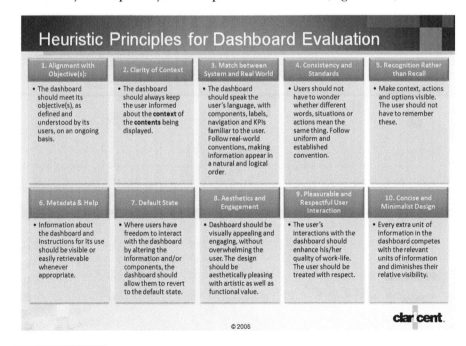

Figure 4.10

Heuristic Evaluation Guide.

[11] Jakob Nielson: http://www.useit.com/papers/heuristic/heuristic_list.html.

Heuristic is often the first tool used by many researchers with limited time and few users against which to test a product. For a true heuristic, however, it is advisable to have at least three people (user or researcher) complete the hueristic individually then combine the results. Each user can then log his or her thoughts and responses in line with the heuristic protocol. Numeric data can also be generated using this method, but such a protocol should be extended to include a larger evaluator size, if you wish to collect more quantitative data.

Competitor Analysis

A competitive analysis, sometimes also called *comparative analysis*, is the process of analyzing products that are similar to or compete with the product being designed in order to generate ideas and assess features and functions—and to understand how the products rank or measure up against each other. Figure 4.11, for example, is a high-level dashboard of Greenpeace's eco-cloud report that can be used as a model for our own reporting and at varying granularity and supported data.

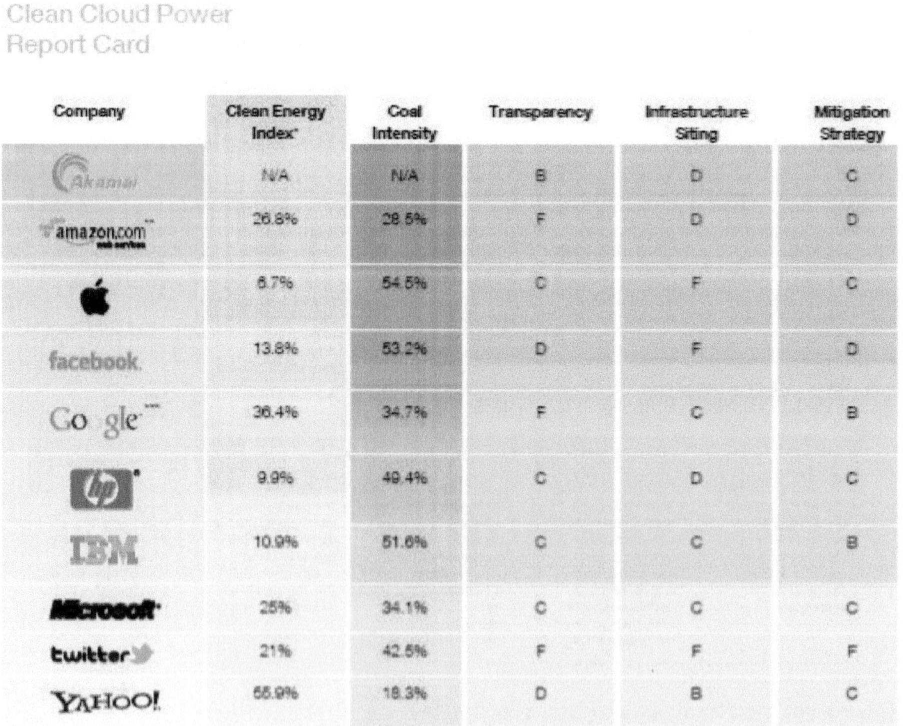

Clean Cloud Power
Report Card

Company	Clean Energy Index*	Coal Intensity	Transparency	Infrastructure Siting	Mitigation Strategy
Akamai	N/A	N/A	B	D	C
amazon.com	26.8%	28.5%	F	D	D
Apple	6.7%	54.5%	C	F	C
facebook.	13.8%	53.2%	D	F	D
Go gle	36.4%	34.7%	F	C	B
hp	9.9%	49.4%	C	D	C
IBM	10.9%	51.6%	C	C	B
Microsoft	25%	34.1%	C	C	C
twitter	21%	42.5%	F	F	F
YAHOO!	56.9%	18.3%	D	B	C

Figure 4.11

Sustainability Competitive Analysis Cloud Computing Providers.

Competitors, or peers, of the product are reviewed to compare against each other and the system being (re)designed. This would usually use a heuristic review as the basis. The method is useful for setting a benchmark but also for collecting design ideas and identifying opportunities for product improvement. In the context of sustainability, some benchmarks can include

- Product energy consumption.
- General use of product data (is product serviceable, for example).
- What expectations users have of a product with regard to sustainable design.
- Best practices to be used as a goal post for less-performing, "must-have" standard features and attributes of a sustainable product (based on product type).

A comprehensive point system can be applied to create the basis for a repetitive analysis (annually etc.) to see how a product has improved over time.

Questionnaires and Surveys

Questionnaires and surveys are good for collecting bulk responses (usually a quantitative method) and for comparison of results over time. Many challenges arise in executing questionnaires because the user's intensions are often not accurately captured, since the questions may be misinterpreted. Hence, all users voting on a point scale may have distinctly different impressions of what is being really asked of them. Given that, it is advisable that surveys also include qualitative data to ensure responses captured are closer to what was truly intended, a better context of the responses.

Panels and Forums

Panels and forums are similar to online surveys, but they are commonly used for market research and use larger sample sizes. Many researchers now use panels in a manner similar to a virtual focus group, with "live" interaction added to the traditional panel method (most often not in real time). The challenge, however, is in ensuring recruitment of the right people with the right motivation and maintaining a high level of energy and attention as users provide insights in product use. In the context of sustainability data, this method can yield tremendous data. In fact, organizations like Green Forums[12] are providing the platform to help users take an active role in contributing to sustainability initiatives.

---

[12]http://www.greenforum.com/.

Fly-on-the-Wall Observation

To be differentiated from a true contextual inquiry, this is a more passive approach and involves going into the field and watching people conduct their normal activities. There is usually no direct contact with the users; otherwise, it would be a contextual inquiry. This method is very effective in environments such as call centers, bank branches, and the like, where customers interact with the organization (assuming the customers observed are doing so with permission by the location of research). This can be very useful in gathering patterns of behavior that can help drive improvement based on what users typically do. Sometimes, assuming an observational position can provide key insight into providing solutions that allow us to come up with smarter designs that lead to more sustainable design practices.

Cultural Probes and Photo Ethnography

Traditional ethnographic techniques involve observing people at their activities over considerable periods of time, often supplemented by video or audio recordings. Cultural probes, however, are one way to access environments that are difficult to observe directly and to capture more of this "felt life," without the intrusion of the researcher's presence. Selected volunteers are given probe packs, like the one in Figure 4.12. The participants use the items in the package over a period of a few weeks and return the completed pack, which is assessed by the user researcher. The items in the pack depend on the circumstances but are all designed to stimulate thought as well as capture experiences. A cultural probe should be combined with interviews before and after use to allow the researcher

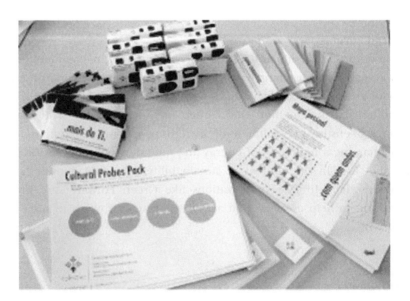

Figure 4.12
Cultural Probe Kit.

to properly explain what is expected and talk the volunteer through what has been recorded.

In many instances and as part of a cultural probe, users are also given cameras with which they can capture images of their daily life. This aspect is called *photo ethnography* and helps researchers gauge a truer picture of the user's visual circumstances and context.

Given the gist of the kinds of data, there are tremendous opportunities for collecting product use data, such as energy use and user's product disposal behavior or reuse, to name a few.

In-House Brainstorm

The reality is that, given the current financial situation of most companies, the preceding methods can also be augmented with small groups of user researchers and designers coming together to review design solutions based on the research. It provides a platform to generate intense discussion based on informed user research already collected. This is most successful in multidisciplinary teams that bring multiple views and can provide a solution that better reflects the worlds of different users. The most important thing about a brainstorming session (Figure 4.13) is what happens after the brainstorm. Of importance is determining

Figure 4.13

In-House Brainstorm Session at Pivot Design Group.

what brainstorming output fits into the larger decisions. In brainstorm sessions, especially comprising creativity and excitement, the challenge is often to sustain the momentum and drive for those solutions deemed suited to a key issue.

QUALITATIVE VERSUS QUANTITATIVE RESEARCH METHODS

When it comes to reporting and segmenting information and data for different audiences, it is important to remember that some stakeholders like to see different types of results. Data, regardless of methodology used, can be either quantitative or qualitative (Figure 4.14). Qualitative research involves analysis of data such as words taken from an interview, whereas quantitative research involves analysis of numeric data, for example, results of a survey using a valid sample size.

For the most part, I have always found that, to gain stakeholder attention and establish stronger credence, pure data often does the trick. Therefore, it is advisable to ensure that any sustainability UX report contains solid numeric information, especially when reporting to top management. Given that, you can utilize either indirect or direct methodologies to gather this type of data. However, as we are at the infancy of an evolving practice, we need to temper reports with impact. In addition, for the most part, it means skewing the report toward quantitative results.

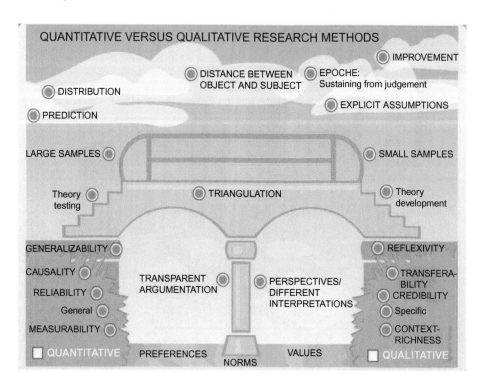

Figure 4.14

Qualitative vs.
Quantitative Method.

FROM FINDINGS TO DATA AND PRESENTATION

At this point, many of you may be thinking, I have the methods as well as some of the questions that I can use to drive data gathering, but what can these data look like? Let us look at some of the kinds of questions we encountered earlier. See Chapter 3 for more detail on these and other types of questions.

a. What do users think of the product's durability?

b. Are users able to service products that are broken?

c. Are products designed to optimize energy use?

d. Are users recycling products as they were intended?

e. Do users feel that companies are providing enough out-of-the-box information about proper disposal of a product if it is not recyclable?

FROM FINDINGS TO USER INTERFACE DESIGN

In general, many of my peers are engaged in projects that include the design of user interfaces alongside hardware products (Figure 4.15).

While writing this book, I had the recurring question of how do we translate the tenets of sustainable design practices and research into designing more sustainable user interfaces.

In Shedroff and Lovins's *Design Is the Problem*, they cite a number of strategies that designers can embrace when achieving more sustainable designs. These include, but are not limited to,

Figure 4.15

Mobile Phone Yesterday and Today.

1. **Dematerialization:** Dematerialization is a reduction of the amount of materials and energy used in a design solution. Miniaturization of a product to use just the amount of materials needed to achieve a design is a new trend in the marketplace. Nowhere has this impact been felt more than in mobile phones, where all leading manufacturers of computers strive to use the lightweight feature of their new tablets as a selling point of the product. Underlying this example is the ideal of dematerialization. Apple, the maker of iPod and iPhone, touts this key marketing element in line with its social responsibility efforts by demonstrating the overall impact miniaturization has had on transportation and Apple's carbon footprint. It explain on its site:

   > "Apple employs teams of design and engineering experts who develop product packaging that's slim and light yet protective. Efficient packaging design not only reduces materials and waste, it also helps reduce the emissions produced during transportation.
   >
   > For example, the packaging for iPhone 4 is 42% smaller than for the original iPhone shipped in 2007. That means that 80% more iPhone 4 boxes fit on each shipping pallet, more pallets fit on each boat and plane, and fewer boats and planes are used—resulting in fewer CO_2 emissions."[13]

2. **Transmaterialization (also known as servicing):** Again, using this strategy, the role of user interface is critical as we transform a product into a service. The Amazon Kindle stands as a perfect example of where good user interface design is providing a platform for turning production of hard copy books into a service.

3. **Informationalization:** This involves sending the information instead of the product. Smarter user interface design can help users adopt information transportation electronically and eliminate traditional means of transportation. Once again, the user interface sits central as a strategy for allowing users to transition from traditional ways of doing things toward more sustainable options. A perfect example is e-billing and e-banking. In recent years, there has been a shift from paper billing and banking to electronic banking. This paradigm shift in how we receive mail (bills) and banking statements may have gone by unnoticed as to why. Today, it is almost becoming standard. This example is also applicable to such annual activities as sending in yearly taxes. User experience is critical in ensuring the successful adaptation of these new standards of communication delivery.

All three of these strategies, combined or alone, are viewed as a direct relationship with user interface design. These strategies have two bottom-line effects: They reduce material and energy usage.

---

[13]http://www.apple.com/environment/.

"We can take heart in the many positive contributions we've already made to the digital world. We design digital transactions and interactions that provide ways for people to conduct their lives with a smaller carbon footprint."[14]

In addition to the preceding strategies, we need to consider our end-users' behavior and the context in which they use the products we design. Interfaces are not only an interaction platform to control or communicate with products, they are also platforms where we can build in game changing intelligence that seamlessly heightens user awareness of sustainability issues while it heightens user experience. We also need to think about user needs in addition to user skills. Therefore, it is important to design solutions that are responsive to the real needs of end users and at the same time strive to encourage more sustainable usage of the products.

Ultimately, a true sustainable design solution lies in a user-centered design strategy for more sustainable end-user behavior. Recognizing opportunities for improved behavior, without imposing unpleasant experiences of forced usability, should be the underlying principle that guides us through a design process.

BOTTOM-LINE IMPACT: SELLING THE SUSTAINABLE USER EXPERIENCE

Climate change and sustainability are two of the top issues business companies face, but how do you sell user experience solutions addressing these issues?

User experience has come a long way from the days of evangelizing to the differentiating ingredient for many products and associated with some of the titans of modern day design (such as the late Steve Jobs). Capturing the attention of key stakeholders within your organization, who have the authority to implement sustainable design change, is yet another hurdle that we face as we evolve as a practice. As was the case when we brought mainstream attention to the fields of human factors, usability, and user centered design, the challenge of introducing another layer (sustainability) should be seen as an evolution rather than an a revolution.

We can demonstrate additional value by showing how consumers have evolved and become more sophisticated in their needs and wants. The pervasiveness of social media is the new straw that can make or break a company and determine whether a product will be a success or not. Coupled with the new buzz word of *sustainability* and related buzz words like *eco chic* and *green*, the imperative for designing with a high level of eco consciousness is not going away.

Combined with the flux in user behavior and the power granted to consumers through virtual spaces, these are powerful reasons for getting stakeholders to

---

[14]Adam Richardson, Frog Design.

think about such things as sustainability and smart design. In Chapter 2, I outlined some of the key drivers that may be integrated into your "sell to management" strategy as you see fit:

1. **Consumer demand for sustainable products and services**: People today are making purchases not only as consumers but also as responsible world citizens. By rejecting the indiscriminate consumption patterns of the past and becoming more selective in their choices, they are signaling a shift in consumer attitudes and behaviors that may significantly affect business profitability and growth.

2. **Stakeholder influence**: Globalization and technology have given customers and citizens a powerful voice. Businesses and public sector organizations need to extend their reach to a new breed of stakeholders that includes nongovernment organizations, media, academics, and the community at large.

3. **Resource depletion**: Economic growth in developing markets combined with high consumption in Western economies has depleted natural resources (especially energy and water). Not surprisingly, there is fierce competition for what remains.

4. **Employee engagement:** Employees' commitment and enthusiasm for sustainability are shaping the way we work and live. As the sustainability mandate expands, organizations committed to social and environmental causes are likely to attract the top talent.

5. **Capital market scrutiny**: Sustainability has crept onto the bottom line. Investors now look at sustainability performance when evaluating a company's potential for future returns.

6. **Regulatory requirements**: Ready or not, government and industry regulations are forcing companies in nearly every industry to take sustainability seriously. If it has not happened yet, it soon will.

The adoption and embracement of sustainability into the design draft rooms is also gaining some traction, as more advanced user experience agencies, like Frog Design, are already integrating it into both strategy and design. The topic has also become a prominent feature of its blog and a growing topic of company principles as they espouse the need to think about the evolution of design.

Adam Richardson, director of product strategy at Frog Design, deliberates on the subject of sustainability as design principle in his article "Tragedy of the Commons," in *Mind*, Frog Design's online magazine. In addition to the traditional factors contributing to product conception and development—business, technological sustainability, and people's goals and desires—Richardson suggests that we should consider a fourth factor—the environment:

> "To quell the ecological damage being caused by our current industrial production system, we must contextualize feature requests within this broader understanding. User desires are no longer justification enough for production. We must add an

Environmental factor to the historical rubric of Business, Technology, and People. Moreover, just as we sideline products and services that fail to adequately meet standards of viability, feasibility, or desirability, so too must we reject initiatives that are not sustainable. Ignoring this "E-factor" should be considered poor business practice and poor design—no matter how much consumers might seem to demand it."

As the mandate to report on product performance in the market (as part of the wider reporting structures and initiative) is realized, the hope is that the field of user-centered design will have a foundation of "sustainability UX" practice embedded in companies where such activities as product sustainability scorecarding becomes the norm. The goal is to move toward a more scientific means of showing how user product interaction can be enhanced by using known research methodology to help guide design to a more sustainable end.

THOUGHTS ON PRODUCT FUNCTIONALITY AND USER EXPERIENCE

As asserted throughout this chapter, there is an established awareness of user experience, but many companies chose to focus on product functionality over user experience, the more holistic end-to-end experience that integrates a sustainable approach to design. At first, this may not seem like an issue but further insight into the two approaches (feature over function) is very revealing.

Take a mobile phone company, for example. Today, it is estimated that nearly 80% of the world's population carry mobile phones.[15] Subscribers use their phone for just about everything from making calls to playing games to browsing the internet; and manufacturers continue to churn out phones loaded with features without thinking of functionality. Today, the average phone has a camera, text messaging, an internet-based instant messenger, internet browser, games, day planners, and an endless variety of downloadable applications. People can micromanage every aspect of their lives with a plastic device that weighs less than a sandwich. In the words of Apple's marketing: "There's an app for that."[16]

While these achievements are great, they also lose sight of what a mobile phone is—it is still a phone. Many mobile phones come loaded with buttons, and features but how many people are going to use them? The more features manufacturers

---

[15]http://mobithinking.com/mobile-marketing-tools/latest-mobile-stats.
[16]A 2009 Apple iphone commercial tagline.

pack into phones, the steeper the learning curve becomes for their users, creating a negative user experience overall. The end question is whether the priority of feature over function results in a sustainable and responsible practice. As a result, a convenient little do-it-all mobile device that should lead to positive user experiences can turn into a serious source of frustration instead, especially for older and novice users. In terms of looking at the issues surrounding product functionality as separate from user goals, we need to consider how functionality that is targeted to meet user goals could be an underlying solution for users getting frustrated with the products they use and disposing of them for the mere fact that it does not meet their needs. This example underscores the importance of implementing a sensible design framework and should be considered when setting design goals.

SUSTAINABILITY DESIGN AND THE CHALLENGE AHEAD

Designing for sustainability frameworks and tools provide important insights for thinking about the outcomes or analytical processes of designing sustainably. What they rarely discuss are the adaptations associated with bringing sustainable design into practice in business organizations. This oversight is notable given that product sustainability

- Extends traditional product relationships into new life-cycle phases, for example, an upstream range of factors to be considered in product design and management, such as eco-toxicity, recyclability or renewability, many of which lie outside the expertise of traditional designers and product managers.
- Has an often overlooked detail, the impact of these changes on the nature and organization of the design function.

Sustainable design informed by a life-cycle perspective can reveal these. A wide range of organizational functions and teams are shaping the design and, therefore, the sustainability of a product. Creating the intelligence and cohesion to design sustainably requires an ability to communicate and coordinate ideals about sustainability among many people. Realistically, we often are limited as designers as to the reach of communication beyond our small circles, but it is a great start in the engagement process as we begin to create levels of appetite and traction for sustainable design practice. In terms of communication, consider the number of activities, as an example, that may require coordination. These may include, but are not limited to,

- User research input.
- Product production planning.

- Manufacturing.
- Social and social responsibility efforts.
- Design and development.
- Brand and marking product strategy.
- Product management.
- Marketing, packaging, and recycling.

People performing these tasks and operating in organization isolation structures may be industrial designers, engineering developers, architects, technical writers, brand managers, manufacturing staff, or biologists. The need to coordinate all these activities is the next stage of full engagement in getting companies to think of sustainability as a companywide initiative. In the spirit of continuous improvement, we can think about the reach we have in our roles and continue to be evangelical as we deliver game changing product design with conscience.

WHAT DOES IT MEAN TO USER EXPERIENCE AND DESIGN PRACTITIONERS?

User experience and user-centered design have the potential to induce more sustainable use of products through design. We need to consider how the existing practice can further cross-pollinate between user-centered design methodologies and the domains of sustainable product design. How we achieve this is through creating pragmatic structures that illustrate the issues surrounding product use and provide recommendations pointed to this issue. In other words, we need to understand existing user behavior, capture the nuanced game changing patterns, and leverage these nuances of known use behavior to create smarter, more sustainable, and socially responsible designs.

WRAPPING UP

As designers, we bear some of the responsibility for the masses of products produced each year. A visible consequence of that responsibility is the growing emphasis on "sustainability" and the fact the word has entered the consciousness of society as well as pervades every vertical market as the reigning buzz word of conference rooms.

We must begin confronting and accepting the assumption that it is possible to create sustainable products and affect change. Products can promote and inspire ecological responsibility by factoring in end users and how they use the products. Strictly speaking, products cannot be "sustainable" in and of themselves. A product can be designed to use more environmentally friendly materials or to consume less energy, but there is no guarantee that this product will somehow find its way back to the manufacturer for reuse, refurbishing, or remanufacturing, unless the system in which it "lives" is designed to capture it, remove it from the waste stage, and reguide it to a more sustainable life path. In short, products are not sustainable, the systems that create them are. As part of the system, designers can take a cyclical view of products from creation to end and think about how we can guide the complete cycle of ensuring more virtuous ends to a product's life span.

To design with a sustainable mindset means that we should think not only about the users but also the products we design. Ensuring that we can capture the information and nuanced user data that achieves more sustainable design should be part of the tempering of the design cycle. As the saying goes, if we cannot measure it, then we cannot change it. A marriage of good user research that embraces new concepts and a translation into smarter designs can be our collective contribution to the wider sustainability initiative.

LOOKING THROUGH THE DESIGN LENS

Reporting on sustainability performance is an important way for us to manage our overall impact on sustainable development. By taking a proactive role within our fields as designers and design researchers is a necessary first step. In this role, we can begin to collect, analyze, and report on firsthand, ground-level research that has realism as a basis for helping companies reduce potential business risk. As part of the experience design cycle, design researchers need to collect the pointed user data that helps them make better products. Situating user experience in this new space, where many at the upper levels of business operations are still seeking answers, begins with creating levels of traction. We can do so through evangelizing and showing how our collective user research bears relevance by connecting to the current sustainability initiatives using evolved user data that considers ecological reporting. We can also start by coming together to evolve our proactive practice through creating frameworks that we can use to measures, track, and improve design to meet a sustainable end.

IN THE NEXT CHAPTER

Chapter 4 provides an intertwined view of user experience concepts to sustainability concepts. Connecting known sustainability phases to the kinds of user research activities we currently use enables us to create a foundation for collecting focused user data and information that can help guide design in an ecologically responsible way. In Chapter 5, we revisit some of the traditional user concepts that factor into our data collection. We also look at some case studies that make the concept of sustainable user experience more tangible for us as researchers and designers.

USABLE AND SUSTAINABLE

INTRODUCTION

In this last chapter, we discussed sustainability as a new factor in the traditional design and development process; we also examined some of the methodologies that can be used to help situate the user experience researcher and designer as key contributors of a metrics- and measures-based design model. Sometimes, designers have to strike a balance among several factors: eco-conscious designs, the constraints of company mandates, and the key principles of our practice. Several questions arise: What does it mean to be sustainable in the context of usability? Does a good user experience conflict with sustainability or are they the same thing? Further, sometimes, we simply need to understand whether a design is in fact purposeful or ethical. Understanding the ideals of sustainable design alongside user experience concepts enables us to navigate comfortably in situations of contradictions A few of the questions we are already faced with include

1. What does it mean for a design to be efficient?
2. What is universal access and how does sustainability factor into this?
3. In the era of sustainability, are the users always right?
4. Should we value ethics over a design's purpose?

5. What are some of the underlying motives of eco-conscious users and the roles they play in design?

6. Where does aesthetics fit in the scheme of sustainable and eco-conscious design?

This chapter discusses such questions and provides some guidance and examples (using case studies) to illustrate some good sustainable design practices at work.

SUSTAINABILITY AND EFFICIENCY, LEARNABILITY, EFFECTIVENESS, AND SATISFACTION

Over the years, we have all encountered the concepts of *efficiency, learnability, effectiveness, memorability*, and *satisfaction* as key principles of designing with users in mind. These ideals also form the foundation for how we collect data and present information on the usability of a product or designs. As sustainability becomes part of the factors affecting design it is important to resocialize these concepts with new lenses to see how our work may be affected by these concepts as a whole.

EFFICIENCY

In the era of sustainability, *efficiency* takes on a loaded meaning and can mean many things at once. Traditionally, we think of efficiency as the extent to which time or effort is well used for an intended task or purpose. However, this definition looks mainly on user task flow efficiency. The term *efficiency* also invokes the notion of energy in product design. Is the product energy efficient? In this section of the book, I refer to *efficiency* as it relates to the ways we work to produce solutions that respond to user needs. Considering our roles in the design process, we need to make products and solutions more efficient, meaning that it responds to users' needs. At the same time, we are called on to practice efficiency in our own work, so that our contribution to the design process is also efficient. It could refer to efficiency in the use of energy usage. It could also mean avoiding the use of materials and other resources that demand many physical iterations of prototypes as we strive for an optimal design.

Autodesk CEO Carl Bass recounts the experience of considering sustainability and efficiency in design. In *GigaOm,*[1] "Green: Net 2011 Live Coverage," a virtual conference focusing on digital energy, he says that trying to re-engineer objects for sustainability and environmentally friendly materials after they are built, even as a prototype, is expensive and time consuming. He also asserts that design decisions are best made "at the beginning of developing a project." In most cases, designers come up with a design and build a physical prototype, then refine the design, build another prototype, and so on, accumulating cost. He pushes for

---

[1]www.gigaom.com.

more digital prototypes that limit the use of materials in the long run. He says that, "With digital prototypes, you can explore options a lot further before you actually have to build a physical prototype."

Employing such design tools is one way to ensure that we are adhering to efficiency along the design continuum in the context of our work.

As we think of efficiency in the context of creating optimal solutions, we can best do so by understanding the circumstances of the target users. Immersion in the user's context gives us insight into how we can design more relevant and responsive solutions, which are more conscious and sustainable. Immersion results in creating "on-point" solutions that require such things as less time, and less energy consumption. When designs are highly responsive to the users' needs, not only are they efficient but also sustainable. Users enjoy using them and the "stickiness" effect kicks in, lessening chances of such things as early disposal as well.

LEARNABILITY

Leveraging the earlier concept of "efficiency," where we design solutions within the users' context as our core, the actual learnability of the system is natural. Understanding user goals and how they expect to use a product creates the opportunity for natural fit solutions, where learnability, once accomplished, is akin to "riding a bike"—once achieved, it is unlikely to be forgotten. The heightened familiarity of learnable concepts comes from the fact that they may follow what is natural, in other words, a metaphor from people's real-world experience. In many respects, a learnable system is one that has in built-in sustainability, as users continue to use products and services that are natural to use.

EFFECTIVENESS

It is difficult not to see a continuous flow in these concepts. As we address the high goal of efficiency, we also by extension tap into the naturalness of solutions that make them both learnable and effective. Effectiveness goes hand in hand with efficiency and learnability and cannot be separated as it is a by-product and key operating concept in the process of user centered design. When solutions are efficient and learning is natural to users, they are also effective. Hence, with efficiency as the base principle, we see a trickle down where effectiveness is a by-product of the user experience.

MEMORABILITY

If *learnability* refers to the ease of onboarding for first time users, then *memorability* refers to how easy it is for returning users to remember how to navigate through the site and accomplish their task. All these usability concepts need to operate at optimal synchronous levels to attain high usability performance. This is why efficiency and memorability also go hand in hand. If an application design is more efficient, there will be fewer steps for the users to go through to accomplish tasks and therefore fewer things to remember, making it easier for them to re-establish proficiency, even after a long period of not using the product. Memorability can be viewed as another intangible product factor that differentiates and adds value, like satisfaction, which many marketers strive for in a world of information overload.

SATISFACTION

Last but not least is the ultimate intangible that many marketers try to capture in the growing struggle to maintain loyalty in a brand-saturated market. With all of the other concepts at optimal levels, users are satisfied with a product's performance.

In the end, tying these concepts to the principles of sustainable design, we can see that "good" design is not a physical object in all its aesthetic wrappings but rather a well-thought-out, strategically crafted solution that meets a purpose and is guided by design consciousness. Designers have to also think about how to infuse sustainable design practices into their own process.

SUSTAINABILITY AND ACCESSIBILITY

Accessibility means that people with disabilities can use the solutions we design. In user experience, we usually think of accessibility in the context of the web. Web accessibility means that people with disabilities can perceive, understand, navigate, and interact with the web, and that they can contribute like those with no disabilities. Accessibility encompasses all disabilities that affect access to the web, including visual, auditory, speech, physical, cognitive, and neurological disabilities. As the definition expands, accessibility can be viewed as the "ability to access" and benefit from a system or a solution. Accessibility is often used to focus on people with disabilities or special needs and their right of access to these systems and solutions, often through use of assistive technology[2] with effectiveness, efficiency, and satisfaction in a specified context of use (ISO standards). The term *accessibility* is also used in the Convention on the Rights of Persons with Disabilities as well as the term *universal design*.

When we consider the two concepts of sustainability and accessibility, we begin to see that, ultimately, sustainable design practices focus on the principle

---

[2]*Assistive technology* (AT) can be defined as any item, piece of equipment, product, or system, whether acquired commercially off the shelf, modified, or customized, that is used to increase, maintain, or improve the functional capabilities of individuals with disabilities (29 U.S.C. Sec 2202(2)). http://standards.gov/assistiveTechnology.cfm#section-1.

of inclusion. Sustainable design should strive to be inclusive and "universal" in its appeal. Through using universal design practices and following those design guidelines, we can practice sustainable design and accessibility in one effort.

"THE USER IS ALWAYS RIGHT" AND SUSTAINABILITY

Inevitably, as a practitioner, you have heard the saying that "the user is always right." This saying has been so entrenched in the user research vernacular that it is also the name of a recently published book by Steve Mulder and Ziv Yaar, *The User Is Always Right: A Practical Guide to Creating and Using Personas for the Web*. The context of this expression is primarily used in research, where the assumption is that, if we fully understand the users and the ways in which they use products, then this should be the basis of our design. In Mulder and Yaar's book, they use personas as a portal to user engagement and inherently purport that a knowledge of a user's psychographic and behavior is the "rightness" that should drive design.

This argument is one that even a usability guru has weighed in on. Mulder and Yaar believe that the user is not always right and we are best served to not listen to users but rather pay attention to what users do and not what they say. He uses a famous example of spinning logo's and drop down menus: features that seems to have faded out with more sophisticated web standards but were quite prominent on many websites not too long ago.

He writes: "A spinning logo might look pretty cool if you don't need to accomplish anything on the page. Another example is the drop-down menu. Users always love the idea: finally a standard user interface widget that they understand and that stays the same on every page. However, while they offer users a sense of power over the design, drop-down menus often have low usability and either confuses users or lead them to unintended parts of the site."

He continues: "To discover which designs work best, watch users as they attempt to perform tasks with the user interface. This method is so simple that many people overlook it, assuming that there must be something more to usability testing. Of course, there are many ways to watch and many tricks to running an optimal user test or field study. But ultimately, the way to get user data boils down to the basic rules of usability:

- Watch what people actually do.
- Do not believe what people say they do.
- Definitely don't believe what people predict they may do in the future."[3]

---

[3]http://www.useit.com/alertbox/20010805.html.

Today, as we enter the era of sustainability, we have to rethink how users factor into the equation. If we think of observing users and using this as the "rightness" to infuse into design processes, we need to fully understand if and when what we observe are in fact sustainable actions. Given that we need to observe with informed eyes and know if behavior is detrimental to the environment at large, we can help curb and counter such actions by building smarter designs that guide users, as if seamlessly, to adopt better usage patterns.

To design the right solution, we need to think of new strategies for driving home an all-points sustainability message in how products and users interact now and in the future. Some of these strategies may seem to collide at times but are necessary to consider when infusing ideals of sustainable design as part of a changing product design life cycle. Thinking in terms of more evolutionary rather than revolutionary efforts to driving home a sustainability agenda with users, here are a number of strategies we can employ:

1. **Contextual mapping and product adaptation:** It is sometimes very difficult to break human habits. Strategically, it is important to think of ways to adapt products and solutions to actual user habits, emphasize positive usage patterns, and minimize the negative ones. Increasing the visibility and convenience of activities with positive impact encourages usage.

2. **Forced usability:** A known staple utilized already by many practitioners, this strategy focuses on making products and solutions autoadapt to changing usage and user circumstances and designs built-in obstacles to prevent unsustainable and negative user behavior.

3. **Eco-awareness messaging:** This strategy is essentially the educational aspect of user engagement. Here, the user is presented with specific information on the impact of his or her current behavior, and it is left to the user to relate this information to his or her own behavior and adapt this behavior.

To illustrate these three strategies, I think specifically of my HTC phone that makes it easy for me to go into a Power Save mode. This habit, collectively employed, has wider impact. It also engages me in a process of energy conservation that I may otherwise ignore if not gently pushed as part of the instrumentation messages of the HTC mobile phone.

This example uses all of the previously listed strategies to gently force a change in user behavior. Granted the product designer using the product as a medium plays a part in how the product is used. However, some credit should also be given to users, as a collective: It is because of the changing value systems that design has had to change to accommodate users' growing eco consciousness. Today, more than ever, consumer activism and demand for ethical brand and product design is driving change at many levels of the manufacturing chain and should receive partial credit for how products are designed and will be designed in the future.

THE CHANGING USER

A recent study on "meaningful brands"[4] conducted from March to June 2011, across 14 markets—France, Spain, the United Kingdom, Germany, Italy, the United States, Mexico, Brazil, Colombia, Chile, Argentina, China, Japan, and India—took into account the views of 50,000 respondents. A number of trends were found that support the growing changes in consumerism and their perceptions of and sentiments on companies and the environment. The survey reported that consumer sentiment continues to shift in the direction of demanding more transparency into company's social responsibility activities. It showed that:

- For the fourth year running, consumers' expectations of companies' responsible behavior continues to rise.
- Nearly 85% of worldwide consumers expect companies to become more actively involved in solving the issues created by poor environmental practices (an increase of 15% from 2010).
- Those consumers are prepared to reward responsible companies by choosing to buy their products, up 11% from last year to more than half of all consumers (51%).
- Those consumers who would pay a 10% premium for a product produced in a responsible way is up once again, from 44% last year to 53% in 2011.
- The percentage of respondents who would punish irresponsible companies has also increased to 44% (from 36% in 2010).
- Only 28% of respondents think that companies today are working hard enough to solve our social and environmental challenges.
- Only 20% trust companies when they communicate about their social or environmental commitments and initiatives.

These trends, among many more, are key drivers in determining how companies need to rethink their role as economic and environmental citizens and also think of the products they design and the relation they have with their customers today and in the coming years.

USER PERCEPTION IN THE CONTEXT OF USER RESEARCH

To provide some further insight into why we need to think about users more than ever, consider the current atmosphere of consumerism today (also see Chapter 4 for other related topics on perceived value). With the growth in eco awareness, companies are experiencing firsthand the full impact of shifting "green" consumer expectations and the overall perception that users have of

---

[4]"Havas Media discusses sustainability and consumer brands" (2011).

their business. The trickle-down effect to user experience design is evident, as we are now in the position to influence the perception that consumers have of a product. In the past, companies may have focused exclusively on the economic performance and rushing quick to market; however, many are now realizing the real impacts of sustainable action is highly critical to the survival of their business. How their products are received in the marketplace is today ever more critical. It can determine a fail or pass with end users.

To add to that is the pervasiveness of social media, which can allow user groups the platform of quick assembly for any cause they deem significant. A user's issue can be as simple as a broken trackball, poor product performance, or even that they cannot fix something that is broken. Some users have issues that go beyond the actual product and may look at the holistic view, the company's business practices as well as the product. For example, a company's supply chain may have a negative environmental impact on whether consumers purchase its products. It is no longer just about the product but the inception and creation as well. Knowing the fuller picture of supply of a product's components is also becoming critical to more and more consumers. Therefore, it is ever more critical to think about the design of products not only at a production level but more at a socioethical level, which looks at a product in context of the system in which it resides. As user experience designers, we can drive change though user engagement and making changes in the design cycle for gain in three spheres: social, economic, and environmental.

GREEN CONSUMERS TO PRODUCT USERS

Environmentalism has experienced a continued upward swing ever since climate change became a hotly debated issue. Though the public is still largely divided over things like fracking,[5] the worldwide dependence on fossil fuels, and climate change, there is a rapidly growing consumer base that continues to evangelize and be active in spreading environmental awareness. Expressions like *carbon footprint* and *carbon neutral* have entered the common vernacular, as consumers work to find ways to minimize their personal impact on the environment. One area that has been seriously affected by this is consumerism. By extension, this impact is one of which we, as user experience designers, need to be acutely aware as well as versed in, if we are to help curb some of the issues surrounding consumerism and thereby users and how they use products.

For the most part, many products users, in their roles as consumers, are fickle; their buying patterns are influenced by many different factors, some of which

---

[5]A method for extracting oil and natural gas.

they may be aware of and some they are not aware of. For example, shoppers encouraged to stay longer and buy more by slow paced music; consumers at movie theaters are encouraged to spend more money with artificial popcorn scents; and consumers in shopping malls are encouraged to stop and visit a store with perfume smells. In the sphere of environmentalism, there's a silent message is also happening, where users are also making purchasing decisions such as buying product in green packaging, with natural looking graphic elements, and think these choices are sound ecologically. The thrust of environmental awareness also is influenced by their desire to support environmentally friendly brands, whether on their own or as part of unspoken social pressure. Some purchasing decisions truly are made on the assumption that a buying decision is a good eco purchase. In some market sectors, sustainability is the price of admission, and brands that lack an eco-friendly image cannot compete with those that do.

Carbon emissions and *carbon footprints* are the terms *du jour* when it comes to the environment. While consumers are fully aware that toxic gases are harmful to air and water quality, recent research into things like climate change, weather patterns, and deforestation indicate that the worst environmental offenders may be gases most consumers typically do not associate with danger, like methane and carbon dioxide. In reaction to our collective growing awareness as consumers, many are opting to self-monitor and curb their own carbon dioxide production. Often, one way they can achieve this is by electing to purchase products that do not contribute significantly to their individual carbon footprint.

What Makes a Product "Green"?

Green products are those that are perceived as being "good" for the environment, either less harmful than conventionally produced goods or directly beneficial in some way or an other. Products that are organically grown, packaged in biodegradable materials, or do not produce a lot of carbon emissions fall into the first category. Products that clean air or water or help remove carbon emissions fall into the second category.

> "There must be a better way to make the things we want, a way that doesn't spoil the sky, or the rain or the land."[6]

Many consumer products, such as mobile phones and computers, generate carbon emissions in three ways: during creation, during shipment, and during use. Half of all products generate the bulk of their emissions during use. This need not be a direct result of how the product functions, either: Everyone knows that

---

[6]Paul McCartney.

cars and trucks generate carbon emissions, but it is easy to forget that electronics can end up consuming electricity from power plants that still rely on fossil fuels. In fact, a sizable chunk of the carbon emissions from First World countries comes from computers. The average laptop computer is capable of producing around 1060 pounds of CO_2 per year with continuous operation, while a desktop can produce over 3500.[7] This created an increased demand for products like Energy Star compliant appliances, which consume less power during their working life, resulting in fewer emissions and a smaller carbon footprint for the end user.

Carbon emissions are not the only environmental concern that is an issue with most consumers today. Landfill space and waste are issues as well. The Western culture legacy of "throwaway" combined with the limited financial resources that we have, collectively drive a large percentage of us to actively seek out user serviceable products, things with replaceable parts that we can service on our own. This helps save money by not forcing us to discard of products once they stop working. Most directly, this helps reduce wasted landfill space by reducing the number of parts that are thrown away.

Last, company business practices and ethics both play an increasing role in how customers choose products. It is not enough for a business to put out attractive, functional, inexpensive products; some customers take extra care to investigate companies before they choose where to spend their money. So, even companies that work to produce low emissions and user serviceable products may find that they still fail to attract green consumers if the rest of their business practices are less eco-friendly.

It behooves modern businesses to make every effort at creating a sustainable production method, avoid violating environmental protection laws, and publicly appear to care as much about the environment as their customers do. More and more consumers are becoming aware of how the things they buy contribute to their overall environmental impact, and this higher degree of eco-awareness is changing their buying patterns across the board.

Sometimes, the distinction between a product that is considered green and one that is not is all about customer perception. This is particularly evident in the textile industry. For example, bamboo is being hailed as a sound environmental option for such things as clothing and flooring, to name only a few uses. The overall argument is that bamboo is natural, takes CO_2 out of the atmosphere during growth, grows quickly, does not require pesticides or herbicides, and performs just as well as less sustainable fabrics and flooring. As a result, green consumers feel positive about buying and using clothing and other fabric or flooring made from bamboo.

---

[7]1060 pounds of CO_2 per year.

However, that does not tell the whole story: Although bamboo is a natural, organic product, most bamboo fibers are turned into bamboo rayon, which must undergo a lot of toxic chemical processing to turn them from plants to fabric. Unlike cotton, which is generally picked, bleached, carded, and spun, bamboo is pulped, soaked in caustic sodium hydroxide, processed with carbon disulfide, separated into sulfuric acid, bleached in a multiphase bleaching process, then spun. The methods to produce bamboo linen rely on natural enzymes instead. This is functionally the same as producing linen from flax, but this method is rarely used because it is difficult and expensive. As a result, the majority of bamboo fabric that is actually produced is rayon not linen and would not qualify as either sustainable or organic. However, this has not yet affected customers' perception of bamboo rayon as green or their experiences buying and using the fabric or flooring made of bamboo.

Sustainability, Consumerism, and Usage Experiences

All consumers have their own values, which vary from shopper to shopper, but these values are what determine the overall customer's experience. Some value designer labels and that is the ultimate positive experience; purchasing the same product in a discount store or buying a knock-off or generic brand is a negative experience for shoppers of a certain mindset. As a rule, customers with a high degree of eco-awareness place great value on not adding to pollution or global warming and opt for the purchase of natural products that are sourced responsibly.

Choosing to buy green products, or shop with companies that practice sustainable production methods, falls in line with green customers' core values. When consumers who self-identify as eco conscious purchase goods that do not align with their values, they experience guilt over their purchasing decisions. Called *cognitive dissonance*, this results from attempting to rationalize two conflicting ideas at the same time. The discomfort results in a negative shopping experience. As mentioned previously, green consumers tend to exhibit a high degree of loyalty to brands they like and whose values align with their own. Given a choice, these customers do not remain loyal to brands whose business practices do not align with their own. For companies to experience long-term growth, there needs to be a strong focus on their customers' buying experience, as well as the eventual usage experience. Brands that create cognitive dissonance in green shoppers ultimately fail in the long run. Another reason that many consumers go green is somewhat more self-preservation driven; they believe that sustainable products are better for them and, in that belief, purchase those products that are thought to be beneficial.

While the average consumer can logically tell the difference between something that is good for the environment versus something that is good for them, one very interesting thing about the true eco-conscious consumer is that many do not make a distinction between the two decision drives while shopping. The two characteristics often go hand in hand, and this has created a perception that green products also somehow provide health benefits to users. In some cases, like organic produce, this perception is easy to justify. In others, like Energy-Star-compliant appliances, it may be more difficult. While improving overall air and water quality does contribute to good public health, most consumers expect health benefits gained from purchasing and using more green products. In either case, the green customer's perception of a brand as being good for the environment, and thus healthier for them, leads to a positive buyer experience as well as usage experience.

Eco-awareness also affects the customers' experience in other ways. Purchasing green products is not the only way that customers reduce their carbon footprints. Between concerns about high oil prices and emissions from cars, many customers are choosing to avoid driving whenever possible. This means that they are more likely to order products over the internet or through catalogs.

Between 2008 and 2009, retail e-commerce saw an increase of 2.1%, from $142 billion dollars to $145 billion.[8] Some businesses seized on this opportunity to help themselves present a "greener" face by setting up sustainable production initiatives that offer customers the option to plant trees to negate the carbon emissions created by packing and shipping their orders. Others advertised their use of recycled packaging or biodegradable packing materials. Though these measures are small and cost very little, they seem to give shoppers a positive buying experience. One such company taking part in such initiatives is Paper Culture, an e-commerce site specializing in eco-friendly products, such as invitations, announcements, and stationery (see Figure 2.12).

Environmental and social awareness go hand in hand, so it stands to reason that there is a large overlap between consumers who feel environmentally responsible and those who feel socially responsible. Though many First World nations are suffering from an economic downturn, this has not deterred green shoppers from expressing a preference for Fair Trade goods. *Fair Trade* is defined as follows: Fair trade is an organized social movement and market-based approach that help producers in developing countries make better trading conditions and promote sustainability. The movement advocates the payment of a higher price to producers as well as higher social and environmental standards during the production of goods. It focuses in particular on exports from developing countries to developed countries, most notably handicrafts, coffee, cocoa, sugar, tea, honey, cotton, as well as more luxurious goods like chocolate, wine, and gold. Concerns about overseas workers being exploited and the desire to own unique, artisan goods helps spur purchases from things like

---

[8]http://www.census.gov/econ/estats/2009/2009reportfinal.pdf.

workers' collectives and Fair Trade farms. Everything from bananas to jewelry is available Fair Trade, and eco-aware shoppers prefer purchasing goods that give workers a livable wage and helps promote ethical, sustainable business practices.

Last, the shopping environment itself is a huge contributor to a customer's experience and brand perception. Many consumers are willing to pay for presentation. They prefer to shop in a quiet store with attractive displays and well-decorated surroundings over a loud, utilitarian big box store, even though it means paying a bit more. When it comes to green consumers, many are willing to try new brands that they come across in their local natural foods market, even though they may overlook that same brand in a big box supermarket. Since increasing numbers of consumers want to avoid driving long distances to larger shopping centers, many turn to small, local retailers. This also contributes to another level of sustainability, and they are supporting local businesses as a socially responsible way to spur on economic growth. As a result, shopping in small, local boutiques produces a more positive customer experience for green shoppers than shopping in larger shopping centers, often out of town centers.

Tying this back to our jobs as user experience designers and researchers, it is important to understand the dynamics and consumer atmosphere and remain conscious of how the experience we build into products affects these seemingly peripheral user factors. For many peers, the awareness of these underlying factors need to be brought to surface, as they are not the motives we think about when we design the users overall experience. But, much like the psychological strands of practice (human factors), within our practice that takes into consideration the psychographic make up of our end users, understanding the complex nature of new eco shoppers who become product users is important. It helps us to better commiserate and think about the optimal solutions that consumers go through before becoming users of products we design.

Product Brand and the User Experience

When it comes to improving customers' experiences with a brand, it is not enough for a company to implement sustainability initiatives if it does not advertise. Advertising about new sustainability practices can help businesses attract green shoppers that had previously overlooked them and give their existing customer base more positive associations with the brand.

A Deloitte study finds that 95% of respondents would prefer to use green products; only 22% actually purchased them in the end.[9] There are a lot of points during the buying experience where green consumers are lost, which companies

---

[9]http://www.ahcgroup.com/mc_images/category/93/deloitte_on_competing_on_green_with_shoppers.pdf.

can use to keep these would-be green customers and develop an eco-aware brand image at the same time.

The first is *information*. Many products are all natural, organic, biodegradable, and sustainably produced, but you would not know it to look at them. Businesses should not assume that customers know that a brand or product is green, even if they are well informed. With the push to create environmentally conscious brand identities, stores and advertisements are clogged with products touting their benefits to the environment. The overall consumer perception is that, if a product or brand is not billing itself as green, it probably is not. As user experience designers, who may be involved in product touch points where we can enable such messages, it is our duty to promote them.

Second is *demonstration*. The industrial age brought about a lot of new developments, one of which was a switch from sustainably produced, cottage industry goods to factory-made products. The irony of the situation is that, now that environmental sustainability is an issue, a lot of green shoppers are looking to return to traditional production methods. As a by-product of this, many customers have an ingrained expectation that green products are not able to outperform their competition: Green appliances do not work as well as high-energy consuming ones, and green cleaning products do not clean as efficiently as harsh chemicals. This critical piece of information is not something that consumers would know unless they are told. Companies should never assume that green brands can stand on their own, especially when they have to compete with the conventional products that consumers already use. Instead, demonstrations, signage, and advertisements demonstrating their products' efficacy are just as important as cultivating a green brand image.

The third is *communication*. Companies need to effectively communicate how their brand contributes to a customer's improved experience. One of the purchasing motivators is guilt avoidance. Therefore, displaying eco information about a brand that helps them feel more confidence in their purchasing decision is yet another way to create positive customer experience. Some companies use their social responsibility sites to showcase their good deeds that overall are good for the environment, whether social, economic, or environmentally sustainable. Some companies do this by advertising their involvement with Fair Trade organizations or in more quantifiable ways by making transparent their own carbon footprints data. Apple, for example, has taken to the latter. However, it must be noted that fair and ethical business proactive green brands must create messages that accurately reflect their true values as well as sustainability performance.

In the long run, the shoppers' experience that retains them as loyal fans; price point and product quality count for only so much. If consumers do not have positive associations with buying and using a product, they will not continue to do so in the future. Green consumers have particular characteristics that differentiate them from other consumers and need to be catered to if their customer experiences are going to be positive ones.

THE SPECIAL CASE OF VISUAL AND INTERACTION DESIGN

With industrial and product design, it is a bit easier to create a sustainability strategy that makes sense, as the products are more tangible. Product designers can create products that are more durable, require less energy to use or produce, and optimize packaging. However, most graphic designers do not produce many physical artifacts, making it a little more challenging to create a meaningful sustainability strategy, and illustrate in tangible means their contribution to sustainable design.

As both visual and interaction designers begin to engage in the wider initiatives of sustainability design practices, we should all begin to consider and embrace some fundamental guiding principles to design. In *About Face 2.0: The Essentials of Interaction Design* (2003), Alan Cooper and Robert Reimann slightly touch on the topic of ethical interaction design, which could be applied here and used as foundational guides to sustainable design. Cooper and Reimann listed four principles that interaction designers can use as guides to design. These principles can also apply to visual designers. The principles in many ways resonate with the sustainability movement and are still relevant. According to Cooper and Reimann, interaction design needs to follow these key principles. They should be

- **Ethical** (considerate, helpful): Do no harm; improve human situations.
- **Purposeful** (useful and useable): Help users achieve their goals and aspirations; accommodate use contexts and capacities.
- **Pragmatic** (viable and feasible): Help commissioning organizations achieve their goals; accommodate business and technical requirements.
- **Elegant** (efficient, artful, affective): Represent the simplest complete solution; possess internal (self-revealing, understandable) coherence and appropriately accommodate and stimulate cognition and emotion.

ETHICAL INTERACTION DESIGN

As Cooper and Reimann point out in *About Face,* sometimes interaction designers are called on to design systems and solutions that are not necessarily the most ethical. Some of these designs have tremendous negative impact. They write,

"Products shouldn't harm anyone, particularly not the users." Possible types of harm they see as a result of unethical interactive system design include

- **Interpersonal harm** (loss of dignity, insult, humiliation).
- **Psychological harm** (confusion, discomfort, frustration, coercion, boredom).
- **Physical harm** (pain, injury, deprivation, death, compromised safety).
- **Environmental harm** (pollution, elimination of biodiversity).
- **Social and societal harm** (exploitation, creation or perpetuation of injustice).

An example of ethical interaction design is sometimes difficult to cite but this is accomplished in many ways. In a later case study, we look at design firms like Eco Lingo, a graphic design not only practicing sustainable activities in its workflow but also taking steps to preserve the environment in its work setting, using wind energy and the like. For interaction design, one of the challenges is situating designers in the activities of sustainable behavior.

The authors go on to state that design should be instrumental increasing positive contribution to the human situation in ways that include

- **Increasing understanding** (individual, social, cultural).
- **Increasing efficiency/effectiveness** of individuals and groups.
- **Improving communication** between individuals and groups.
- **Reducing sociocultural tensions** between individuals and groups.
- **Improving equity** (financial, social, legal).
- **Balancing cultural diversity with social cohesion.**

Using this as a guide, we can begin to think about how a workflow is defined on a protocol of universal access, for example, ensuring that content has universal appeal and is well localized to respect other cultures. A few years back, I had the occasion to work on a localized mobile device for a Middle Eastern population. Research indicated that, while to Westerners the color green holds little sacred quality, it was a color imbued with local sacredness and the usage of it was reserved for things in the realm of religion.[10] In design, respecting these ideas and beliefs is practicing an act of universal inclusion and wider universality that unites rather than disrupts. In terms of day-to-day work, we can also chose to use virtual boards in communicating concepts over printing out designs that often require much iteration.

The authors' contributions are ever more relevant today and can form a strong basis that interaction designers can use in designing sustainable solutions.

---

[10]The color green in Middle East is sacred, tied to the idea of Heaven, and used to stand for certain Islamic beliefs and ideas.

PURPOSEFUL INTERACTION DESIGN

Purposeful design is goal-directed; it helps designers create products that support users. Throughout this book, we emphasize how important it is to understanding the changing context of users as they use products and solutions. Crafting solutions in the physical world is a little easier than in the virtual world, where interaction design resides. However, this does not mean that the contribution of interaction design in driving purposeful design is lessened. When we think of the experiences that users have in the virtual world, be it in interacting with a power-saving interface or an efficient virtual translation of a physical activity, interaction design is central to the user's interface with such solutions. Creating purposeful solutions and systems is instrumental in allowing for adoption of the solution by users, and interaction design drives this experience from start to finish in the users' overall experience.

In terms of purposeful design, this is rooted in the idea of not simply designing for design sake. Many companies are still of the mind that they need to create new designs to keep market interests even though a product they have is still relevant and functional.

Coming up with new design, it must serve a good purpose. As designers, we have a responsibility to make sure that designs meet a need and do not exist for the sake of existing.

PRAGMATIC INTERACTION DESIGN

Cooper and Reimann's third guideline is "pragmatic" design. They write, "A design must get built to be of value." This third principle proposed by the authors speaks to the need for design practicality. They go on to marry concepts of pragmatism to business and technical feasibility:

> "Once built, it needs to be deployed in the world. And once deployed, it needs to generate profitable revenue for its owners. It is critical that business goals and technical requirements be taken into account in the course of design. This doesn't imply that designers necessarily need to take everything they are told by their stakeholders and developers at face value: There needs to be an active dialog between the business, engineering, and design groups about where the boundaries are and what areas are flexible."

Given this description of what it means to be pragmatic, I would like to add that, while business and technical goals are central to the execution of design, they must be tempered with social responsibility as a guiding principle. While the design may be profitable and feasible technically, we also need to consider its pragmatism from an environmental standpoint. Given that the authors also preface this third guideline with the point of "ethical consideration," it goes without saying that they view all four principles operate in unison (ethical, purposeful, pragmatic, and elegant) to drive home a "sustainable design."

ELEGANT INTERACTION DESIGN

The last principle is *elegance* in interaction design. Cooper and Reimann define *elegance* as a "gracefulness and restrained beauty of style" and as "scientific precision, neatness, and simplicity." Cooper and Reimann believe that elegance in design, or at least interaction design, incorporates both of these ideals. Exemplifying the previously discussed principles, a number of interaction and graphic design firms are contributing to sustainability by embracing a more holistic approach to design as part of their processes. They include but are not limited to design shops like Creative Slice and Eco Lingo.

Creative Slice is an Arizona-based "green website design" agency that integrates sustainability at the forefront of its marketing and business plans. The "Green Choices" page on its site details its efforts in lowering their energy consumption. While the company does not necessarily make a tangible product, what is important here is the growing consciousness and engagement of visual design peers in understanding their role in the thrust for ecologically conscious design practices. Taken from the company's website (Figure 5.1) are mentions of the firm's other initiatives and contribution to sustainable choices in which nondesigners can also engage. Some of their indirectly work-related activities are

Figure 5.1
Creative Slice Website.

- "We purchase solar power through the GreenWatts program with Tucson Electric Power."
- "We get our office drinking water (and many lunches) from the close-by Community Food Co-Op."
- "We use LCD monitors and laptops, helping to lower our energy consumption."
- "We use a Kill-A-Watt device[11] to determine energy loads from our devices and keep them to a minimum."
- "We participated in the One Laptop Per Child project to provide learning tools to children in developing countries."
- "We're now selling GREEN CHOICE stainless steel reusable bottles!"
- "The majority of our meetings are done via email or phone which means our clients and contractors don't need to drive as often."
- "Our office uses 100% natural light during working hours. In fact, our light switch could use a dusting."
- "Our office is part of a co-working space Spoke6 (which we founded) located just North of Downtown Tucson."
- "We generally commute via bicycle to our office and Tim Bowen[12] bicycled more miles than he drove in 2008."
- "All of our office paper is 100% recycled (though we rarely even use the printer and generally it's powered off)."
- "We recycle paper, plastic, cans, glass, etc."
- "We are members of the 1% For The Planet program and donate 1% of all our profits to eco-friendly organizations."
- "We are part of Local First Arizona as well as Green America."
- "We support our local community radio station (KXCI) with a yearly donation."
- "We support the Sonoran Institute and The Nature Conservancy with a yearly donation."

Eco Lingo is another design firm that practices eco-conscious graphic design and has green themes integrated throughout most of its website (Figure 5.2), including a description of its philosophy in the "Integrate" section. The company lays out some of its eco practices that provide support for its social responsibility claims: The company is powered by solar and wind energy; Eco Lingo also purchases renewable energy from a local utility company. In terms of design, the company places emphasis on using paperless and virtual workflows, including product management software that allows the customers and design team to share and collaborate easily.

---

[11]Kill-A-Watt is an electricity usage monitor from P3 International. It features a large LCD display and it enables cost forecasting.
[12]Founder of Creative Slice.

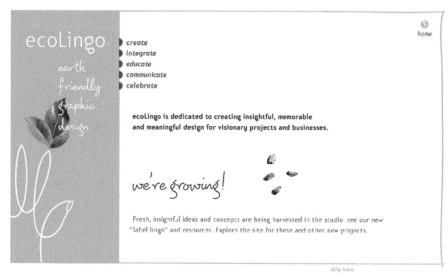

Figure 5.2
ecoLingo Website.

Many more examples of eco-conscious design firms are cited in "Ten Examples of Sustainability Plans for Graphic Designers,"[13] which also showcases a number of eco-friendly design studios and architectural firms.

Beyond these efforts from the practices of visual and interaction designers are other little ways, which if we add up the collective impact mean incremental savings, for example, designing images, icons, and graphics so that they do not guzzle up memory.

Interaction designers can promote the design of more efficient task flows that can help save battery life. For example, after speaking to a nonphone contact on Blackberry, there is no way to "on the fly" add the details of the person in Contacts; by comparison, this function is standard on the Android HTC phone, where on completion of a call, a user has immediate quick "add contact" choices. The Blackberry workflow means extra steps for users, which basically means more battery life.

In addition, interaction designers should think about removal of workflow redundancies in the system, not too many or not too few ways of doing the same thing. Focusing on the optimization of user task flows is another way that inter-action design can contribute to the general goal of efficiency that affects such things as power use. As a personal example, I recall not too many months ago, before getting rid of a mobile device, the overall frustration I had as I tried to simply change a ringtone and assign individual ringtones to important callers.

---

[13]http://www.pushingsnowballs.com/sustainability/10-examples-of-sustainability-plans-for-graphic-designers/.

This activity took me half an hour. Today, on a more advanced mobile phone, I am able to efficiently change a ringtone for important callers and my significant other.

The Context: Designing to Last

Throughout this book, I provide sideline Context inserts to give each chapter some focus. In this last chapter, I pay attention to the ideals of designing for sustainability in all its aspects (durability, efficiency, usability, ethics, and all the other elements that come together to define what it means to be sustainable).

As a by-product of First, Second, and Third World upbringing combined, my views on design is shaped by seeing first hand what it means to design not only for aesthetics and universal access but also what it means to design for durability.

As a child first growing up in a Third World country, the buying decisions of my parents, grandparents, and neighbors boiled down to one thing, buying things that lasted and were serviceable. In our household, brands like Toyota, Siemens, General Electric, Johnson and Johnson, Whirlpool, and Sony were equated with "built to last." These were the brands, for better or worse, that left impressions on my childhood consciousness and affect some of my buying decision to this day.

Somehow a bond has been created with these brands, and whether true or imagined, their products seems to meet the primary need that maps to my own value systems within a Third World and Second World nation, where I later resided. Products that were long-lasting, products that did the job and were serviceable survived; and those that did not were fleeting brands in the Second and Third World buying activities. Since then, now living in a First World nation, many other brands have left similar impressions on me, for example, Doc Martens and Kitchen Aid. What they all seem to have in common is that the products last and are reparable if they should wear and tear.

In the case of Doc Marten, the craftsmanship was so well done that it pained me to see a new looking pair of shoes meet its end even after 13 years, just because the over used soles were wearing thin. The shoes stood up to serviceability and may very well last another 5 years.

The same goes for the Kitchen Aid stand mixer I purchased over 14 years ago. Friends come over and are shocked when I tell them that the appliances are in fact 14 years old. The classic designs of the mixers do not make me feel the need to purchase a new one. And some of the appliances are modular, meaning that I can add extra functionality in some cases. The standard packages provide a bowl, whisk, dough hook, paddle mixer, and assorted shredders. For example, the stand mixer, with a few added parts, can be morphed into a sausage stuffer. Some other add-ons include a fruit and vegetable grinder, a juicer, a grain mill, and an ice cream maker.

(Continued)

At a good level of depth, I engage with these products because I know that I will not be purchasing the same product again anytime soon. These kinds of products contribute to the sustainability initiative, in that they are not engaged as much as their counterparts in the practice of planned obsolescence, meaning that they do not use up as many materials in the long run.

With the value shifts in the marketplace (customer advocacy, social responsibility, etc.,) and a playing ground where brands are fleeting, it is ever more crucial that designers think about more than the design of hardware. We need to rethink design in the context of wider world and environmental issues, making design decisions that are human centric and respectful to our collective diminishing resources. From a business standpoint, all these factors are more of a reason to differentiate products beyond what is now commoditized. The transcendent product quality that gives business the edge is sustainability in its manifold definition. Products should go beyond just being aesthetically pleasing; they should also be purposeful, ethical, and pragmatic as well. In the finality, all these qualities serve to move toward a general respect for our users as well as our environment.

CASE STUDIES IN SUSTAINABILITY

Sometimes, as we learn new concepts, it is difficult to form a full level of engagement until concrete examples are provided to illustrate working sustainable design concepts and solutions. Following are a number of case studies in sustainability aimed at providing some level of identification for those of use in the field:

1. Buffalo bicycles, a maintenance-free bike.
2. Green pizza packaging for utility.
3. Software as a service.
4. Apple's sustainability initiative.
5. *The Oxford English Dictionary.*
6. The compact detergent box.
7. Citizen-centric services.
8. Herman Miller's Mirra chair.
9. Electronic paperless banking solutions.

All of these case studies meet some sustainability goal, which was intentional in design.

CASE STUDIES IN SUSTAINABILITY: BUFFALO BICYCLES, A MAINTENANCE-FREE BIKE

Green Options Buffalo is a not-for-profit organization dedicated to healthy, environmentally sustainable and community-friendly transportation. They created the Buffalo Blue Bicycle program in 2006 to help affect social change and provide mobility options for those most in need. Their recycled metallic blue bicycles are accumulated through local donations, police auctions, and roadside collections from garbage. Remodeling and refurbishing these bikes provides sustainable transportation options that helps make a difference in some of the poorest countries in the world. The key to the bike's success is the underlying impact it has on the socioeconomic conditions of many in Third World countries as well as people of varying sizes (Figure 5.3).

The bike is designed to be comfortable for people of different heights, and it allows both men and women to ride the bike with the same degree of comfort; women are able to ride while wearing dresses. The frame of the bike is made of 16-gauge steel, creating solidity in the bike. In an interview with Fast Company's environmental online magazine *Co. Exist*,[14] Michael Collins the company's CCO describes it as "more of a truck" and says "it is built to last with no maintenance for more than 5 years." The sealed-off brake is also hidden in the rear hub, shielding it from dirt and water. Another key feature of the bicycle, Collins says, is that all its parts are compatible with local parts. So,

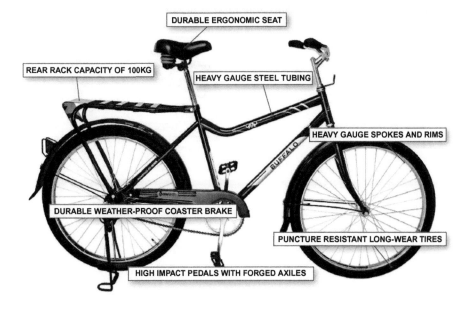

Figure 5.3

World Bicycle Relief's Buffalo Bike.

[14]http://www.fastcoexist.com/.

if a spoke snaps, a local replacement will fit. "The decision to ship these bikes over Western bikes considered that if the bike needed parts they could easily be found locally."

This solution is a sustainable transportation system that achieves the need for mobility through equitable, affordable, and efficient options with limited impact on the environment. Buffalo bikes are also durable, in that they will not break down as easily as other models. And, if they do, they are easily maintained and serviced. Overall, bike riding over car use contributes to sustainability goals by offering a low-cost and low-pollution option to all.

Sustainability points: equitability, affordability, durability, energy efficiency, universal access, serviceability, efficiency, social consciousness.

CASE STUDIES IN SUSTAINABILITY: GREEN PIZZA PACKAGING FOR UTILITY

When we think of the end-to-end product life cycle, packaging is one of the key areas where user experience designers can have an impact. The package is the first instance of user engagement and can either attract or repel the user. Packaging solutions that meet real users' contexts can set the stage for new standards and replace solutions we have come to accept as status quo. Take for example the clever design of Pizza Hut's green pizza boxes (Figure 5.4).

In Costa Rica, Pizza Hut introduced a multifunctional pizza box, which can be separated into individual plates and a small container for leftovers. Using the box eliminates the need for disposable plates and ancillary storage materials like

Figure 5.4
Green Pizza Box.

aluminum foil and plastic wrap, not to mention the energy and water cost savings of dirty dishes, if we think en masse. The box, designed in partnership with a Central American packaging manufacturer SigmaQ, uses patented GreenBox technology. ECOvention believes that this solution is not only convenient but also environmentally sustainable for its customers. Pizza Hut Costa Rica's pizza boxes have already received positive responses from its customers, as evidenced by an increase in sales since the product's launch, according to *Prensa Libre,* one of Central America's leading newspapers. This packaging solution is just one of many innovative packaging solutions. And, there is a growing trend by manufacturers to self-differentiate with innovative packaging.

In Scott Boylston's *Designing Sustainable Packaging,* a practical book on creating packaging that reflects sustainable and ecologically sound principles, he provides guidance on how to design a sustainable package. The book challenges graphic designers to re-envision packaging design as a less environmentally destructive practice than it presently is and examines an array of techniques and methodologies for creating innovative and sustainable packaging designs, from first concept to final production. Further, given the example of the pizza box, it demonstrates the power of ethnography and how observing how people consume take-out pizza can benefit from repackaging.

The Sustainable Packaging Coalition (SPC),[15] an organization dedicated to sustainable packaging also provides guidelines for designers and developers:

- **Design sustainability:** This means applying the theories and driving for inclusion of them in our work.
- **Design for transport:** This involves thinking of how to use less, reducing transportation cost overall.
- **Design for environmental best practices:** Best practices are out there, and these should be sought as input to similar work.
- **Design for fair labor and trade practices:** This involves the social and economic consciousness of our work, ensuring ethical design choices are made that do not take away from those in developing countries who, too, are a part of the production supply chain and need to be fairly compensated for their work.
- **Design from renewable virgin materials:** This considers the mass impact of material usage. Can the materials used in a design be easily restored to the planet, for example, bamboo? See earlier examples used.

---

[15]The Sustainable Packaging Coalition® is an industry working group dedicated to a more robust environmental vision for packaging. Through strong member support, an informed and science-based approach, supply chain collaborations, and continuous outreach, SPC endeavors to build packaging systems that encourage economic prosperity and a sustainable flow of materials. The SPC is a project of GreenBlue®, a nonprofit organization that equips business with the science and resources to make products more sustainable.

- **Design for reuse:** Can the components of the design be reused for other things? For example, in a recent privately commissioned study conducted by a few of my peers on packaging, HTC packaging was voted as "best packaging" by users. Most female participants mention using the black phone bag for their jewelry or other prized items.
- **Design for recycling:** Ensure that the design's by-products are easily recycled after use. Provide guidance to users on how to recycle, and if your company has a take-back program, help redirect users to use such programs with out-of-the-box information. Another thing that can be done is designing future messages that guide users to recycling and restoration options as their product's life comes to an end, either by email or on devices.
- **Design for composting:** Using compostable materials in a design enables later composting of used packaging.

Using these principles can help achieve packaging solutions that are responsive not only to marketing and transport but also thinking about the full life cycle of product containers and how they can be reused, for other purposes.

Sustainability points: equitability, multifunctional utility (saves on water), recyclability, dematerialization, affordability, universal access, social consciousness.

CASE STUDIES IN SUSTAINABILITY: SOFTWARE AS A SERVICE

As consumers of software, we do not often stop to think about the leaps and bounds we have made from the days where we needed a CD to install a piece of software to the current practice of going to a website to download the same software. In this case study, I want to underscore the value that user experience and interaction design has played in humanizing and modernizing the process of downloading and installing software (Figure 5.5). Software as a Service (SaaS)

Figure 5.5

Lexmark Old and New Printer Driver Download.

provides software application vendors a web-based delivery model to serve a large number of customers. I also include here the production of electronically transferred and purchased services, such as music and reading material that limit our use of CDs and books, though not explicitly stated in this case study.

SaaS is a prime example that contributes to a reduction in the usage of hard CDs and other materials and ancillary hardware needed to produce and serve customers. In this example, I do not cite a specific product example but rather the paradigmatic shift we have made as a society from the use of hard CDs to using the web as a means of software delivery. This example is significant, as we practitioners can provide direction for how companies can design such solutions that in the end are more sustainable options.

Sustainability points: dematerialization, absence of waste, efficiency, reduction in the use of transportation and packaging.

"Modern technology owes ecology an apology."[16]

CASE STUDIES IN SUSTAINABILITY: APPLE'S SUSTAINABILITY INITIATIVE

In Chapters 3 and 4, I cite Apple as an illustrative example to engage readers in thinking of user experience design. This case study is more about Apple's initiative to make sustainability simple for end users and consumers. Apple's website clearly details the company's carbon footprint, which totaled 14.8 million metric tons of greenhouse gas emissions in 2010.

In 2011, the company is among the top five companies on Greenpeace Green Electronics review as it continues to make an effort in communicating its impact. According to the company's report from 2010, this footprint breaks down as follows: (46%), transportation (2%), product use (45%), recycling (1%), and facilities (2%).

When analyzing the components of its carbon footprint (Figure 5.6), 98% are related to the product's life cycle, from manufacturing to recycling.

Some highlights of Apple's efforts in the key phases in the product manufacturing follow:

■ **Manufacturing:** Apple eliminated brominated flame retardants (BFRs), lead, PVCs, mercury, and other harmful toxins from its products. Some product components no longer contain chlorine, arsenic, or elemental bromine. Second, many products are smaller and thinner, using fewer materials. For example, the second generation iPad was 33% thinner than the original.

---

[16]Alan M. Eddison.

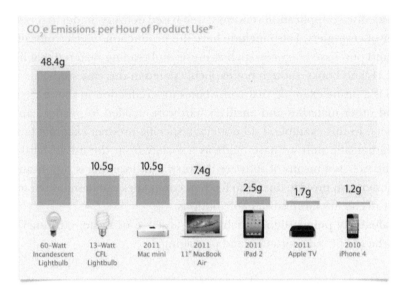

Figure 5.6
Apple and Sustainability.

- **Transportation:** Packaging is also becoming smaller, which makes transportation of the products more efficient. For example, in terms of transportation, the packaging on the iPhone 4 is 42% smaller than the original iPhone.
- **Recycling:** Apple exceeded its goal of 70% worldwide recycling of its products in 2010. The company attempts to use recyclable materials in its products and packaging wherever possible. The MacBook Pro battery can be recharged up to 1000 times, producing less waste than other, shorter-lived laptop batteries. Apple does not ship e-waste to other countries for disposal, also adding to its ethical practices of universal respect for those in less fortunate conditions that have a history of being the recipient of much of the worlds' waste.
- **Facilities:** The company also reports on their website that three of its facilities are powered by 100% renewable energy. It has also offered commuter programs, such as biodiesel commuter coaches, that eliminated the carbon dioxide equivalent of 1906 single-occupancy vehicles from the roads each day.
- **Product use:** All of Apple's products continue to exceed Energy Star specifications. Products labeled with Energy Star meet the requirements set forth by the Environmental Protection Agency, which include standards for energy efficiency, energy savings, and quality.

No doubt, today, the company ranks among the top brands in the world. Apple accomplished this by incorporating energy-saving features into its products. For example, certain Macs have light sensors that adjust the brightness of the display, saving energy when the room is already well lit. Similarly, the battery efficiency automatically adjusts to the power of the graphics, using less energy when viewing simple graphics, such as email.

Overall, the company stands as a gold standard for many other electronics makers. While the company does not claim to have achieved its sustainability goals, its transparency makes for an interesting study in sustainability.

Sustainability points: transparency, equitability, reduction of hazardous material, energy efficiency, cube optimization, miniaturization (use less), recyclability, dematerialization, social consciousness.

CASE STUDIES IN SUSTAINABILITY: THE OXFORD ENGLISH DICTIONARY

This case study is the *Oxford English Dictionary* (Figure 5.7). In August 2010, Oxford University Press, the dictionary's publisher, stated that, since so many people prefer to look up words using its online product, it is uncertain whether the 126-year-old dictionary's next edition will be printed on paper at all. From a design and user experience perspective, we are on the verge of something very exciting. We are well situated to think about how many virtual experiences will be designed as physical ones phase out. What we are not always conscious of is that this is part of the mandate of eco awareness, as we live in a world with less and less resources to go around. These are essentially some of the core tenets of what it means to begin the process of waste elimination.

In this example, the *Oxford English Dictionary* helps reduce the need for physical paper- and plastic-based objects by reproducing the dictionary as a subscription-based service, starting off with free access for basic usage. The effort of the publisher is well noted and contributes toward a dematerialization effort. Further, in a world where neologisms are the norm, the virtual dictionary provides the opportunity for on-the-fly updates.

On the one hand, the efforts of the publisher are suited for First and Second World nations, where the internet is very pervasive. The solution can be classified as a sustainable one, because at its core is the cost savings from cutting down trees

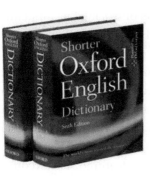

Figure 5.7

Oxford English Dictionary, *Then and Now.*

for paper and eliminating the need to buy new versions of a book that often sits on bookshelves collecting dust, due to the advent of the more readily available web for many users. Today, there are even mobile dictionary applications that make using them much quicker than locating the actual physical dictionary to seek out the meaning of a word.

While the *Oxford English Dictionary* is cited here as a case study, it must be tempered with some other aspects of what it means to be sustainable in the fuller picture, designing for universal access.

The challenge that the publisher now faces is how to design its dictionary for universal access. Consider, then, how we can make the solutions that allow the world's unwired masses to have the same degree of access that we have in more technologically advanced nations. Such a solution needs to consider factors along the product design continuum:

■ Designing for portability.
■ Designing for durability.
■ Designing for energy efficiency.
■ Design for serviceability and maintenance.
■ Designing ethically and with purpose.
■ Selecting an appropriate form to fit the content (material selection etc.).

These are but a few of the factors we need to consider in designing for a more sustainable world.

Sustainability points: equitability, dematerialization, affordability, universal access, social consciousness, paperless.

CASE STUDIES IN SUSTAINABILITY: THE COMPACT DETERGENT BOX

In recent years, there has been a trend in the detergent manufacturing market to optimizing packaging of detergents. To most end users, this silent shift in packaging may have gone unnoticed, but for those observers of sustainability initiatives and social responsibility, it is a great advance toward the wider initiative of lowering carbon emissions. The traditional boxes were often quite large and went along with a high transportation cost. While many companies are taking the steps to lower their overall carbon footprint, this case study focuses on one such company, Proctor and Gamble (Figure 5.8). I ask that readers disregard other issues surrounding product contents, as the issue of ecological detergent is one that stirs the sustainability pot and can become contentious at times. Consider only the step toward cube optimization; companies, such as the one featured, have reduced packaging size by concentrating detergent in both liquid or powder form.

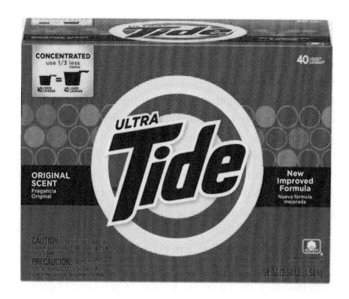

Figure 5.8
Tide Detergent Packaging Optimization.

In February 2011, Procter and Gamble (P&G) announced it is compacting its entire U.S. and Canadian portfolio of powder laundry detergents. For many in the field of sustainability, this came as great news. The new, compacted detergents join other products in the P&G Future Friendly portfolio, such as Tide ColdWater, PUR, and Cascade Action Pacs, that help reduce waste, save energy, or save water while offering value and outstanding performance.

The new, compacted detergents provide users with the same number of loads in a detergent carton that is smaller, resulting in a convenient product that is easy to handle and store. The compacted formulas and smaller cartons also allow for increased efficiency including reduced fuel consumption and a reduction in packaging. Len Sauers, vice president of sustainability, P&G, asserts that powder compaction is a win-win from operations all the way through consumer use. He also believes that powder compaction delivers meaningful benefits for the environment. By compacting its entire carton powder laundry detergent lineup, if consumers do as recommended, P&G could help save up to 4 million gigajoules (GJs) of energy each year, or the equivalent of the energy needed to provide 34,000 average homes with electricity for a year.

"As Future Friendly products, concentrated powder detergents show how simple choices can lead to meaningful results," offers Maurice Coffey, marketing director, P&G Future Friendly. "By taking this small step with our consumer, we can create benefits for the environment and ultimately improve consumers' lives."

The company has taken these consumer benefits one step further. Tide for traditional top-loading machines now has improved stain-fighting power, while Gain, another one of the products in their portfolio, delivers a "joyful scent" experience with more freshness.

In recognition of P&G's long-term and continued commitment to sustainability and its real achievements, the Dow Jones Sustainability Index (DJSI) includes P&G on the listing of sustainable companies. P&G has been on the list since the inception of DJSI. Further, the Financial Times and Just Means[17] honored P&G with the 2008/2009 Social Innovation Award. *Corporate Knights*[18] also ranked P&G in the top 15 of its 2010 Global 100 Most Sustainable Corporations in the World list.

P&G makes this list of case studies to illustrate the use of packaging redesign as well as to optimize delivery of a product. An example such as this is inspiring to designers to think about how they can replicate such successes in their respective fields.

Sustainability points: reduced cost of transportation, cube optimization, dematerialization, energy efficiency (detergent optimized for cold water).

CASE STUDIES IN SUSTAINABILITY: CITIZEN-CENTRIC SERVICES

Today, the term *citizen-centric services* (sometimes referred to as *e-government services*) is popular with many world governments as they strive to reconnect with the community and deliver services that meet or exceed the public's needs as well as their expectations. In the past, governments delivered services to their citizens through a programmatic business model that required face-to-face contact to administer a citizen's request. For example, citizens who applied for business permits or dog licenses had to commute to the physical office location, along with the entire necessary documents to get this task done. Moreover, if they required another document from another department, this required another physical engagement. In addition, if they were applying on the same day, it created a sense of redundancies in many instances, as the same basic information is often needed for many of these applications. Planning applications, for example, may involve many departments—planning, licensing and building services; today, this can be done using e-government services, all of which, are made possible through a single online portal. Further, these services can even be made proactive, using push technology services to notify citizens on the progress and status of their activities as they go through the government systems.

---

[17]A one stop shop on Corporate Social Responsibility: http://www.justmeans.com/.
[18]Corporate Knights, a self-described magazine focused on clean capitalism.

One key benefit of this form of service offering is the convenience it provides as citizens can complete these applications from the comfort of their homes.

In their traditional forms, these services required a citizen to

Step 1. Call the offices to check the application requirements.

Step 2. Commute to the offices.

Step 3. Retrieve a number (in paper form).

Step 4. Wait in line.

Step 5. Complete the application; unsuccessful attempts have to repeat the process if documents are missing.

Step 6. Commute home.

Step 7. Wait for the document to arrive in the mail.

Today, as the thrust of sustainability is in full swing, a citizen-centric solution is now becoming the normal mode of operation for many government organizations. Service is provided either by telephone, kiosk, or in the form of web portals, where citizens can complete once complicated applications over the web.

In this virtual form, the task flow is as follows:

Step 1. Citizens log onto the website.

Step 2. All documents are assembled.

Step 3. Online forms are completed.

Step 4. Scanned documents are uploaded, where needed.

Step 5. Application is submitted.

Step 6: Citizen receives an e-copy (via email or downloadable document) of confirmation.

Application instances that require original government identification cards or certification documents be mailed out to citizens are still done so using traditional means until more security is built in to prevent fraudulent activities from occurring.

Today, it is fair to say, with the onslaught and pervasiveness of the web, many people have come to expect from government the same level of service they experience in the private sector and are demanding streamlined and efficient service. Apart from the role that user experience can play here in creating efficient workflow that retain the user base and deter citizens from reverting to traditional mean, citizen-centric services are sustainable for a number of reasons. They are:

■ Limit the number of commuters who need to travel for the purpose of engagement at government office and limits the cost of energy and carbon emissions from commuting.

Figure 5.9

Citizenship and Immigration Canada's Self-Service Website.

Electronic access to municipal departments means fewer vehicle trips. For example, in deploying an e-permitting system, Connecticut's Capital Region estimates that it comes at a cost savings of 111,000 miles driven and 98,000 kg of CO_2 per year.

■ Cut back on the paper work needed to complete these process, paperless service-based operation model. Less paper used means fewer trees cut and less paper to be thrown away.

■ Create social benefits for citizens, who are given a sense of self-empowerment.

To make a citizen-centric approach effective and sustainable, good user-centric design practices must be embedded into the way policy and services are developed and delivered. Further, in terms of universal access and long-term sustenance of e-government and other citizen-centric types of services, the challenges include

1. Digital inclusion and citizen-centric services: ensuring access for all and helping citizens become confident users of new technology and online services.
2. Transforming the goal of the service by focusing and prioritizing citizen goals over government goals.

However, headway is to be made in implementing such services by allowing citizens to apply for such things as health cards and social security numbers. This is especially the case in Canada (Figure 5.9), where past fraudulent activities in the health care system has dictated an in-person application.

As well, in the case of such things as first time driver's licenses and passports, we may take a long time to get to e-services, given some of the 21st century challenges with privacy and security. However, with tightened budgets forcing many governments to find better long-term solutions, this may be in the pipeline, as many governments, from local to federal, move in the direction of e governing. In many respects, e-government programs are about infrastructure planning and modernization; but in implementation, they are in themselves an irrefutable and quantifiable gain in terms of sustainable progress.

Sustainability points: paperless, dematerialization, affordability, universal access, social consciousness.

CASE STUDIES IN SUSTAINABILITY: HERMAN MILLER'S MIRRA CHAIR

Launched in 2003, the Mirra chair (Figure 5.10) was developed with a design protocol rooted in recyclability, reduced toxicity, and renewability. The chair itself was designed by Designed by Studio 7.5 for Herman Miller. The result is the best-selling chair that is made from 96% recyclable materials. It contains no

Figure 5.10

Herman Miller Mirra Chair.

polyvinyl chloride.[19] The chair can be disassembled in less than 20 minutes using simple tools, meaning it is serviceable as well.

The journey to sustainable design began many years earlier, when the environmental department of Herman Miller launched a pollution prevention project to reduce formaldehyde emissions from the wood-finishing products used at that time. This initial interdepartmental collaboration led to the formation, in 1989, of a cross-functional Environmental Quality Advisory Team (EQAT), an internal working group that draws together middle managers and experts from around the company.

Over time, this forum grew, focusing on setting environmental strategy. Building on this collaborative model, in the early 1990s, Herman Miller launched an offshoot Design for Environment (DfE)[20] team to take the lead in product redesign. Today, design is front and center in any Herman Miller undertaking, from the point of material sourcing to the planning of product to life cycle.

Amalgamating talent from various departments, including development, manufacturing, and environmental functions, the DfE team followed a corporate goal to send zero waste to landfills as a guiding principle of design. One of the outcomes from this project was the momentum for other projects. By the late 1990s, Herman Miller developed interest in a cradle-to-cradle approach to product design, and it dedicated staff in the environmental department to build the DfE capability.

Examining the "materials chemistry" of its products, Herman Miller catalogued every material in every product, an extensive investment in sustainability learning that resulted in well-documented data that the company has since published and continues to share with interested companies and other manufacturers. The company teamed up with McDonough Braungart Design Chemistry (MBDC; see Chapter 2) to help examine material options to drive the cradle-to-cradle mandate they set out to meet.

The protocol guides consideration of sustainability through

- A materials recycling evaluation to improve the recycled content in its products as well as to enable material recycling from them.
- A materials chemistry analysis.
- A product ease-of-disassembly review.

---

[19]PVC is a synthetic material sourced from natural resources (oil and salt) and is the third most widely produced plastic, after polyethylene and polypropylene. PVC pipes are widely used in construction because PVC cheap, durable, and easy to use. According to a market study (Ceresana Research), PVC production is expected to exceed 40 million tonnes by 2016. According to IUPAC, polyvinyl chloride should be named poly(chloroethanediyl), but this name found no widespread use.
[20]The U.S. EPA's Design for the Environment program helps consumers, businesses, and institutional buyers identify cleaning and other products that perform well, are cost effective, and are safer for the environment.

Herman Miller has integrated the cradle-to-cradle protocol into its new product design process, a move that assures all products are screened for sustainability. Working through its implementation issues and strategizing environmental goals around it has helped Herman Miller identify gaps in occupational literacy and need for knowledge-sharing tools to replicate sustainable design success across products.

Herman Miller is now working externally to build bridges and apply its sustainable design lessons in other projects. As part of its corporate responsibility mandate, the company committed to treating sustainability as a common good rather than a market competition and began sharing its best practices with interested parties, including other companies. It does so by giving presentations at targeted conferences and working to build sustainable design standards through trade associations.

Sustainability points: dematerialization, no waste (cradle to cradle), elimination of hazardous material, ethical material sourcing, social consciousness, efficiency (process), total beauty (inside and out).

"The nation behaves well if it treats the natural resources as assets, which it must turn over to the next generation increased, and not impaired in value."[21]

CASE STUDIES IN SUSTAINABILITY: ELECTRONIC PAPERLESS BANKING SOLUTIONS

These days, almost all banks offer paperless options and online account access. Besides being environmentally friendly, paperless banking is convenient. Bank customers have easy to access to their account information wherever there is a safe and secure internet connection. Customers are now also able to do a myriad of tasks, such as

- Bill payment.
- E-money transfers.
- Checking balances.
- Applying for loans and overdraft protection.

Customers are also able to store and file their electronic statements as well as sort them for later accounting purposes. The case of e-banking (Figure 5.11) is very similar to e-government, where the savings are relatively equivalent in terms of eco impact. Customers are saved from going to the bank to do such activities

---

[21]Theodore Roosevelt.

Figure 5.11

TD Waterhouse Electronic Banking.

as paying bills, which before demanded a physical bank visit. Don Shafer, of the small bank consulting company BancVue,[22] estimates that banks spend between $1.50 and $3.50 per customer printing and mailing monthly statements. With e-banking, customers can reduce their carbon footprint at the same time, making it not only financially and environmentally beneficial but also socially beneficial, a true sustainable solution.

These similar sustainability practices go beyond banking. They foster environmentally friendly behavior everywhere. Some banks even provide the forum to give their customers opportunities to network with each other and exchange ideas, financial and otherwise. Green Choice Bank is headquartered at the Green Exchange in Chicago. Formerly a factory, this LEED certified building has a green roof, a high-efficiency heating and cooling system, low-toxin (VOC) paint, and even a rainwater capturing system for irrigation. The bank's Houston location donates to the environmental or social organization of customers' choice when they open a business account. While the move to paperless banking is a good step that many banks have embraced, the activities of such banks as Green Bank is noteworthy, making it a perfect case study. What lies at the root is that, as banks transition to providing more virtual solutions, engagement of user experienced designers is once again at the forefront of creating optimal solutions that will engage users and keep them as e-customers.

---

[22]The company is located in Texas.

Sustainability points: paperless, dematerialization, affordability, universal access, social consciousness.

CASE STUDIES IN SUSTAINABILITY: MEKA CONTAINER HOMES

MEKA is a Toronto-based company designing modular luxury housing out of used shipping containers; MEKA stands for modular, environmental, kinetic, and assembly and, as the name infers, is modular and can be connected to create larger living structures (Figure 5.12). Partly inspired by the hidden costs that homebuilders face, the MEKA homes are shipped completely built and, in many respects, is like a finished designed product, once received by the new owners. An example of the house is located in New York City Manhattan's West Village; the one on display is about 320 square feet and surprisingly spacious; it receives many visitors daily. Its appeal, beyond its high aesthetic, is its affordability, as many people can look at it and think of being able to afford it, given the high prices of homes in the city. Not only is it a high attraction sight, it has received a lot of press worldwide, as it is aligned with wider sustainability initiatives and such things as the Small House Movement.[23]

This case study departs from the previous ones in that it is not a common consumer item, though the company's founder Michael de Jong would likely agree that it is an example of good product design. In an interview with the *Wall Street Journal*, he is noted: "It's a product design, not a housing design." The houses are priced reasonably, from $39,000 up to $128,000. They also meet the mark on a beautiful design both on the inside and outside, meeting

Figure 5.12
MEKA Container Homes.

---

[23]The Small House Movement focuses on smaller living spaces that foster sustainable living for individuals, families, and communities worldwide.

the requirements of many of the frameworks we encountered so far, particularly the total beauty framework. While we may not be able to speak to the original material sourcing gone into the container, we can assert that it meets the mark of being.

1. **Cyclic:** It closes the loop in material sourcing. The structures are recycled for use after their utility is met in their previous use as shipping containers.
2. **Solar:** MEKA homes use solar power to power the houses.
3. **Safe:** The shipping container in its refurbished form presents to its inhabitants a safe living environment.
4. **Efficient:** Compared to the cost it would take homebuilders to build from scratch, there is no comparison with a prefabricated home, modified and beautified for human habitation.
5. **Socially responsible:** The product is manufactured under Fair Labor conditions and in terms of social responsibility, it also meets the mark on universal design. It allows many to think of home ownership due to the lowered housing cost.

Sustainability points: equitability, affordability, durability, energy efficiency, universal access, serviceability, social consciousness.

WRAPPING UP

Today, building in a good user experience alongside a design are the key competitive differentiators across companies. If you think about it at a concrete level, consider the world of electronics, where the physicality of products is now commoditized. On the surface, it is all beginning to look the same, and while some products still focus on a comparative feature listing of their products, now more than ever the emphasis is on the "user experience." For many companies, this means responding to the user's changing environment and an attunement to the zeitgeist. The late Apple CEO Steve Jobs, a champion of experience design, has often espoused the virtues of understanding the full context of humans, as we design. He asserted, on many occasions, the need to see not only the user's solo context but the wider human environment as we design.

> "To design something really well you have to get it. You have to really grok what it's all about. It takes a passionate commitment to thoroughly understand something—chew it up, not just quickly swallow it. Most people do not take the time to do that. The broader one understands of the human experience, the better designs we will have."

Sustainability, as an added ingredient in the human experience pot, presents an opportunity for user experience practitioners to contribute at high levels in their organizations, helping to set product strategy and business goals at the same time. Taking what we know and use today as tools of our trade and engaging with the wider sustainability initiative is one step closer in understanding the fuller context of what it means to design for users and to do so sustainably.

LOOKING THROUGH THE DESIGN LENS

As user experience practitioners, we must understand what this means for design and the contributions that we can make in the design process along the continuum of a product life cycle. Putting on our business hats, we need to also evangelize and socialize sustainability to our respective management teams by showing real value and that we can engage with users to have impact, leading to tangible and improved solutions. How do we make products and services that are well engineered, profitable, aesthetically pleasing, and enjoyable to use and at the same time ensure that they are also purposeful and ethical? This question in a nutshell is the crux of our challenge. The response includes

- Evangelizing and selling the merits of sustainability within our organizations.
- Socializing these principles with peers.
- Showing value of user experience design by presenting data that speak to the values of sustainable design.
- Infusing sustainable design thinking, as part of the product development life cycle.
- Designing and developing sustainable products (taking theory to practice).

At the end of the day, taking the theories of sustainable design into practice is the goal of driving change and having impact in the changing world, where ecological consciousness is and will continue to be the mode of operation. Also, focusing on ways to capture the baseline data we need to build on is essential. We need to be able to measure it, before we can change what it is.

GENERAL RESOURCES

1. *The Secret of Things* (video): http://www.thesecretlifeofthings.com/. *The Secret Life of Things* is a set of short animated videos exploring the hidden environmental impacts of everyday things. Each video comes with a free pack of learning resources to inspire and engage budding designers and product developers with life cycle thinking and eco design.

2. Networkedblogs.com (blog portal): **http://www.networkedblogs.com/topic/sustainability**, a one-stop shop portal into the sustainability blogs on the web.

3. ESP Design.org (organization): **http://www.espdesign.org/sustainable-design-resources/sustainable-design-videos/**. ESP Design provides practical information to aid the design of more sustainable products.

4. *Sustainability Dictionary* (dictionary): **http://www.sustainabilitydictionary.com/**. This is an online resource for learning the lingo of sustainability.

5. The Centre for Sustainable Design (organization): **http://cfsd.org.uk/resources/:** The Centre for Sustainable Design (CfSD) was established in 1995 in Farnham, Surrey, UK, at what is now the University for the Creative Arts. The centre has led and participated in a range of high-quality research projects and organized more than a hundred conferences, workshops, and training courses focused on sustainable innovation and product sustainability. CfSD is recognized worldwide for its knowledge and expertise, having worked closely with business, policymaking, and research communities for two decades.

6. Design Can Change.org (organization): **http://www.designcanchange.org/#resources/design**. The site is dedicated to providing designers with a wide range of information regarding sustainable business practices. Through case studies, interviews, resources, and discourse, the site encourages and supports designers as they incorporate sustainable thinking into their professional lives.

7. Demi (organization): **www.demi.org.uk**. This website contains lots of information on design for sustainability.

8. Green Biz (organization): **http://www.greenbiz.com**. Green Biz is an excellent, regularly updated source of eco-news and resources for corporations. Be sure to subscribe to its email newsletter and check out the business toolbox, for information about the implications of sustainability for business and industry.

9. Sustainable Life Media (organization): **http://www.sustainablebrands.com**/. Sustainable Brands is a learning, collaboration, and commerce community of forward-thinking sustainability, brand, and design professionals who are working to leverage sustainability as a driver of business and brand value.

10. Independent Designers Network (network organization): **http://www.indes .net/eco-ref**. Compiled by the Independent Designers Network, this is an extensive list for print and packaging designers, including material selection links, marketing and labeling laws, environmental impact, and waste stream links.

11. The International Center for Creativity (learning organization): **http: //www.icisfoundation.org**. The International Center for Creativity, Innovation and Sustainability holds eco-design master classes (in Europe) and has some good lists of links on its site.

SUSTAINABILITY BOOKS FOR DESIGNERS AND RESEARCHERS

1. *In the Bubble: Designing in a Complex World*, by John Thackara.
2. *Cradle to Cradle: Remaking the Way We Make Things*, by William McDonough and Michael Braungart.
3. *Design for the Real World*, by Victor Papanek.
4. *The Green Imperative*, by Victor Papanek.
5. *Eternally Yours: Time in Design*, by Brian Eno and John Thackara.
6. *Biomimicry: Innovation Inspired by Nature*, by Janine M. Benyus.
7. *Design Is the Problem*, by Nathan Shedroff.
8. *Design for the Real World: Human Ecology and Social Change: The Designer's Atlas of Sustainability* (2nd Edition), by Ann Thorpe.
9. *Cats' Paws and Catapults: Mechanical Worlds of Nature and People*, by Steven Vogel and Kathryn K. Davis.
10. *Sustainable Solutions: Developing Products and Services for the Future*, by Martin Charter.
11. *Natural Capitalism*, by P. Hawken, A. B. Lovins, and L. H. Lovins.
12. *The Ecology of Commerce*, by P. Hawken.
13. *Green Design for the Environment*, by Dorothy MacKenzie.

SUSTAINABILITY FRAMEWORKS

1. *Biomimicry,* Janine Benyus: http://biomimicry.net/.
2. *Cradle to Cradle,* William McDonough and Michael Braungart: http://www .mcdonough.com/cradle_to_cradle.htm.
3. *Natural Capitalism,* P. Hawken, A. B. Lovins, and L. H. Lovins: www.natcap .org/.
4. *The Natural Step,* Brian Nattrass and Mary Altomore: http://www .naturalstep.org/.
5. *The Total Beauty of Sustainable Products,* Edwin Datchefski: http://www .biothinking.com/.

REFERENCES

Alexander, C., Ishikawa, S., Silverstein, M., 1977. A pattern language: Towns, buildings, construction. Oxford University Press, New York.

Apple. (n.d.). The story behind Apple's environmental footprint. http://www.apple.com/ environment/ (accessed 10.08.11).

Arndt, R. (n.d.). A maintenance-free bike to give Africans some mobility. www.fastcoexist .com/1678778/a-maintenance-free-bike-to-give-africans-some-mobility (accessed 16.11.11).

Benyus, J.M., 1997. Biomimicry: Innovation inspired by nature. Morrow, New York.

Benyus, J.M., 2002. Biomimicry. Harper Perennial, New York.

Biotech Products. (n.d.). *Biotech products.* http://www.biotech-products.net (accessed 13.12.11).

Brundtland, G.H., 1988. Our common future: [report by the] World Commission on Environment and Development, chairman: Gro Harlem Brundtland. Oxford University Press, Oxford.

Business at its best: Driving sustainable value creation. (n.d.). www.accenture.com/ SiteCollectionDocuments/PDF/Accenture_Business_at_its_Best.pdf (accessed 10.10.10).

Carson, Rachel, Lois Darling, and Louis Darling. Silent spring. Boston: Houghton Mifflin, 1962. Print.

Cooper, Alan, and Robert Reimann. *About Face 2.0: The Essentials of Interaction Design.* New York: Wiley, 2003. Print.

Creative Slice. (n.d.). Tucson Green Web Design WordPress Website Development. http:// www.creativeslice.com (accessed 11.12.11).

Datschefski, E. (n.d.). HAVEN: Deep ecology, total beauty. http://www.haven.net/live/ beyond/edwin_d.htm (accessed 14.12.11).

Datschefski, Edwin. The Total Beauty of Sustainable Products. Crans-Près-Céligny, Switzerland: RotoVision, 2001. Print.

Dow Jones Sustainability Indexes. (n.d.). http://www.sustainability-index.com/ (accessed 13.12.11).

Easy Ways to Go Green, 2008. Green symbols guide: An environmental symbols resource. http://www.easywaystogogreen.com/green-guides/guide-to-green-symbols/ (accessed 13.12.11).

ecoLingo. (n.d.). Earth friendly graphic design. http://ecolingo.com/ecoLingo.htm (accessed 13.12.11).

FedCenter—Home. (n.d.). http://www.fedcenter.gov (accessed 13.12.11).

Fehrenbacher, K. (n.d.). GigaOM. http://www.gigaom.com (accessed 13.12.11).

Finding the green in today's shoppers. (n.d.). http://www.ahcgroup.com/mc_images/category/93/deloitte_on_competing_on_green_with_shoppers.pdf (accessed 23.11.11).

Forum for the Future. (n.d.). About us, *Action for a Sustainable World*. http://www.forumforthefuture.org/about (accessed 13.12.11).

Global Reporting Initiative. (n.d.a) *GRI reporting guidelines*. www.globalreporting.org/ReportingFramework/G3Online/ (accessed 07.08.11).

Global Reporting Initiative. (n.d.b). *Global reporting initiative*. https://www.globalreporting.org (accessed 10.10.11).

Global Reporting Initiative. (n.d.c). Report Services List. www.globalreporting.org/ReportServices/GRIReportsList/ (accessed 14.09.10).

Global mobile statistics 2011: All quality mobile marketing research, mobile Web stats, subscribers, ad revenue, usage, trends. (n.d.). *Mobithinking*. http://mobithinking.com/mobile-marketing-tools/latest-mobile-stats (accessed 13.12.11).

Green Forums. (n.d.). http://www.greenforum.com/ (accessed 13.12.11).

Greenpeace International. (n.d.). Guide to greener electronics. http://www.greenpeace.org/international/en/campaigns/climate-change/cool-it/Guide-to-Greener-Electronics/?id= (accessed 13.12.11).

Havas Media discusses sustainability and consumer brands. (2011). *Environmental Management and Energy News: Environmental Leader*. http://www.environmentalleader.com/2011/03/10/havas-media-discusses-sustainability-and-consumer-brands/ (accessed 13.12.11).

Hawken, P., Lovins, A.B., Lovins, L.H., 1999. Natural capitalism: Creating the next industrial revolution. Little, Brown and Co, Boston.

Idea: Planned obsolescence, 2009. *The Economist: World News, Politics, Economics, Business & Finance*. http://www.economist.com/node/13354332 (accessed 13.12.11).

IKEA, 2010. Sustainability Report. www.ikea.com/ms/en_US/about_ikea/pdf/ikea_ser_2010.pdf (accessed 24.06.11).

IKEA bins bags in bid to make stores greener, 2007. Business: *The Observer*. http://www.guardian.co.uk/business/2007/jul/08/theobserver.observerbusiness3 (accessed 10.10.11).

ISO Organization. (n.d.). www.iso.org/iso/iso_catalogue/management_and_leadership_standards/environmental_management/the_iso_14000_family.htm (accessed 01.09.11).

Janine Benyus shares nature's designs. (n.d.). *TED: Ideas Worth Spreading* (video). http://www.ted.com/talks/janine_benyus_shares_nature_s_designs.html (accessed 13.12.11).

Johnson & Johnson. (n.d.). *Health care products and pharmaceuticals*. http://www.jnj.com/connect/caring/environment-protection/health-planet (accessed 13.12.11).

Lovelock, James, and Lynn Margulis. "Gaia Theory Homepage." Gaia Theory Homepage. N.p., n.d. Web. 10 Aug. 2011. http://www.gaiatheory.org/

Matthews, R., 2011. *Greenpeace green electronics guide*. www.greenpeace.org/international/Global/international/publications/climate/2011/Cool%20IT/greener-guide-nov-2011/guide-to-greener-electronics-nov-2011.pdf (accessed 05.12.11).

McDonough, W., Braungart, M., 2002. Cradle to cradle: Remaking the way we make things. North Point Press, New York.

Mines, C., 2007. In search of green technology consumers—Forrester Research. http://www.forrester.com/rb/Research/in_search_of_green_technology_consumers/q/id/43729/t/2 (accessed 13.12.11).

Modular luxury buildings. (n.d.). *MEKA World.* http://mekaworld.com (accessed 13.12.11).

Mulder, Steve, and Ziv Yaar. The User Is Always Right: A Practical Guide to Creating and Using Personas for the Web. Berkeley, CA: New Riders, 2007. Print.

Naik, S., Ward, M., Godfrey, G., Hanifan, G. (n.d.). Simultaneous sustainability and savings. *Accenture.* www.accenture.com/SiteCollectionDocuments/PDF/Accenture_Simultaneous_Sustainability_and_Savings.pdf (accessed 12.12.10).

Nattrass, B., Mary Altomore, M. (n.d.). *The Natural Step.* http://www.thenaturalstep.org (accessed 13.12.11).

Nielsen, J. (n.d.). Ten heuristics for user interface design. http://www.useit.com/papers/heuristic/heuristic_list.html (accessed 13.12.11).

Oxford Dictionaries Online. (n.d.). http://oxforddictionaries.com/ (accessed 14.12.11).

Papanek, V.J., 1971. *Design for the real world: Human ecology and social change* (1st American ed.). Pantheon Books, New York.

Richardson, Adam. "Tragedy of the Commons | Page 3 of 3 | design mind." design mind | business. technology. design. Frog Design, n.d. Web. 26 Feb. 2012. http://designmind.frogdesign.com/articles/tragedy-of-the-commons.html?page=2

Robischon, N., 2009. What is ethonomics? www.fastcompany.com/blog/noah-robischon/editors-desk/what-ethonomics (accessed 20.09.11).

Saatchi, W.A., Saatchi S - Landing. (n.d.). *Landing.* http://www.saatchis.com/ (accessed 13.12.11).

Shedroff, N., Lovins, L.H., 2009. Design is the problem: The future of design must be sustainable. Rosenfeld Media, Brooklyn, NY.

SROI Network. (n.d.). http://www.thesroinetwork.org/ (accessed 13.12.11).

Standards.gov. (n.d.). *Assistive technology.* http://standards.gov/assistiveTechnology.cfm#section-1 (accessed 14.12.11).

Strategy for Sustainability. (n.d.). The Book. http://www.strategyforsustainability.com/book/ (accessed 14.09.11).

Ten examples of sustainability plans for graphic designers.(n.d.). *Pushing Snowballs: Marketing for Creative Businesses.* http://www.pushingsnowballs.com/sustainability/10-examples-of-sustainability-plans-for-graphic-designers/ (accessed 13.12.11).

The Plastic Bag vs. Paper Bag Facts, 2009. http://www.biotech-products.net/documents/The Plastic Bag vs. Paper Bag Facts.pdf (accessed 12.07.11).

The Sustainable Design Toolbox, 2010. http://www.thesustainabledesigntoolbox.typepad.com (accessed 13.12.11).

Transport. (n.d.). *Adidas Group.* www.adidas-group.com/en/sustainability/Environment/transport/default.aspx (accessed 07.06.11).

U.S. Census Bureau, 2011. 2009 report—final. www.census.gov/econ/estats/2009/2009reportfinal.pdf (accessed 08.12.11).

Wal-Mart. Sustainability. (n.d.). http://walmartstores.com/sustainability/ (accessed 14.08.11).

Werbach, A., 2008. *The Birth of blue.* www.saatchis.com/birthofblue/birthofblue.pdf (accessed 10.10.10).

Werbach, A., 2009. Strategy for sustainability: A business manifesto. Harvard Business Press, Boston, MA.

INDEX

Page numbers followed by *f* indicates a figure and *t* indicates a table.

Printed and bound by CPI Group (UK) Ltd, Croydon, CR0 4YY

03/10/2024

01040311-0004